DATE DUE

Demco, Inc. 38-293

GRIEG
MUSIC, LANDSCAPE
AND NORWEGIAN IDENTITY

To Ingrid

Grieg

Music, Landscape
and Norwegian Identity

Daniel M. Grimley

THE BOYDELL PRESS

First published 2006
The Boydell Press, Woodbridge

Transferred to digital printing

ISBN 978-1-84383-210-2

The Boydell Press is an imprint of Boydell & Brewer Ltd
PO Box 9, Woodbridge, Suffolk IP12 3DF, UK
and of Boydell & Brewer Inc.
668 Mt Hope Avenue, Rochester, NY 14620, USA
website: www.boydellandbrewer.com

A CiP catalogue record for this book is available
from the British Library

This publication is printed on acid-free paper

CONTENTS

MUSICAL EXAMPLES

ILLUSTRATIONS

PREFACE

This book concerns Grieg's music and its relationship with landscape, the role which music and landscape played in the formation of Norwegian cultural identity in the nineteenth century, and the function that landscape has performed in the critical reception of Grieg's work. It is not intended as a comprehensive history of Norwegian music, nor as a life-and-works study of Grieg. Critical reconsideration of Grieg's work, however, is timely for a number of reasons. Grieg's music continues to enjoy a prominent place in the concert hall and recording catalogues, but has yet to attract sustained analytical attention in Anglo-American scholarship. Historians such as Benedict Anderson and John Hutchinson have stressed the constructed (or imagined) nature of nationalist discourses, encouraging a more theoretical and contextualised engagement with the issue of national identity in music. Similarly, though representations of landscape have long been a focus for study in cultural geography and other disciplines, they are only just beginning to be the subject of musicological criticism. Previously, landscape has often been associated loosely with programme music, a problematic trend given the historical emphasis on the autonomy of the musical work that has shaped much musicological writing. But just as the notion of aesthetic autonomy seems increasingly untenable, so the idea of landscape in music becomes a more discursive concept. Grieg's music offers an especially compelling and hitherto underexplored area for such research. Furthermore, recent work in musicology has stressed the way in which music histories have been written along exclusive and canonic (especially Austro-German) lines, so that a reappraisal of supposedly peripheral repertoires such as Norwegian music can be undertaken in a more pluralistic disciplinary context.

My book uses Grieg's work as a case study to try and develop new perspectives on the relationships between music, landscape and identity. The tension in Grieg's work between competing musical discourses, the folklorist, the nationalist and the modernist, offers one of the most vivid narratives in late-nineteenth and early-twentieth-century music, and suggests that Grieg is a more complex and challenging historical figure than his critical reception has often appeared to suggest. It is through the contested category of landscape, I will argue, that these tensions can be contextualised and ultimately, through analytical enquiry, resolved.

Grieg's writings, diaries and correspondence have been widely published and edited in excellent collections edited by Finn Benestad and others.

Though much of this material has been translated into English, I have generally preferred to use my own translations when quoting from Norwegian sources, and all translations in this book are mine unless otherwise acknowledged. Any faults or inaccuracies which occur are therefore entirely my own responsibility. Norwegian spelling and orthography are highly variant, not least because there are two different official Norwegian languages: *bokmål* (or *riksmål*), and *nynorsk* (or *landsmål*) and also because of subsequent spelling reforms (for example in 1907–9, 1917 and 1934–6), including attempts to produce a common Norwegian (*samnorsk*). Though these differences may be confusing to a non-Norwegian reader, I have not attempted to standardise spelling or usage in this study, but retain the original form as used in the relevant source material. Exceptions to this rule include the titles of Grieg's pieces (which generally follow the form used by the critical edition, *Grieg samlede verker*), and the relatively infrequent occasions where I have not had access to material in its original language. The relationship between Grieg's music and these different forms of spoken and written Norwegian is itself one of the topics of discussion in Chapter 3.

Music examples are provided as frequently as possible to support the analytical discussions throughout the book. However, the reader may find it useful to consult scores of the *Lyric Pieces*, the folk-song arrangements op. 17 and op. 66, the song-cycle *Haugtussa* ('The Mountain Maid'), op. 67, and the *Slåtter* ('Norwegian Peasant Dances'), op. 72, all of which are widely available in reliable and inexpensive editions. Where detailed reference is made to musical pitches, the Helmholtz system of registral designation is used (middle c = c¹); capital letters are used to refer to pitch classes with no fixed registral position.

Many people have assisted me during the writing of this book, and I regret that I cannot thank them all individually by name. Work on the project was completed principally in two stages, both supported by the Arts and Humanities Research Board: a preliminary research visit to Bergen to consult material in the Grieg Archive, Bergen Public Library (Bergen Offentlige Bibliotek), funded by an Arts and Humanities Research Board small grant; and a writing-up period of matching research leave in spring to summer 2005. I am grateful to the University of Nottingham Research Committee for an initial period of leave in autumn to winter 2004, which enabled the writing-up process to begin, and to my colleagues in the Department of Music for shouldering the additional administrative and teaching burden that my leave created.

Any book on this period of Norwegian music must acknowledge the foundation laid by Norwegian scholars themselves, especially Finn Benestad, Dag Schjelderup-Ebbe and Nils Grinde. I am particularly grateful to Harald Herresthal and Ståle Kleiberg for their generous comments on my work; I have freely drawn on their writing throughout this study. Though I only had the opportunity to read Peer Findeisen's fine study of Grieg's folk-music arrangements after I had arrived in Bergen, his work has been tremendously stimulating. The origin of this book was a class on 'Klokkeklang' that I attended as an undergraduate in Cambridge, taken by my future doctoral supervisor, W. Dean Sutcliffe, which prompted my first critical thoughts on Grieg. I am immensely grateful for his continuing critical guidance and support. In Norway, I wish to thank Siren Steen, curator of the Grieg Samling, Bergen Offentlige Bibliotek, for her guidance through the collection and her friendship during my stay in Bergen, as well as her invaluable assistance with photographic material during the book's production process; the Grieg Academy, who provided very generous academic support and a warm welcome (especially Ragna Sofie Grung Moe, who helped with many arrangements for my visit); Ingrid Gjertsen, curator of the Arne Bjørndal collection; Monica Jangaard and Erling Dahl, jr, at Troldhaugen; the Troldhaugen foundation.

I am also grateful to Julian Rushton, David Fanning, Jeffrey Kallberg and Julian Johnson, who have been tremendously supportive of my work throughout the project. My readers were Harald Herresthal and Benjamin Walton (Chapter 1); Robert Adlington (Chapter 2); W. Dean Sutcliffe and Judith Jesch (Chapter 3); and Ståle Kleiberg (Chapters 4 and 5). They suggested many corrections and improvements to my text, without which the book would have been poorer, and I am indebted to them for their critical scrutiny. Barry Peter Ould of the Grainger Society has been of great assistance with copyright and source material issues during my work on Grainger in Chapter 5. I am grateful to Caroline Palmer at Boydell & Brewer, and their agent Bruce Phillips, both of whom have overseen the project with enthusiasm, and to Clive Tolley, who copy-edited the book with considerable insight and precision. Parts of the book have been presented at conferences or seminars at the Universities of Cambridge, East Anglia, Surrey, Melbourne, Glasgow, Nottingham and King's College, London, and at the Annual Meeting of the American Musicological Society in Columbus, Ohio. My thanks go to the many friends and colleagues who have commented on this material in its various stages of development or have helped in some other way with the book, including Byron Adams, Daniel Chua, Martin Dixon, Stephen Downes, Sarah Hibberd, Tomi Mäkelä, Svend Ravnkilde, Alexander Rehding, Edward Rushton, Jim Samson, Sam Smith, Sue and Steve Sykes and Andrew Taylor.

Finally, I wish to thank my parents and my sister, Carla, whose support is central to every aspect of my work. This book is dedicated to my partner, Ingrid, a brilliant scholar and soulmate, with all my love.

The National Composer as Miniaturist

Composers' final resting places can often provide valuable insights into their historical reception and the context in which their music was originally created. Grieg's grave is a case in point.[1] It consists of a simple stone tablet with a heavy lintel, set into the dark granite of a cliff below his villa, Troldhaugen ('Troll Hill'), looking out over the waters of Nordåsvatnet towards the outer skerries and the open sea. Designed by Grieg's cousin, architect Schak Bull (nephew of the internationally renowned Bergen-born violin virtuoso Ole Bull), Grieg's name is carved in stylised runic letters across the face of the stone, evoking the Golden Age of Norway's Viking past. In some senses, the grave is an 'anti-memorial', an object that, initially at least, appears to resist its conventional cultural function. By comparison with the popular image of Grieg outside Norway, an idealisation of the composer surrounded by picturesque fjordland scenery promulgated most notoriously perhaps by the Broadway musical *Song of Norway*,[2] the grave seems strikingly abstract and non-representational. There is no image or statue of the composer, and no attempt to soften the stark geometric lines of Bull's design. The contrast with the familiar vernacular style of the villa above, and Grieg's little composing hut set quaintly beside the water, could not be greater. In other ways, however, the grave literally sets in stone a particular strand of Grieg reception, namely his music's perceived association with the Norwegian landscape. Bull's design grounds Grieg's creativity in the Norwegian soil. It strongly reinforces the metaphorical links between Grieg's music and western Norwegian topography. Furthermore, it invokes one of the most powerful images in Norwegian folk culture, which Grieg often felt drawn towards in his work: the myth of a subterranean supernatural music that enchants or bewitches passers-by. The grave site therefore

---

[1] A photograph of the grave with a short accompanying description can be accessed via the Troldhaugen website. The English-language version is at http://www.troldhaugen.no/default.asp?kat=66&sp=2.
[2] The musical was adapted from the novel by Milton Lazarus and written by George Forrest and Robert Wright. It opened on 21 August 1944 at the Imperial Theatre on Broadway and ran for over eight hundred performances before travelling to London, where it was staged at the Palace Theatre. In 1970 it was turned into a film directed by Andrew L. Stone and starring Toralv Maurstad.

combines a number of important cultural tropes: a sense of remoteness and inaccessibility that serves as a symbol of perceived Norwegian isolation (felt particularly perhaps in the Westland); the definition of nationhood in terms of landscape; the formation of a national culture through its association with the natural environment; and the mythic origins of musical creativity in the (super)natural world. The grave is also emblematic of a form of acoustic ecology. Listen, it suggests, and it becomes possible to hear the inspiration for Grieg's work in the sound of the wind among the pine trees on the cliff top above or the waves on the shore below. Significantly, given the title of one of Grieg's own works, *Den Bergtekne* ('The Mountain Thrall'), op. 32, on contemplating Grieg's grave it is Grieg himself who ultimately appears to have been 'taken into the mountain'.

This book is concerned with the nature and function of landscape in Grieg's music. It is concerned partly with issues in critical reception, but its aim is also to analyse the ways in which landscape is represented in the sound of Grieg's work. Conventionally, landscape has been used to prettify his work: the images of lakes, fjords and snow-capped mountains that often accompany his music in the media have served to make his work more amenable to popular consumption. This raises a particular problem regarding the critical status of Grieg's work. From a scholarly perspective outside Scandinavia, Grieg appears to have suffered more than many composers from changes in musical fashion. Though the success of his pedagogical piano series, the *Lyric Pieces*, ensured that Grieg became an international household name during his own lifetime when the market for such music was at its height, his reputation has since shifted as the tradition of domestic piano playing has declined. His work now hovers uneasily on the edge of the canon. That is not to imply that his music is necessarily unheard. The concert suites drawn from his incidental music for Ibsen's *Peer Gynt*, op. 46 and 55 (1874–92), the Piano Concerto, op. 16 (1868–72), and the arrangement for strings of the *Holberg Suite*, op. 40 (1885), continue to be staples of the orchestral repertoire. In recent years, they have also begun to find an even more prolific medium for dissemination, albeit of an anonymous kind, through their adoption for numerous television soundtracks, playovers and advertisements. Few classical composers, in that sense, can have reached so wide and diverse an audience.

As with many 'popular classics', however, commercial success has often been associated with the idea of the aesthetically commonplace, so that Grieg's music can easily seem over-exposed. Consequently, many of Grieg's most significant and stylistically progressive works, particularly his folk-music arrangements, have yet to attract sustained critical attention in Anglo-American scholarship. Though the songs have always been admired by a small group of *cognoscenti* (and have been the subject of two monographs in English since 1990)[3] they are relative rarities in the concert hall. Singers outside Scandinavia are increasingly reluctant to include unusual items (particularly those in a challenging and unfamiliar language) in their recital repertoire. The folk-music arrangements have arguably suffered even more severely, and, with the exception of Peer Findeisen's fine study (in German),[4] have not yet been the subject of substantial critical discussion beyond their brief coverage in Finn Benestad's and Dag Schjelderup-Ebbe's biography.[5] When we think of Grieg as a popular or even overly familiar musical figure, therefore, it is only with a selective and unrepresentative range of his work in mind.

Landscape has often been used to promote the image of Grieg as the 'founding father' of Norwegian music. But this role is a historically contestable category on many levels, particularly since it reinforces a perception of his work outside Norway as a composer of merely 'local' significance working on the edge of the mainstream late-Romantic Austro-German tradition. The broader importance of Grieg's work has consequently remained under-appreciated. His work lies tantalisingly just outside the sweep of the grand narratives, such as 'the emancipation of the dissonance' or 'the birth of modernism', that have conventionally shaped our view of nineteenth and early-twentieth-century musical history. Compared with Chopin, for instance, Grieg's approach to large-scale form often appears symmetrical and four-square. Likewise, though Grieg's treatment of folk material is acknowledged as innovative, works such as the *Slåtter* have been broadly overshadowed by the music of later figures such as Béla Bartók who articulated a more consistently professional interest in ethnomusicological research and whose work seems more clearly attuned to developments in twentieth-century art-music. In this respect, Grieg's folk-song arrangements have become little more than historical precursors to a perceived 'full-blown' folk modernism that emerged only later in the twentieth century. In spite of energetic attempts in much recent writing to dismantle such fixed patterns of historical thought, Grieg has remained on the periphery of academic musical debate.[6] Indeed, if anything, Grieg's work seems even further beyond reach than before. He is neither 'exotic' enough to appeal to

---

[3] The two studies are Beryl Foster, *The Songs of Edvard Grieg* (Aldershot: Scolar, 1990), and Sandra Jarrett, *Edvard Grieg and His Songs* (Aldershot: Ashgate, 2003).

[4] Peer Findeisen, *Instrumentale Folklorestilisierung bei Edvard Grieg und bei Béla Bartók: vergleichende Studie zur Typik der Volksmusikbearbeitung im 19. versus 20. Jahrhundert* (Frankfurt am Main: Peter Lang, 1998).

[5] Finn Benestad and Dag Schjelderup-Ebbe, *Edvard Grieg: The Man and the Artist*, trans. William H. Halvorson and Leland B. Sateren (Gloucester: Alan Sutton, 1988). Originally published as *Edvard Grieg: mennesket og kunsteren* (Oslo: Aschehoug, 1980).

[6] For a useful contemporary summary of the concerns of the so-called 'new musicology', including its attempts to deconstruct received canons of musical inquiry, see Jann Pasler's article, 'Directions in Musicology', *Acta Musicologica* 69 (1997), 16–21, originally read at the round-table discussion on the state of the discipline at a meeting of the International Musicological Society, London, 1997.

interdisciplinary scholarship, nor a significantly central part of the Western canon to justify the employment of urgent rescue attempts from the supposedly totalising claims of structuralist analysis or historical positivism as has been the case with other more clearly mainstream figures.

One of the most pervasive ways in which landscape has operated in Grieg's historical reception is by strengthening the image of the 'little master'. Accounts of Grieg's physically diminutive stature and weak constitution have merged imperceptibly with his perceived inability to deal with the compositional demands of large-scale musical structures such as sonatas, symphonies or Grand Opera. This miniaturist theme lies deeply buried in Grieg reception. In a survey of his orchestral music in Gerald Abraham's landmark 1948 collection of Grieg essays, for example, Hubert Foss remarked that 'never touched in his manhood by the *kolossal*, Grieg was determined, content, to be a small master: his deliberate smallness is one of his greatest virtues'.[7] In the same anthology, Kathleen Dale suggests that the reason why Grieg 'wrote so few long works and so many short ones is due to the fact that he was essentially a lyricist'. In the case of later figures such as Anton Webern, however, lyrical intensity has more usually been associated with expressive depth rather than structural-aesthetic failure, whereas the opposite often seems to have been held true for Grieg.[8] Dale concludes that, far from being a conscious aesthetic or compositional decision, Grieg's miniaturism was determined inadvertently by his physical condition. 'Never robust in health', she reminds us, Grieg apparently 'lacked the necessary staying power to wrestle with the larger problems of form and balance.'[9] Historically this interpretation may have been partly true: Grieg certainly suffered from poor health throughout his adult life and the cumulative demands of maintaining an international performing career, with its associated administration and correspondence, must inevitably have had a negative impact on his creative output. In a covering letter to his publisher Hinrichsen dated 28 February 1903 sent with the manuscript of the *Slåtter*, Grieg wrote: 'I can well understand that you would rather have had an original work from me. It will come. You need only provide me with a bit of good health.'[10] But physical well-being cannot surely have been the sole reason for Grieg's decision not to undertake large-scale compositional projects more frequently, and it would be unwise to extrapolate a general principle from such circumstantial evidence alone.

[7] 'The Orchestral Music', *Grieg: A Symposium*, ed. Gerald Abraham (London: Lindsey Drummond, 1948), 16–25, here 16.
[8] See, for example, Christopher Wintle's article, 'Webern's Lyric Character', in *Webern Studies*, ed. Kathryn Bailey (Cambridge: Cambridge University Press, 1996), 229–63.
[9] 'The Piano Music', in Abraham, *Grieg: A Symposium*, 45–70, here 45.
[10] Quoted in the critical commentary to the Henle Edition of op. 72 edited by Einar Steen-Nøkleberg (Munich, 1994), 63.

Not all critics have shared this view of Grieg's miniaturism. In his volume for the Master Musicians series, for instance, John Horton despairingly complains that

> The conventional portrait of Grieg as a man and musician, derived from an uncritical reproduction of the statements and opinions of his earliest biographers, represents him as a frail, dreamy recluse set against a background of tourist-brochure scenery, with such talents as he possessed fully extended in the production of salon pieces and orchestral works, mostly of a programmatic kind, whose appeal is continually waning.[11]

Horton regards the songs as Grieg's most significant work, and adds that 'the fact that most of them lie outside, or on the periphery, of the German *Lied* tradition should not in itself diminish their importance'.[12] Nevertheless, aspects of miniaturism still occasionally surface in more recent critical work on Grieg, often close to metaphors of landscape. The defence offered by Benestad and Schjelderup-Ebbe in their discussion of *Haugtussa*, for example, becomes potentially self-defeating in this regard. They begin positively, by acknowledging that 'Music historians sometimes speak disparagingly of Grieg as a miniaturist', but their subsequent claim, that '*The Mountain Maid* stands as eloquent proof of the fact that excellence is not a function of length or of demanding and restrictive forms. Great art can equally well be found in that which is small', only partially succeeds in creating new critical space for Grieg's work. They conclude that we have to understand *Haugtussa* as a large-scale cyclic work in order to appreciate its real aesthetic value. Hence, '*The Mountain Maid* should, if possible, always be performed as a complete cycle; and it should be judged as a totality, not merely as a collection of individual songs. Only so does the true greatness of his work come fully into view.'[13] The selective process by which Grieg arrived at the final structure of the cycle could be seen as a deliberately assimilative act: as Beryl Foster has observed, the narrative design of the set inevitably invites comparison with pre-existant canonic models such as Schubert's *Die schöne Müllerin* or Schumann's *Dichterliebe*.[14] However, Grieg's work need not be heard solely in terms of such canonic archetypes. The brief, almost telegrammatic quality of the songs, and their simple strophic design, could be equally well heard as both an intensified response to the text, and a reaction against what Grieg perceived as the distastefully 'anatomical' character of contemporary Austro-

---

[11] John Horton, *Edvard Grieg* (London: Dent, 1974), 196.

[12] Ibid., 198.

[13] Finn Benestad and Schjelderup-Ebbe, *Edvard Grieg*, 344–5.

[14] Foster 1990: 240–1. The most extensive discussion of *Haugtussa* as a cycle is to be found in James Massengale's '*Haugtussa*: from Garborg to Grieg', *Scandinavian Studies* 53 (1981), 131–53, the first article to consider the musical significance of the songs that Grieg chose to omit from his final published selection. This topic is returned to in Chapter 3 below.

German music.[15] Rather than being an indicator of technical deficiency, the individual scale of the songs has become a sign of greater compositional control and refinement. If reading *Haugtussa* as a 'small work' does not automatically constitute a 'downgrading' of its aesthetic or historical importance then, similarly, we need not feel uncomfortable according his folk-music arrangements a level of critical attention that has normally been reserved for the large-scale symphonic repertoire.

Grieg himself contributed significantly to his own reception as a miniaturist. Much of his correspondence complains about his perceived lack of skill in dealing with the large forms. These difficulties seem to have been particularly acute when Grieg was working on his String Quartet in the summer of 1877. In a letter to the Danish composer Gottfred Matthison-Hansen dated 13 August, for instance, he wrote:

> I must do something for my art. Day after day I become more
> dissatisfied with myself. Nothing I do pleases me, and even if
> I seem to have ideas there is neither fluency nor form when I
> proceed to the working out of anything greater. It is beyond
> reason – and yet I know where it comes from. It is due to lack
> of practice, and also to lack of technique, because I have never
> managed to get beyond composing in fits and starts. But there
> must now be an end of that. I want to battle myself through the
> larger forms, cost what it may. If I become mad in the process,
> you now know the reason.[16]

Both the String Quartet and other large-scale works, such as the planned opera on the life of Olav Trygvason with Bjørnstjerne Bjørnson that never materialised,[17] seemed to have assumed an almost totemic significance for

[15] See, for example, Grieg's letter to Johan Halvorsen written from Leipzig on 26 January 1897, barely six months after working on the *Haugtussa* songs: 'Down here art is all too much just art – and not nature. Therefore I long for the great nature back home, which more than anything is related to great art. German art now – especially the performed, perhaps – is either *School* art or the art of *guts*! Both lack the higher purer level and therefore smell as though they belong in the school room or anatomy chamber.' ('Det er dette hernede at Kunsten så altfor meget er bare Kunst – og ikke Natur. Derfor længes jeg mod den store Natur hjemme, der mere end noget Andet er i Slægt med den store Kunst. Tydskernes Kunst nu – især den udførende kanske – er enten *Skole*kunst eller *Indvolds*kunst! Begge savner det høje rene Niveau og lugter derfor således som det gjør i et Skolerum og Anatomikammer.') Quoted in Grieg, *Brev i utvalg 1862–1907*, ed. Finn Benestad, 2 vols (Oslo: Aschehoug, 1998), I, 357 (hereafter *Brev*).

[16] 'Noget må jeg gjøre for min Kunst. Dag for Dag bliver jeg mere utilfreds med mig selv. Intet af hvad jeg gjør, tilfredsstiller mig, og om jeg end synes, jeg har Tanker, så bliver der hverken Flugt eller Form, når jeg skrider til Uarbejdelse af noget Større. Det er tilat tabe Forstanden over – og jeg ved nok, hvoraf det kommer. Det er Mangel på Øvelse, altså Mangel på Teknik, fordi jeg aldrig har drevet det videre end til at komponere rykkevis. Men det skal nu have en Ende. Jeg vil kjæmpe mig igjennem de store Former, det koste hvad det vil. Bliver jeg forrykt på Vejen, så ved Du nu Grunden.' *Brev*, II, 145.

[17] Bjørnson began working on the libretto for *Olav Trygvason* in 1872, but finished little more than the first three scenes before breaking off from the project. See Benestad and Schjelderup-Ebbe, *Edvard Grieg*, 157–71, for a full account.

Grieg, a ritualised symbol of his supposed creative weakness. Later that month, having managed to complete the quartet, Grieg wrote of his need to 'tackle another chamber music work', as though referring to a fitness regime, and complained of 'too much folkiness'.[18] Such comments do not simply implicate Grieg in some of the less positive aspects of his own reception history. Rather, they point to a complex set of late-nineteenth-century critical standards in which national identity was often linked to a perceived inability to operate successfully within the mainstream tradition of large-scale chamber and orchestral music. They also serve to draw attention repeatedly to Grieg's own sense of peripheralisation, his concern that it is 'as though the mountains have no more to tell me',[19] an act of self-isolation in which metaphors of landscape and the natural world are once again prominent.

One of the central threads in this book is an attempt to relocate the idea of landscape in Grieg's music through analytical enquiry and by placing it in its historical context. The intention is to try to investigate landscape as a 'topic' in Grieg's music, and consider the wider issues that it raises for the interpretation of his work. The first chapter considers the role of folklorism in the formation and popularisation of an independent Norwegian cultural identity in the nineteenth century. Norwegian scholars such as Harald Herresthal have shown how folklorism and music became especially powerful nationalist discourses with broad popular appeal. The pioneering work of collectors such as Ludvig Mathias Lindeman provided a creative resource to which composers such as Halfdan Kjerulf and Edvard Grieg increasingly turned. Earlier nineteenth-century musicians, such as Waldemar Thrane and Ole Bull, had assimilated folk music in order to articulate a sense of popular Norwegian musical style, for consumption both in Norway and abroad. Grieg's achievement, in his folk-song settings op. 17 and op. 66, was to develop this folklorist discourse allied to an increasingly focused sense of structural syntax that ultimately points towards a more objective, writerly or modernist musical aesthetic. The chapter begins with a survey of musicological writing on nationalism, before proceeding to an analysis of the rise of folklorism in Norway in the nineteenth century. The discussion concludes with a brief comparative analysis of two of Grieg's earliest folk-song settings, the 'Springdans' and the 'Jølstring' from his *25 norske Folkeviser og Danser* ('Twenty-five Norwegian Folk Songs and Dances'), op. 17.

The second chapter argues that landscape in Grieg's music invokes dualities of gender, national and ethnic identity, authenticity and musical purity

---

[18] Letter to Matthison-Hansen, 10 February 1878, *Brev*, II, 147. Benestad suggests that the other chamber music work may have been a movement, Andante con moto, from a Piano Trio that Grieg never completed. The piece was published in the Grieg Critical Edition (*Samlede verker*, IX, 1978).
[19] 'som om Fjeldene Intet mere havde at fortælle mig', from a letter to Gerhard Schjelderup, 18 September 1903, *Brev*, I, 613.

which were especially urgent given contemporary debates about language and political independence in Norway at the end of the nineteenth century. Closer study of Grieg's *19 norske Folkeviser* ('19 Norwegian Folk Songs'), op. 66, suggests that landscape can also be understood from a more abstract perspective. In common with the music of other contemporary Nordic composers such as Sibelius and Carl Nielsen, landscape often functions as a static, contemplative musical object that plays a central role within the internal structural discourse of Grieg's work. For Grieg, landscape is not only concerned with pictorial evocation, but is a defining element of what W. Dean Sutcliffe has called his 'ideology or culture of sound'.[20]

Grieg's song-cycle, *Haugtussa*, based on the verse-novella by Arne Garborg, was written at a pivotal point in both Grieg's musical development and the emergence of an independent Norwegian cultural identity. Garborg was at the forefront of the language debate in the second half of the nineteenth century between *riksmål*, the official Danish-Norwegian language, and *nynorsk*, a linguistic synthesis of different western Norwegian dialects. The subject matter of Garborg's work is also significant: the story of Veslemøy, the mountain maid, draws on themes and topics from western Norwegian myth and the local landscape. Grieg's choice of text was far from neutral, and the composition of *Haugtussa* cannot be understood outside its immediate historical context as a form of *Heimatkunst*. But *Haugtussa* also invites other possible readings, which are explored in the third chapter. The final number 'Ved Gjætle-bekken' ('By Goat Brook'), in particular, responds to Grieg's notion of landscape as structure as explored in the previous chapter, by playing with through-composed and strophic musical forms and different levels of musical perspective. This chapter examines *Haugtussa*'s ambivalent relationship with both the folklorism promoted by Garborg, and Grieg's emergent sense of modernist syntax.

Grieg's most ambitious and radical response to Norwegian folk music is perhaps the *Slåtter*. Grieg wrote the pieces based on Hardanger-fiddle tunes, using transcriptions prepared by Johan Halvorsen from the playing of Knut Dahle, a fiddler from Telemark in southern Norway. Grieg himself pointed to a tension between different musical cultures: the mainstream Austro-German tradition of which he was essentially a product (through his training at the Leipzig conservatoire), and the Norwegian folk tradition to which he felt he more properly belonged. The creative tension in Grieg's music is not the result of an inability to meet the demands of large-scale symphonic form, as his critical reception has often suggested, but the product of a linguistic conflict between the deliberately primitivist treatment of musical material and an increasingly abstract sense of syntax and structure. The fourth chapter

[20] W. Dean Sutcliffe, 'Grieg's Fifth: The Linguistic Battleground of "Klokkeklang"', *The Musical Quarterly* 80/1 (Spring 1996), 161–81.

summarises the compositional history of the *Slåtter*, including Grieg's early attempts to notate Hardanger-fiddle music, and examines the intricate rhythmic characteristics of selected dances from the set. Commentators have often commented on the *Slåtter*'s rigorously modal harmonic language, but close reading of dances such as 'Knut Luråsen's Halling II' suggests a more complex relationship with diatonic and modal systems. Consideration will also be given to recent attempts to 'reclaim' the so-called 'Grieg Slåtter' by contemporary folk musicians and ethnomusicologists such as Sven Nyhus. Within Norway, at least, Grieg's most sustained engagement with a particular folk repertoire remains a problematic and controversial work.

As the reception of the *Slåtter* suggests, the influence of Grieg's folk-song arrangements on twentieth-century music has been ambivalent. Later Norwegian composers, such as Fartein Valen, sometimes sought to retreat or distance themselves from the seemingly overt nationalism of Grieg's work, whereas others, such as David Monrad Johansen and Geirr Tveitt, more readily embraced Grieg's enthusiasm for Norwegian folk music. Perhaps the most powerful example of Grieg's influence on later music can be seen in the work of Percy Grainger. Grainger first met Grieg during his tour of England in May 1906 and after Grieg's death in 1907 Grainger became one of the leading international exponents of his music. For Grainger, Grieg's music embodied the aesthetics of rugged, physical purity (allied to problematic assumptions regarding race, gender and linguistic character) that he perceived and admired in Nordic folk music. The final chapter considers two case studies, David Monrad Johansen and Grainger, and suggests that the influence of Grieg's work is more anxious and ambivalent than the simple notion of emulation might initially suggest. The role of landscape, both in writing about Grieg's work and in musical attempts to come to terms with his compositional legacy, here begins to assume a darker significance.

Thinking about the influence of Grieg's folk-music arrangements, particularly on composers after Grieg's death, brings us back to his tomb in the grounds of Troldhaugen. Grieg's grave crystallises some of the most powerful ways in which landscape and music have been related in his historical reception. It draws on mythic accounts of the origins of music in the sounds of the natural environment, locating his work in the western Norwegian topography. At the same time, however, through its resistance to conventional forms of representation, the grave points towards music's supposedly abstract, autonomous character. Finally, it reinforces the symbolic associations between images of landscape and death that are part of a broader European aesthetic tradition, in particular the representation of an earthly vision of Arcadia that is ultimately a reflection of human mortality. In its conjunction of the local, national and universal, the natural and the artificial, and the subjective and objective, Grieg's grave becomes a focal point for embedding his music's cultural meaning and for beginning to problematise the relationship between sound and landscape.

CHAPTER ONE

National Contexts: Grieg and Folklorism
in Nineteenth-Century Norway

Defining musical nationalism

Grieg has been widely acknowledged as a central figure in the emergence of a distinctively Scandinavian tone in nineteenth-century music. The precise nature of his 'Norwegianness', however, is less clearly understood. This is partly because the relationship between music and nationalism remains a problematic issue. As Celia Applegate has suggested, the difficulty is partly one of definition: 'the meanings of the key terms in the debate, nation and nationalism, are by no means self-evident, particularly when one descends to the ground of specific historical experience'.[1] In any such discussion, there is inevitably a tension between different levels of historical experience. To what extent can we regard Norway as a special case study, as opposed to part of a broader European phenomenon? Even more fundamentally, perhaps, it is unclear how such tensions could be articulated in Grieg's music, and how justified we are in retrospectively hearing Grieg's work as the individual expression of a collective Norwegian musical identity. Given the complexity of these questions, a brief survey of recent writing on nationalism and associated forms of cultural practice is necessary before we can proceed to more detailed consideration of folklorism and landscape in nineteenth-century Norway and their influence on Grieg's music. The aim is not to offer a comprehensive critique of the concept of national identity in music, since such a project is arguably beyond the scope of any single book. Rather, the intention is to create a clearer sense of critical and historical context that can form the basis for further discussion.

Given the prevalence of the term in historical scholarship, attempts to outline a single unified definition of nationalism have proved surprisingly difficult. As Anthony D. Smith has noted, 'at best the idea of the nation has

---

[1] Celia Applegate, 'How German is It? Nationalism and the Idea of Serious Music in the Early Nineteenth Century', *Nineteenth-Century Music* 21/3 (1998), 274–96, here 275.

11

appeared sketchy and elusive, at worst absurd and contradictory'.[2] Previous writers on nationalism such as Elie Kedourie have argued that the concept is essentially a modernist phenomenon.[3] For them, the emergence of the nation state as the primary unit of political organisation in the nineteenth century is ultimately attributable to both the notion of citizenhood (embodied in the Enlightenment ideals of *liberté*, *egalité* and *fraternité*) that underpinned the French Revolution, and the process of industrialisation that transformed the Western economy in the early half of the century. A crucial step in the advancement of this trend, Eric Hobsbawm maintains, was the nineteenth-century elision of two separate concepts: that of the nation (defined as a collective identity or community through a shared ethnic, linguistic or cultural heritage), and of the nation state (defined as a political unit with precise territorial boundaries). The nation state was seen as both an organic entity, the 'natural' development of human society along evolutionary lines that lent itself readily to metaphors of growth or flowering, and as a historical imperative, the supposedly logical outcome of a scientific process of progressive social advancement. The apparent contradiction between these positions, the natural (organic) and scientific (mechanistic), Hobsbawm suggests, was unproblematic for nineteenth-century nationalists.[4] Indeed, this dualism reflects what Benedict Anderson has described as the temporal nature of the nation state: 'If nation-states are widely conceded to be "new" and "historical", the nations to which they give political expression always loom out of an immemorial past, and, still more important, glide into a limitless future.'[5]

Central to the operation of this temporal vision, Anderson and Hobsbawm maintain, is a collective process of *invention*. For Anderson, the process of invention through which a nation imagines itself is one of the defining features of nationhood: 'communities are to be distinguished, not by their falsity/genuineness, but by the style in which they are imagined'.[6]

[2] Anthony D. Smith, *National Identity* (London: Penguin, 1991), 17.

[3] See, for example, Elie Kedourie, *Nationalism* (4th, expanded edn, Oxford: Blackwell, 1993), especially 2–4, and Ernest Gellner, *Nations and Nationalism* (Oxford: Blackwell, 1983).

[4] Eric Hobsbawm, *The Age of Capital: 1848–1875* (London: Abacus, 1997, repr. 2003). Hobsbawm observes (105): 'Surely the Englishman knew what being English was, the Frenchman, German, Italian or Russian had no doubt about their collective identity? Perhaps not, but in the age of nation-building this was believed to imply the logically necessary, as well as desirable transformations of "nations" into sovereign nation-states, with a coherent territory defined by the area settled by members of a "nation", which was in turn defined by its past history, its common culture, its ethnic composition and, increasingly, its language. But there is nothing logical about this implication. If the existence of differing groups of men, distinguishing themselves from other groups by a variety of criteria is both undeniable and as old as history, the fact that they imply what the nineteenth-century regarded as "nationhood" is not.'

[5] Benedict Anderson, *Imagined Communities: Reflections on the Origin and Spread of Nationalism* (rev. edn, London: Verso, 1991), 11.

[6] Anderson, *Imagined Communities*, 6.

Anderson argues that it is through the development of mass-media forms of communication, specifically print culture, that this national imagination can be disseminated. Certainly, it could be claimed that pamphleteering had as great an influence on the development of nineteenth-century nationalism in Norway as revolutionary politics or military action. For Hobsbawm, this process of invention is allied to the idea of a national tradition, 'a set of practices, normally governed by overtly or tacitly accepted rules and of a ritual or symbolic nature, which seek to inculcate certain values and norms of behaviour by repetition, which automatically implies continuity with the past',[7] and hence with the temporal vision of nationhood identified by Anderson. By demonstrating links with a historical past, Hobsbawm suggests, this process of invention gave rise to a nationalist historiography that simultaneously created a sense of community through a shared common heritage, and also provided a precedent or basis for the continued political existence of the nation state in the present. Furthermore, as Svetlana Boym has observed, the invention of a national tradition was in many senses a response to a sense of incompleteness: 'Invented tradition does not mean a creation *ex nihilo* or a pure act of social constructivism; rather, it builds on the sense of loss of community and cohesion and offers a comforting collective script for individual longing'.[8]

Many historians therefore agree that the idea of invention was crucial to the formation of national communities in the nineteenth century on many levels. This becomes particularly apparent as the nature and tone of nineteenth-century European nationalism shifted in the years following the 1848 revolutions. During this period, Hobsbawm suggests, the liberal concept of the nation state as a democratic union of individuals was replaced by a more radical (often right-wing) definition of the nation in ethnic or increasingly racialist terms.[9] In the light of this historical shift, not all commentators have felt comfortable with the idea of invention as an unmediated category for understanding the process of nation-building in the nineteenth century. Nina Witoszek, for example, argues that 'the postulate that nations are invented reduces history to an ideological construction that serves the particular interests of particular groups', since it is subject to insufficient ideological critique. 'Nationalism, in this reading, becomes a mere cognitive error to be exposed by analytical demystification.'[10] In other words, 'invention' can seem too neutral a term unless we ask who is doing

---

[7] Eric Hobsbawm and Terence Ranger (eds), *The Invention of Tradition* (Cambridge: Cambridge University Press, 1983, repr. 1995), 1.

[8] Svetlana Boym, *The Future of Nostalgia* (New York: Basic Books, 2001), 42–3.

[9] Eric Hobsbawm, *The Age of Empire: 1875–1914* (London: Abacus, 1995, repr. 2001), 146.

[10] Nina Witoszek, 'Nationalism, Postmodernity and Ireland', in *Nationalism in Small European Nations*, ed. Øystein Sørensen, KULT skriftserie no. 47 (Oslo: Noregs Forskningsråd, 1996), 101–21, here 104–5 (note).

the inventing, when, and what purpose their invention ultimately serves. This does not necessarily negate the concept altogether, but rather suggests that it should be employed with a greater sense of local context. Anthony Smith, similarly, claims that 'Nations and nationalism are no more "invented" than other kinds of culture, social organisation or ideology'.[11] The invention of a national tradition, Witoszek and Smith suggest, must therefore be understood as a political act, even as we draw attention to the fictitious or imagined nature of such nationalisms.

In spite of this emphasis on invention, nineteenth-century nationalism has conventionally been understood as a socio-economic phenomenon, a reading that has left relatively economically weak nations such as Norway out in the cold.[12] But both Smith and another recent commentator, John Hutchinson, have sought to shift critical attention away from what Friedrich Meinecke first described in 1908 as the formation of the *Staatsnation* (the nation state, or, more broadly, political nationalism), towards that of the *Kulturnation* (cultural nation).[13] For Hutchinson in particular, the distinction between these two kinds of nationalism is fundamental, 'for they articulate different, even competing conceptions of the nation'.[14] Hutchinson's argument rests on the observation that political nationalism has usually been seen as the more progressive, modernist form of the two, while cultural nationalism has been regarded as a more primitive or preliminary form of national expression. This has resulted in a form of historical peripheralism, since:

> The consensus is that cultural nationalism is a regressive force, a product of intellectuals from backward societies, who, when confronted by more scientifically advanced cultures, compensate for feelings of inferiority by retreating into history to claim descent from a once great civilisation. Somehow or other, cultural nationalism, it is argued, is functional for the formation of nations in such backward cultures, but in itself cannot shape their path to socio-political modernisation.[15]

Hence, Hutchinson concludes, the familiar historical narrative is that during the process of nation building, an initial period of 'cultural awakening' is followed by the goal of political self-determination. Cultural expression

---

[11] Smith, *National Identity*, 71.

[12] This is, arguably, the basis for most of Hobsbawm's work, and holds true equally for writers such as Hans Kohn and Gellner.

[13] Smith, *National Identity*, 8. See also Peter Alter's discussion in his *Nationalism*, trans. Stuart McKinnon-Evans (London: Edward Arnold, 1989), 14.

[14] John Hutchinson, 'Cultural Nationalism and Moral Regeneration', in Hutchinson and Anthony D. Smith (eds), *Nationalism: A Reader* (Oxford: Oxford University Press, 1994), 122. For an application of Hutchinson's model to aspects of late-nineteenth-century Norwegian nationalism, see Morten Haug Frøyen, 'Kulturell og politisk nasjonalisme hos Arne Garborg', in *Arne Garborgs kulturnasjonalisme*, KULT skriftserie no. 61 (Oslo: Noregs Forskningsråd, 1996), 7–103, especially 15–16.

[15] Hutchinson, 'Cultural Nationalism', 127.

therefore becomes subordinate to political will. Though, as Miroslav Hroch's work suggests,[16] this model may well apply broadly in many cases, including Norway, during the nineteenth century, Hutchinson argues that it is too one-dimensional to be an accurate reflection of all local historical contexts. Furthermore, the relative weighting of cultural and political forms of nationalism in much historical writing is a contentious one. 'Kohn and Gellner are surely right to identify cultural nationalism as a defensive response by educated elites to the impact of exogenous modernisation on existing status orders', Hutchinson suggests, 'but they are wrong to perceive the celebration of the folk as a retreat into an isolated agrarian simplicity free from all the disorders of civilisation.' Underlying the 'celebration of the folk' which dominates many forms of cultural nationalism, Hutchinson argues, lies 'first, a dynamic vision of the nation as high civilisation with a unique place in the development of humanity and, secondly, a corresponding drive to recreate this nation which, integrating the traditional and the modern on a higher level, will again rise to the forefront of world progress'.[17] Whether or not it succeeds, cultural nationalism therefore emerges as a progressive, modernist process, one concerned with precisely the dual temporal vision of nationhood identified by Anderson and not simply a regressive return to an anachronistic state of pre-industrialisation.

Hutchinson's analysis is useful for many reasons, not least for the way in which it decentralises much historical writing and allows us to re-evaluate the importance of forms of cultural practice, particularly music, that have not always received substantial attention in critical discussions of nationalism. But perhaps it also suggests why musicologists have often seemed reluctant to engage with nationalism as a subject of historical inquiry. If cultural nationalism has not been valued particularly highly by scholars working within the historical sciences, why should it occupy those working within the arts and humanities? Over and above such disciplinary differences, however, discussions of nationalism in musicology appear to have operated with a different set of political agendas. For Celia Applegate, the relative absence of discussions of musical nationalism in historical musicology reflects a nationalist bias within the discipline itself. In particular, she suggests, the alignment of territorial boundaries with the notion of a 'national school' common to much historical writing on music has reinforced the assumption that nineteenth-century nationalism was a

---

[16] See, for example, Miroslav Hroch, 'Specific Features of the Nation-Forming Process in the Circumstances of Small Nations', in Sørensen, *Nationalism*, 7–28 (especially 13–14). Hroch proposes a three-phase model of national self-determination for small nations during the nineteenth century, beginning with a process of self-identification as a community (through ethnic, linguistic or other factors), followed by a series of challenges (social demands; linguistic and cultural demands; political demands), and leading towards the achievement of full political independence.

[17] Hutchinson, 'Cultural Nationalism', 128.

stylistic category that only applied to countries outside the mainstream Austro-German canon. Joseph Kerman, she suggests, sees the 'nationalist blindness' of musicology as the legacy of both the discipline's origins in *Musikwissenschaft*, which presupposed and hence advanced the universality of Austro-German music, and the 'long reign of analytical musicology', a sub-discipline that has supposedly reified the Austro-German canon.[18] Even if Kerman's views now seem overly exaggerated or generalised (particularly as regards the influence and extent of such analytical positivism), there is nevertheless a strong sense that, despite recent developments in the field, familiar canonic patterns of historical thought are not easily deconstructed.

Though Applegate welcomes the extent to which recent scholars have drawn on theories of reception, postmodernism and literary criticism to dismantle earlier fixed notions of nationalism in music, she argues that nationalism is not always as standardised or as institutionalised as it initially appears. Furthermore, she finds much scholarship coloured by a prophetic pessimism in the light of future events: 'not all nationalisms are state-seeking, not all forms of nation-building are state-building or state-centred, and therefore, sometimes a symphony is just a symphony'.[19] Hence, nationalism in music need not be an absolute category, and is certainly never a stable one. Applegate does not wish to deny the fundamental importance of nationalism in nineteenth-century thought, but merely suggest that it is a more complex, and variant, phenomenon than we have often assumed. Nationalism can therefore be reconceived as 'a way of ordering experience, of looking at the world and making sense of one's place and identity in it – in Bourdieu's terms, a mode of "vision and division" of the world'.[20] For Applegate, nineteenth-century nationalism served an essentially localised function. In German-speaking lands the rise of institutions such as the public symphony concert and attempts to theorise the aesthetic of absolute music, both hitherto associated with the formation of a German musical nationalism, more locally reflected a crisis in the status of the professional musician. The aesthetic of musical autonomy that was fundamental to the idea of nineteenth-century Austro-German symphonic music 'referred back to the need, the desire, and the struggle for professional autonomy of the practicing musician'.[21] As we shall see, similar tensions underpinned the rise of folk music in nineteenth-century Norway, in particular the 'professionalisation' of folk musicians through the institution of the fiddle competitions, a development which adds a further dimension to Grieg's folk-song arrangements. But Grieg's music can also be regarded as a form

[18] Applegate, 'How German is It?', 277.
[19] Ibid., 280.
[20] Ibid., 281.
[21] Ibid., 286–7.

of 'vision and division'. Images of the Norwegian landscape in particular are both an integral part of his critical reception, and an aspect of his music's representation or meaning.

If Applegate's work suggests that nationalism can only be understood in the diversity of its local forms, a more unified genealogy of musical nationalism has nevertheless been presented by Richard Taruskin.[22] One of the principal aims of Taruskin's argument is to dismantle the hegemonic status of Austro-German music in writing about nineteenth-century musical history. For Taruskin, nationalism is properly defined as a 'condition or attitude'.[23] Similarly, the definition of nationhood upon which such a sense of collective identity is based is not a neutral or natural category, but (variously) takes account of linguistic, geological, geographical, political, cultural and religious boundaries. Nationalism is hence a secondary phenomenon, albeit one which achieves self-definition through a perception of shared communal experience (a perception that, as Taruskin notes, may itself be illusory). Taruskin traces a strong historical narrative from the origins of collective musical identity in renaissance Europe through the dissemination of printed vernacular song (a technologically driven change that echoes Anderson's work on the importance of mass media) to the supposed dissolution of musical nationalism following the end of the Cold War. But the focus of his discussion falls on the emergence of cultural nationalism in the context of German Romanticism, and the ideological factors brought into play by the rise of musical folklorism. It was the search for an authentic form of national musical expression, allied to a vertically defined linguistic or ethnic community, Taruskin argues, which led nationalism from being associated with a democratic liberalism at the start of the nineteenth century, towards more exclusive right-wing ideologies of musical nationhood after 1848. This shift, in which Wagner's writing on music played an important role, parallels the darkening tone of nineteenth-century political nationalism identified by Hobsbawm, and offers a powerful example of the way in which cultural nationalism became a political act.

Though Taruskin turns to Russian music as a counter-example, there is a danger that his attempt to unpack the nationalist assumptions that underpin the myth of German musical universality inadvertently reinforces the geocentrism that his critique seeks to deconstruct. Certainly, the music of 'peripheral' nations such as Spain, Finland or Norway does not figure prominently in his account. As a result, some sense of their local contexts,

[22] Richard Taruskin, 'Nationalism', in *The Revised New Grove Dictionary of Music and Musicians*, ed. Stanley Sadie and John Tyrrell, XVII (Basingstoke: Macmillan, 2001), 687–706. Note the use of the singular in the title of Taruskin's entry; Jim Samson prefers the plural form in the first section of his article, 'Nations and Nationalism', in *The Cambridge History of Nineteenth-Century Music*, ed. Samson (Cambridge: Cambridge University Press, 2001), 568–600.
[23] Taruskin, 'Nationalism', 689.

and hence of the full diversity of musical nationalisms, is inevitably absent. Furthermore, though Taruskin argues persuasively that the reception of Tchaikovsky reveals how such canonic patterns of critical thought have become embedded in musicological writing, there is little discussion of the way in which musicians from smaller nations on the 'edge' of Europe oriented themselves towards perceived mainstream centres of musical development. From this perspective, it becomes difficult to conceive nationalism as a process of dialogue in which notions of periphery and mainstream are not presented as absolute historical categories but developed as part of a more discursive sense of cultural practice.[24] A stronger sense of this dialectical relationship between perceived centre and periphery is reflected in Carl Dahlhaus's writing on musical nationalism, particularly his essay 'Nationalism and Music' in the collection *Between Romanticism and Modernism*.[25] As James Hepokoski has observed, Dahlhaus's work dates from a period when writing about nationalism and music history in Germany seemed especially problematic.[26] Significantly, Dahlhaus approaches the subject from the opposite end to that adopted by Hobsbawm and most other historians, not seeking to establish a single unified definition of the nation from the outset, but rather stressing its ideological character. The fact that the nineteenth-century nation cannot be reduced to a single definable set of criteria in no way diminishes the importance of nationalism as a historical idea, Dahlhaus maintains, since 'ideas are historical facts too', a remark directed as much towards certain kinds of historical or analytical positivism as post-Marxist theory.[27] For Dahlhaus, Johann Gottfried Herder's idea of the *Volksgeist* (spirit of the people) provided a means of justifying or accounting for the sense of collective identity fundamental to the formation of nationhood. Particularly when allied to a Hegelian notion of historical self-determination in nineteenth-century historiography, the *Volksgeist* hypothesis became a powerful model for the expression, or celebration, of national identity: the Romantic image of the nation state as organic being identified by Hobsbawm and others. But, for Dahlhaus, the *Volksgeist* hypothesis also introduced a

[24] Jim Samson writes ('Nations and Nationalism', 591): 'Historical justice is hard to come by as we assess the cultures of Europe's periphery. We may skew the plot in favour of the values of a dominant culture, writing a kind of assimilationist history which draws the more highly valued figures into a canon of European romanticism or modernism, while ignoring measures of difference. Alternatively (and this is probably the greater danger) we may fetishise what we perceive to be the difference. In either case we run the risk of undervaluing, or misunderstanding, the constitutive role of Western Europe as an historical "presence" in those cultures which sought to establish their separateness. Dialogues with the West were fundamental to the quest for a voice in the East, the South-east, the North, and the far West.'

[25] *Between Romanticism and Modernism: Four Studies in the Music of the Later Nineteenth Century*, trans. Mary Whittall (Berkeley: University of California Press, 1980, repr. 1989), 79–101.

[26] James Hepokoski, 'The Dahlhaus Project and its Extra-Musicological Sources', *Nineteenth-Century Music* 14/3 (1991), 221–46, especially 222–3.

[27] Carl Dahlhaus, 'Nationalism and Music', 79.

fundamental tension between individual expression and collective will, since 'according to this idea, it was the spirit of the people of Norway that demanded musical expression in and through Edvard Grieg, and not Grieg (as an individual rather than as the representative of his nation) who first created what is thought to be quintessentially Norwegian in music'.[28] Hence, Dahlhaus asks, 'do individual characteristics proceed out of the national substance, or is the concept of what is national formed by generalisation on the basis of individual characteristics?' As a problem of historical reception, this tension is probably unresolvable. It is difficult to conceive of a study, however comprehensive, that could prove conclusively whether Grieg's critical status as Norway's 'national composer' was entirely either *sui generis* or retrospective: Grieg's adoption of elements from Norwegian folk music, from this perspective, only serves to complicate the issue.

The tension between the individual and the collective need not be resolved at the level of reception in any case, since, for Dahlhaus,

> A distinction between national style as a musical fact and nationalism as a creed imposed on music from without is far too crude to be an accurate reflection of the historical and aesthetic reality. For a musical fact is not something pieced together from precise, unambiguous components but the result of the categorical formation of an acoustic substratum, a formation which presupposes or includes aesthetic and ideological elements as well as structural and syntactical factors.[29]

It is nevertheless necessary to pause and consider exactly what Dahlhaus intends by such terms as 'acoustic substratum', or what meaning he seeks to attach to structural or syntactical factors (and what precisely those structural factors constitute). Recent musicology, after all, has become increasingly suspicious of overly determined readings that emphasise solely details of musical structure or syntax, or documentary historical evidence, without some kind of critical interrogation. Dahlhaus suggests that the problem is partly one of intention:

> If a composer intended a piece of music to be national in character and the hearers believe it to be so, that is something which the historian must accept as an aesthetic fact, even if stylistic analysis – the attempt to 'verify' the aesthetic premise by reference to musical features – fails to produce any evidence.[30]

Nationalism therefore cannot be identifed by systematic analysis alone. Tomi Mäkelä argues that 'almost any stylistic feature can be nationalistic,

[28] Ibid., 81–2.
[29] Ibid., 85–6.
[30] Ibid., 86–7.

if a composer uses it consciously and for nationalist reasons. Nationalism has to be regarded as a category of reception and intention rather than as something technically musical: nationalism is always primarily an ideology which may have artistic consequences.'[31] Even here, however, issues of authorial control and transmission prevent any attempt to reach a definite point of conclusion. How can we verify what Grieg's intentions were, for example, when he adapted Norwegian folk music in his arrangements? Furthermore, though a history of nineteenth-century listening might seem like an attractive means of identifying how audiences understood national character in Grieg's work, it cannot ultimately provide a fully contextual account of the way in which Grieg's music was heard without betraying some element of our own contemporary critical perspective.

Dahlhaus also identifies other problems within musical constructions of nationalism that are relevant to Grieg's folk-song arrangements. Laying temporarily aside the issues of intentionality identified above, Dahlhaus turns to the status of folk-music borrowing in art-music contexts as a carrier of national meaning. At one level, Dahlhaus argues, folk music simply serves in such works as a sign of difference or alterity, and is not linked to any particular idea of nationhood. 'When it comes to invoking or imitating a model', Dahlhaus argues, 'folklorism – though national in inspiration – is no different in principle from the exoticism or historicism of the nineteenth century.'[32] Hence,

> It is not clear how far the 'ethnic raw material' in which nineteenth-century nationalism purported to discover the roots of national musical styles belongs of its original nature in the category of national at all. The assumption that folk music is always and above all the music of a nation – a view which was taken to be self-evidently true in the nineteenth century – is questionable and ill-founded.[33]

Though presumably derived from the same sense of collective identification as Herder's *Volksgeist* hypothesis, the category of folk music itself, Dahlhaus implies, is a potentially contestable one. It functions as an 'exotic' element only by sounding against a normative universal style, a definition that, as we shall see, is itself the product of a particular nationalist perspective. As Dahlhaus notes, such 'universality' was ultimately the prerogative of the 'central' musical nations, a point that forms the basis for Taruskin's discussion of musical nationalism. By the same definition, however, fixed distinctions

---

[31] Tomi Mäkelä, 'Towards a Theory of Internationalism, Europeanism, Nationalism and "Co-nationalism" in Twentieth-Century Music', in *Music and Nationalism in Twentieth-Century Great Britain and Finland*, ed. Tomi Mäkelä (Hamburg: von Bockel, 1997), 10.
[32] Dahlhaus, 'Music and Nationalism', 99.
[33] Ibid., 92.

between folk and art musics are also collapsible, since they similarly rely upon the assumed authority of one musical style over another: the concept of the folk is no less constructed or imagined than other nationalist categories. The notion of an 'ethnic raw material', for example, is itself a mediated one. At this point, Dahlhaus again shifts attention from problems of intention (such as who decides where to draw the boundaries between the normative and the exotic, or between folk and art musics), to the idea of reception as aesthetic arbiter:

> To write off the nationalist interpretation of folk music as an aesthetic error which is now being set right by empirical research would also be a mistake: a misuse of the categories. Aesthetically it is perfectly legitimate to call bagpipe drones and sharpened fourths typically Polish when they occur in Chopin and typically Norwegian when they occur in Grieg, even if some historians are irritated by the paradox of something which is common to national music generally and yet is felt to be specifically national in the consciousness of the individual nations.[34]

In other words, musical context becomes the most important parameter, even if it remains unclear exactly how far or wide such contexts should be drawn. It is not certain, for example, whether bagpipe drones and sharpened fourths always denote Norwegianness in Grieg's music, or whether their meaning remains constant across all of Grieg's work. Dahlhaus suggests that all folk-music references at least share a sense of archaism, of removal from contemporary art music, so that their 'exotic' quality is one of temporality (the listener's perception of the passing of time) as much as the result of their modal or harmonic characteristics. The implications of this pattern of temporal disjunction for understanding Grieg's folk-song arrangements are powerful, and will be explored further below. Such archaism, Dahlhaus maintains, is linked to nationalism through a 'denial of the universal'. It also reinforces Anderson's definition of the nation as both pre-ordained and natural through a sense of the musical work as something both primordial (through its association with the folk) and simultaneously progressive. 'Local reinterpretation in this fashion', Dahlhaus argues, 'is a historical process and creates its own aesthetic legitimacy.'[35] But, frustratingly, it is not clear exactly how or why this legitimisation is achieved. Is it purely a function of reception, or achieved through what might be called structural means? Though much of Dahlhaus's argument suggests the former (that music becomes 'national' only through a process of critical reception), his discussion ultimately turns more towards the latter. Hence, Dahlhaus claims, 'the harmonic style of

---

[34] Ibid., 95.
[35] Ibid., 97.

Tristan, governed by the dominant and coloured by a chromaticism which derives from harmonic ambiguity, is confronted, in works like Grieg's *Slåtter*, with a modally based harmonic style and with a chromaticism determined primarily by melodic, contrapuntal features'.[36] Here, the opposition of *Tristan* and the *Slåtter* is no less retrospective, or artificial, than that of folk and art-music elements within op. 72. And the issues of intentionality and reception are no less problematic when we consider Grieg's sense of his own peripheral relationship with both Wagner's work and Norwegian folk music.

Potentially therefore, Dahlhaus's analysis collapses the binary oppositions on which many critical readings of nationalism rest, since it suggests that such dualisms cannot remain stable or balanced beyond their immediate historical context. Dahlhaus's work nonetheless provides a vital framework for further investigation, and remains a central thread throughout much of this book. In particular, focusing on the tensions inherent within constructions of musical nationalism, between individual versus collective musical expression, universal versus local models of musical style, and between intention and reception, opens up a series of interpretative perspectives on Grieg's work that can yield fruitful results. And even if, ultimately for Dahlhaus and other more recent writers, nationalism in music becomes an infinite vanishing point rather than an absolute historical category, this sense of contingency can only benefit scholarly discussion of Grieg's folk-music arrangements as we seek to place them in a broader critical context and address the topic of landscape.

Music, folklorism and Norwegian national identity

Most commentators on nineteenth-century European nationalisms agree that sustained interest in folk culture dates from the late eighteenth century under the influence of Enlightenment thinking. A 'return to the folk' was seen as an idyllic, idealised state of community achieved through a purer state of individuality. But the perceived links between folklore and nationalism which developed in the nineteenth century were more philosophically and ideologically driven. Hegel, like Herder, believed that nationhood was expressed through a common spirit which articulated a powerful sense of community through shared language, folk customs and a profound sense of spiritual belonging. This Hegelian model appealed to a higher level form of nationhood, founded on ideals of universality and shared culture. Interest in folk culture was also driven by more localised political agendas, through struggles for national independence and cultural self-determination. It seems ironic given this trajectory that folklorism began as essentially an

[36] Ibid., 97.

22

antiquarian or elite aesthetic pursuit. Jim Samson observes that 'it was in the realm of high culture rather than folk culture that the spirit of nationalism made itself felt', and that 'folk culture had in reality little, if anything, to do with the nation, though it was often expressive of a sense of place: a locality'.[37] The Romantic obsession with folklorism was initially expressed through the work of folk collectors such as Arnim von Brentano, the Brothers Grimm, and, in Norway, the fairy tales of Asbjørnsen and Moe. But by the 1840s folklorism had become part of a more explicitly nationalist discourse adopted by various groups across Europe, including Norway and Finland, in order to serve specifically political agendas. There is a further irony that folklorism began as a primarily Germanic pursuit, part of a broader shift towards creation of a unified German state. Although towards the end of the nineteenth century folklorism was associated more with nations on the 'periphery' of Europe (Eastern Europe, Russia and Scandinavia), Øyvind Østerud notes that

> The early Norwegian folklorists, in search of the 'hidden Norway', were explicitly inspired by European, particularly German, Romanticism. This meant more than a model of scholarship. It also implied an interpretation of the substance, meaning that Norwegian folklore, myths and fairy tales had absorbed, moulded and adapted foreign cultural influences to a Norwegian context. It was the configuration that made non-national inputs Norwegian, and the early cultural nationalists were quite explicit about these relationships.[38]

The adoption of a Germanic mode of discourse, in other words, can be understood retrospectively as integral to a Norwegian process of self-definition. The assimilation of an apparently extra-territorial discourse itself became a nationalist strategy. Indeed, the tension between such assimilationist and isolationist elements within Norwegian nationalism only became increasingly intense as the nineteenth century progressed. As Østerud observes, one of the later pioneers of Norwegian nationalism, the linguist Moltke Moe, who coined the term 'the national breakthrough', cited Rousseau, the Ossianic ballads of James MacPherson, Herder and the Brothers Grimm as important 'foreign pioneers' for the creation of a distinctively Norwegian national cultural practice.[39]

The rise of folklorism in nineteenth-century Norway can therefore be seen as part of a larger narrative of social and political self-determination

---

[37] Samson, 'Nations and Nationalism', 570.

[38] Øyvind Østerud, 'Norwegian Nationalism in a European Context', in Sørensen, *Nationalism*, 29–39, here 31.

[39] Ibid., 31. The title of Moe's general survey of Norwegian literature was 'Det nationale gjennembrud og dets mænd' ('The National Breakthrough and Its Men').

that reflects many of the tensions in other comparable European states. But what were the local factors that defined Norwegian nationalism? The idea of a sovereign Norwegian nation state arguably dated back to the early medieval period, but at the start of the nineteenth century Norway had been a Danish principality for over four hundred years (since the Union of Kalmar in 1389). Norway was therefore peripheralised on at least two levels: both from continental Europe through its relative geographical isolation, and as a subject of the Danish crown. The drive for an independent Norwegian cultural and political identity in the nineteenth century became what Østerud calls a 'counter-culture', or form of resistance.[40] Following Denmark's support for Napoleon, Norway was ceded to Sweden at the treaty of Kiel in 1814. Though the Danish crown prince Christian Frederik made an abortive attempt to create an independent Norwegian assembly and declared a 'free, independent and indivisible realm' in the democratic Eidsvoll constitution of 17 May, Norway only achieved full political independence in 1905. During this period, Norway did not undergo the same large-scale industrialisation as other major European nation states, and it was not directly involved in any significant military conflict, though Sweden's refusal to intercede in the 1864 Schleswig-Holstein war between Denmark and Prussia was the cause of significant political unease within Norway. It was this event in particular, as Dag Thorkildsen notes, which revealed the moderate idea of a Pan-Scandinavian alliance of Nordic states as little more than a political fiction.[41]

The other major factor potentially affecting the development of Norwegian cultural nationalism in the nineteenth century was the process of large-scale emigration, which had a significant impact, particularly in rural areas. Norway again seems comparable with other 'peripheralised' European nations such as Ireland, which suffered similar patterns of population loss. Hobsbawm suggests that approximately two-thirds of the population increase in Norway during the middle of the nineteenth century emigrated to the United States, mostly from rural districts in southern and western Norway.[42] As Chris Goertzen notes, over 29,000 Norwegians emigrated in one single year alone (1882), a trend that was unsustainable over the long term given the small-scale family basis of the Norwegian rural economy.[43] For Hobsbawm, emigration had an ambivalent effect upon the development of nationalism in such countries, serving as both a stimulant to modernist

---

[40] Ibid., 34–5.
[41] Dag Thorkildsen, 'Skandinavismen – en historisk oversikt', in *Nasjonal identitet – et kunstprodukt?*, ed. Øystein Sørensen, KULT skriftserie no. 30, Nasjonal identitet no. 5 (Oslo: Noregs Forskningsråd, 1994), 191–209.
[42] Hobsbawm, *The Age of Capital*, 230.
[43] Chris Goertzen, *Fiddling for Norway: Revival and Identity* (Chicago: Chicago University Press, 1997), 6.

progress (in an attempt to arrest perceived social-economic decline), and inspiring a reactionary celebration of the folk in a mood of nostalgic retro-spection. Hobsbawm suggests cautiously that:

> The mutual aid and protection of emigrants may have contributed to the growth of nationalism in their nations, but it is not enough to explain it. However, in so far as it rested on an ambiguous and double-edged nostalgia for the old ways emigrants had left behind, it had something in common with a force which undoubtedly fostered nationalism at home, especially in the smaller nations. This was neo-traditionalism, a defensive or conservative reaction against the disruption of the old social order by the advancing epidemic of modernity, capitalism, cities and industry, not forgetting the proletarian socialism which was their logical outcome.[44]

Elements of neo-traditionalism and conservatism can certainly be traced in late nineteenth-century Norway, not least through the political ascendancy of a party representing the interests of rural smallholders. But the election victory of *Venstre* in 1882 was a crucial step forward in the advancement of Norwegian independence, and coincided with the most intense period of emigration.[45] Nevertheless, Hobsbawm's analysis of cultural national-ism seems overly pessimistic and one-sided. Not all folklorisms need be as inward-looking as his comments imply. Nor, despite their celebration of eth-nic and linguistic purity, were such movements entirely right-wing in politi-cal orientation. John Hutchinson's call for a more balanced view of forms of cultural nationalism which sought 'to challenge ossified political and cultural elites and to inspire a rising educated generation to campaign to "recreate" the idea of the nation as a living principle in the lives of people'[46] stresses the extent to which such movements were also emancipatory. In Norway this meant a political shift away from the *Embedsmannstat* ('civil-serv-ant state'), a term coined by Jens Arup Seip to describe the conservative liberalism which dominated the first half of the nineteenth century,[47] and the elevation of a folk culture which was both progressive and retrospective in outlook.

Recent Norwegian scholarship has stressed the centrality of folklorism to the definition and popularisation of an independent Norwegian cultural identity in the nineteenth century. Harald Herresthal's rich historical account of nineteenth-century Norwegian music, for example, has shown how folklorism and music became especially powerful nationalist discourses

---

[44] Hobsbawm, *The Age of Empire*, 155.
[45] T. K. Derry, *A Modern History of Norway, 1814–1972* (Oxford: Clarendon, 1973), 206–11.
[46] Hutchinson, 'Cultural Nationalism', 124.
[47] Øystein Sørensen, 'The Development of a Norwegian National Identity during the Nineteenth Century: Some Aspects and Problems', in *Nordic Paths to National Identity in the Nineteenth Century*, ed. Sørensen, KULT skriftserie no. 22, Nasjonal identitet no. 1 (Oslo: Noregs Forskningsråd, 1994), 17.

with broad popular appeal.[48] The idea of 'national song' was vital to the formation of this discourse. Herresthal identifies *Det norske Selskab*, a group of students and intellectuals that met in Copenhagen cafés in the 1770s whose songs embodied both nostalgia for the homeland and a form of resistance to the political domination of Denmark in Norwegian culture, as among the earliest expressions of Norwegian cultural difference.[49] After 1814, however, the issue of national song appears to have risen up the political agenda. Lars Roverud's account of music-making in Norway, *Et Blik på Musikens Tilstand i Norge* ('A Look at the Condition of Music in Norway', 1815), paralleled developments in contemporary German periodicals which argued that music education could become a form of national self-improvement, and hence both emancipatory and creative. Roverud was scandalised that Norway should have to rely on imported musicians (particularly from the Royal Chapel in Denmark) when he believed there was so much indigenous talent, especially among the rural farming class (*bondestanden*). He argued that national song should celebrate Norwegian nature, as well as the notions of fellowship and community.[50] These ideals were elevated in songs such as Henrik Anker Bjerregaard's text, *Sønner av Norge* ('Sons of Norway') to Christian Blom's melody, the first 'national hymn', which became a popular hit at Constitution Day celebrations on 17 May, one of the most symbolically powerful ritual events in the Norwegian national calendar.[51]

If nationalism in Norway can be understood as emancipatory, creative and ritualistic, features common to other forms of nationalism in nine-teenth-century Europe, it also shared their preoccupation with images of landscape and nature. The nationalist desire for local colour finds one of its earliest expressions in Norwegian music in Waldemar Thrane's *syngespil* (comic opera), *Fjeldeventyret* ('The Mountain Tale'), to a libretto by H. A. Bjerregaard (1825). Thrane had studied in Paris with Anton Reicha between 1817 and 1818, during which time he had the opportunity to acquaint him-self with the latest developments in French opera; *Fjeldeventyret*, composed on his return to Norway, was Thrane's only stage work. Herresthal and Nils Grinde accord *Fjeldeventyret* a privileged place in the historical development of Norwegian music.[52] Herresthal writes that 'both contemporaries and

[48] Harald Herresthal, *Med spark i gulvet og quinter i bassen: musikalske og politiske bilder fra nasjonalromantikkens gjennombrudd i Norge* (Oslo: Universitetsforlaget, 1993).
[49] Ibid., 14.
[50] Ibid., 19.
[51] Ibid., 22–3. On the quasi-religious character of ritual in the formation of national identities, see Jim Samson, 'Nations and Nationalism', 570. Samson suggests: 'Like its sacred counterpart, the nation needed its ceremonies, anthologies and its validating myths', which gave rise to events such as the Constitution Day ceremonies in Norway.
[52] Herresthal, *Med spark i gulvet*, 30–7; Nils Grinde, *A History of Norwegian Music*, trans. William H. Halvorson and Leland B. Sateren (Lincoln: University of Nebraska Press, 1991, originally published as *Norsk Musikkhistorie* (Oslo: Universitetsforlaget, 1981)), 126–31.

following generations experienced it as a breakthrough for Norwegian composition and the first convincing attempt to give Norwegian music a national colour'.[53] Prominent among such contemporary accounts of *Fjeldeventyret's* perceived Norwegianness was an anonymous article entitled 'Nogle Ord om Nationalmusik' ('Some Words on National Music'), published in a Norwegian periodical three years after Thrane's death in 1828.[54] For Herresthal, the article reveals that the question of national music 'was an important topic of debate, and that the opinions could turn from cultural openness to national isolation'.[55] The article may have been intended partly as a tribute to a newly deceased composer, but it also served (more importantly) as an aesthetic discourse on the nature of Norwegian music. The essay's lament that 'had Thrane lived, and our poets worked in association with him, he would surely have given us many musical works, which would have been an adornment for our Fatherland' is not merely a monument or memorial but betrays an overwhelming desire for the creation of a national musical tradition.[56] Nevertheless, for Herresthal the historical status of *Fjeldeventyret* as a 'national work' is potentially ambivalent, 'since musicologists from our time experience the stylistic features from the period's European music as more prominent than the typically Norwegian'.[57] The solution to this problem, Herresthal suggests, is to understand *Fjeldeventyret* in its historical context:

> The characteristic feature of Thrane's technique was that he let the townspeople sing in a European tonal language, while the mountain people were characterised with the help of *lur* [mountain horn] tones, *hallings* and folk-like melodies. This form of 'local colour' is a technique we can find in both Mozart and the work of Thrane's teacher, Anton Reicha. Thrane had not therefore sought to create a Norwegian musical language throughout his *syngespil*. In the same way that Bjerregaard had used Norwegian dialect within the Danish language where it seemed natural, Thrane had created a corresponding local colour within the contemporary European musical style. For conditions at the time, the Norwegianness in *Fjeldeventyret* was more than sufficient.[58]

[53] 'både samtiden og de følgende generasjoner opplevde som et gjennombrudd for den norske tonekunst og som det første overbevisende forsøk på å gi norsk musikk en nasjonal farge.' Herresthal, *Med spark i gulvet*, 31.

[54] *Almindeligt norsk Maanedskrift* 11/12 (1831), 468–98. The article is discussed in Herresthal, *Med spark i gulvet*, 31–5.

[55] 'nasjonalmusikk var et viktig debatt-tema og at synspunktene kunne svige fra kulturell åpenhet til nasjonal avsondring.' Herresthal, *Med spark i gulvet*, 31.

[56] 'Havde Thrane levet, og vore Digtere arbeidet i Forening med ham, så havde han sikkerligen givet os flere musikalske Værker, der vilde have været en Prydelse for vort Fædreland.', 'Nogle Ord', 484 (quoted in Herresthal, *Med spark i gulvet*, 31).

[57] 'fordi musikkforskerne i vår tid opplever stiltrekkene fra datidens europeiske musikktradisjoner som mer fremtredende enn de typisk norske.' Herresthal, *Med spark i gulvet*, 30.

[58] 'Det karakteristiske ved Thranes teknikk er at han lar bybefolkningen synge på et europeisk tonespråk,

The apparently radical sense of Norwegianness advanced in *Fjeldeventyret* was therefore in fact a dialogue between Norwegian and European elements, a pattern that was to remain a constant theme in Norwegian music throughout the nineteenth century. And, as we shall see in later chapters, this polarisation of European and Norwegian musical styles foreshadows one of the fundamental structural tensions in Grieg's work.

This dialogue, between Norwegian and European elements, reveals itself in *Fjeldeventyret* through the *syngespil*'s play with operatic convention. Two numbers in particular stand out: the Overture, and 'Aagots Fjeldsang' ('Aagot's Mountain Song') (Exx. 1.1 and 1.2). Both numbers begin with the stylised sound of the *lur*, a folk horn traditionally used for herding calls on high mountain pastures.[59] The pitch material associated with this instrument is largely triadic, although the Overture hints at a modally variant fourth scale degree (in bar 3, for example), a familiar sign of ethnic 'otherness' in Western music even in 1825. 'Aagots Fjeldsang' is more remarkable, since the *lur* prelude is followed by an extended unaccompanied *kulokk* (cow-lure or herding song), where the modally variant interval is much more prominent and exposed.[60] The function of Aagot's *kulokk* is to intensify

Example 1.1. Waldemar Thrane: *Fjeldeventyret*, overture

mens fjellfolket karakteriseres ved hjelp av lurtoner, hallinger og folketonepregede melodier. Denne form for «couleur locale» er en teknikk vi både kan finne hos Mozart og i verker av Waldemar Thranes lærer, Anton Reicha. Thrane har altså ikke forsøkt å skape et gjennomgående norsk tonespråk i syngespillet sitt. På samme måte som Bjerregaard innenfor det danske språk benyttet norsk dialekt der det falt naturlig, skapte Thrane en tilsvarende lokalkoloritt innenfor tidens europeiske musikkstil. For datidens kondisjonerte var norskeheten i *Fjeldeventyret* mer enn nok.' Ibid., 31.

[59] See Grinde, *A History of Norwegian Music*, 87.

[60] An interesting musical detail is the boundary play around the pitch cells $g\sharp^2$–a^2. Though the $g\sharp$ is dissonant, it is left unresolved at the end of the *kulokk*.

the sense of distance, the impression of open space conveyed both by the music's literal spatial displacement (it is sung offstage, 'udenfor Scenen', and presumably remains hidden from view), and by its associations with the Norwegian countryside. Other landscape devices include the music's static harmonic texture, the lack of dynamic harmonic movement serving as a

Example 1.2. Waldemar Thrane: *Fjeldeventyret*, 'Aagots Fjeldsang'

conventionalised symbol of the pastoral, and the series of repeated triadic calls that suggest a mountain echo. The *kulokk* then frames a simple strophic arietta in contrasting antique style (in the stern 'Nordic' key of D minor),[61] in which Aagot sings of night drawing on and her lost love. As Herresthal suggests above, both here and in the preceding *kulokk*, Bjerregaard employs dialect, rather than official Danish-Norwegian, to represent Aagot's peasant origins, adding an additional layer of supposed realism to the opera's construction of Norwegianness.

The evocation of local colour in *Fjeldeventyret* satisfied two requirements: first, the need to provide an authentic sense of location for a specifically Norwegian audience in order to intensify (or respond to) nascent feelings of nationhood; and second, to engage in a wider European operatic discourse in which such local colour had become a conventional expectation. The *kulokk* which frames 'Aagots Fjeldsang' is also a *ranz des vaches*: a musical form that could serve as both indigenously Norwegian and, by the early nineteenth century, as a more cosmopolitan European image of the 'folk'. By appealing to this cosmopolitan spirit, the *kulokk* transcended the Danish colonial influence that was felt by many to pervade Norwegian musical life during the *Embedsmannstat*. Furthermore, it could also be heard to embody the democratic ideals of individual freedom and liberty with which the *ranz des vaches* was associated, hence reinforcing its role as a symbol of an independent Norwegian identity.[62] For Rousseau, whose *Dictionnaire de musique* provided the most standard reference source for the melody, the *ranz des vaches* was an idealised type of folk utterance, in which 'the music does not act exactly like Music, but as a sign to aid memory'.[63] Its function in *Fjeldeventyret* is not just to create a sense of spatial distance, therefore, but also to open up a sense of temporal space, which, through feelings of nostalgia or retrospection, is ultimately connected with the idea of longing for a (Norwegian) homeland. This sense of displacement is a common property of the Romantic landscape, one upon which Grieg's music particularly dwells. But it also invokes the dual temporality which Benedict Anderson and others have identified as a crucial component of nineteenth-century nationalist discourses: the belief that the nation was both a primordial site of shared origins and a future state of political community. Musically, however, the shift in temporality is arguably achieved less through the *kulokk*'s individual characteristics, the use of dialect, modal inflections and folk instruments or idioms, but rather through its sense of difference. As Dahlhaus's analysis of musical nationalisms

---

[61] The author of 'Some Words on National Music' maintained that D minor was Norway's 'fundamental tone' (*grunntone*), whereas Italian music was properly in A minor (Herresthal, *Med spark i gulvet*, 35).
[62] For a discussion of the *ranz* in its nineteenth-century French context, see Benjamin Walton, 'Looking for the Revolution in Rossini's *Guillaume Tell*', *Cambridge Opera Journal* 15/2 (2003), 127–51, especially 135–9.
[63] Quoted by Walton, 'Looking for the Revolution', 138.

suggests, its affective function is ultimately the result of its exotic quality, not the specificity of its local colour.

The sense of Norwegianness in *Fjeldeventyret* is therefore constructed on a series of binary dualisms: the opposition of peasant dialect and the official Danish-Norwegian language; the stylised evocation of Norwegian folk music with nature associations versus a normative contemporary European musical discourse; a rural folk milieu versus an urban audience; retrospective versus prospective visions of Norwegian nationhood; isolationist versus assimilationist nationalist tendencies. The fact that these oppositions are unable to be resolved or synthesised into a single unified definition does not detract from their potency as symbols of Norwegian musical identity. As the anonymous author of 'Some Words on National Music' suggested in 1831, 'the piece was genuinely Norwegian, the composer was genuinely Norwegian, and so for us all the wonderful and well-known music for *Fjeldeventyret* became genuinely Norwegian too'.[64] In this sense, *Fjeldeventyret* confirms Dahlhaus's thesis that nationalism is first and foremost a product of its contemporary critical reception. Our analysis of 'Aagots Fjeldsang' also suggests that such critical reception cannot be fully understood without some reference to musical context and convention. In particular, the play between 'generalised folk idioms' and other more 'mainstream' musical discourses appears to be a central thread in such patterns of reception, and it forms a basic framework for understanding the formation of a Norwegian musical style during this period.

The idealisation of the Norwegian landscape that figured prominently in *Fjeldeventyret* was an important strategy in the definition of an independent self-identity. It was one that also engaged in a dialectical process of isolation and assimilation with perceived mainstream continental European traditions. Indeed, the relationship between music and landscape in *Fjeldeventyret* can be understood as forming a basic model for Norwegian cultural nationalism throughout the nineteenth century. In chapters 2 and 3, we shall consider how Grieg's music shifted the representation of landscape from the purely pictorial to a more structuralist domain, and assess the implications of this process of abstraction for an analytical reading of his work. In the remainder of this chapter, however, we shall turn our attention to the way in which the binary oppositions between centre and periphery, folk and high art, which underpinned the images of Norwegian landscape in *Fjeldeventyret* shaped the formation of another aspect of Norwegian folklorism, namely the antiquarian and artistic interest in folk song.

---

[64] 'Stykket var ægte norsk, Komponisten var ægte norsk, og ægte norsk blev da også den os alle så velbekjendte underskjønne Musik til Fjeldeventyret.' 'Nogle Ord', 482 (quoted in Herresthal, *Med spark i gulvet*, 35).

Grieg and the 'invention' of Norwegian folk music

Mid-way through his discussion of *Fjeldeventyret*, the author of 'Some Words on National Music' wonders wistfully 'whether among our mountains and valleys some remnants of the melodies our Fathers used to hum could not be found, and whether it would not be worthwhile to arrange them according to artistic principles and then, refined, reintroduce them into the folk life'.[65] The invocation of the dual temporal vision of the nation identified by Anderson is crucial to this argument. Folk music was defined as shared cultural property, a repertory of ancient and (usually) anonymous melodies whose origins were supposedly timeless. The association of this repertory with a particular ancestral group (here referred to simply as 'the melodies our Fathers used to hum') reinforced the image of the nation as a biological entity or family, as much as a political territory. This strategy was both inclusive and exclusive, inviting readers to associate themselves with the same mythic origins as those invoked by the writer (the collective reference to '*our* Fathers'), and linking notions of common ancestry with national topography ('*our* mountains and valleys'). But the discussion is also ambivalent, since a narrative twist is provided by the implication that the folk repertory is in some sense lost or concealed, and that it must be reawakened or, even more urgently, saved from oblivion. It is only through modern or progressive 'artistic principles', however, that folk music can be re-integrated into the national consciousness. Such a process is nevertheless a historical imperative, the essay suggests, since it is vital to the formation of a distinctively Norwegian musical identity. Only through the revival of a dormant cultural tradition can the modern nation achieve complete self-determination.

This form of folklorist thinking is common to many nineteenth-century nationalisms, and hence Norway emerges again as an exemplar of a broader European phenomenon. But this folklorist trend has not always been viewed favourably by critical commentators. John Hutchinson remarks that, for modernist historians such as Hans Kohn and Ernest Gellner, such folklorism is perceived as a defensive or reactionary response. It is understood as 'the creation of intellectuals in backward societies, who, threatened by the advance of an exotic scientific-industrial culture with which they find it difficult to compete, advocate a nostalgic return to the pristine integrated world of the folk and engage in linguistic and cultural reconstruction'. Hutchinson disagrees with this analysis, and argues that Kohn and Gellner 'are wrong to perceive the celebration of the folk as a retreat into an isolated agrarian simplicity free from all the disorders of civilisation'. Rather, 'behind

---

[65] 'Om der ikke iblant vore Fjelde og Dale skulde findes Levninger af de Melodier som vore Fædre nynnede, og om det ikke skulde være Umagen værd, at behandle dem efter Kunstens Regler og således, forædlede, atter at føre dem ind i Folklivet.' 'Nogle Ord', 474 (quoted in Herresthal, *Med spark i gulvet*, 32–3.)

this evocation of the folk on the part of intellectuals and the intelligentsia is, first, a dynamic vision of the nation as high civilisation with a unique place in the development of humanity and, secondly, a corresponding drive to recreate this nation which, integrating the traditional and the modern on a higher level, will again rise to the forefront of world progress'.[66] In 'Some Words on National Music', this tension between retrospective (organicist) and prospective (synthetic) notions of a folk-music tradition in turn reflects an aesthetic tension between conservative and progressive impulses. As Herresthal observes, folk music is ultimately perceived as being in an incomplete state of development. Though the essay is willing to grant that folk instruments possess a unique (*eiendommelig*) and 'idyllic' sound, it is the simplicity of the folk melody alone that is privileged as the defining characteristic of ethnic raw material in need of refinement.[67] This process of refinement seeks to elevate both the musical material to the level of high art, and intensify (or legitimate) a sense of national musical identity. Hence, following John Hutchinson's model, though the initial aim is the creation of 'a revived folk community', based on the recovery of a hidden musical repertory, 'what results is rather a modern science-based culture with native idioms'.

Thrane's use of local colour in *Fjeldeventyret* was believed to have begun to achieve this synthesis of folk music and contemporary modern idioms.[68] But Thrane's early death presumably ensured that *Fjeldeventyret* did not immediately lead to the formation of a distinctively Norwegian musical style, even if it reflected the growing popular appeal of Norwegian folk culture. Hitherto, many of the earliest printed sources for Norwegian folk music had been published outside Norway. Nils Grinde, for example, lists Johann Mattheson's pamphlet *Etwas Neues unter den Sonnen! Das unterirrdische Klippen-Koncert in Norwegen* ('Something New under the Sun! The Netherwordly Cliff-Concert in Norway', Hamburg, 1740), which includes a fiddle melody with the characteristics of a *halling* (an athletic moderately paced dance in duple time) on its title page.[69] One of the accompanying accounts of this netherwordly concert printed by Mattheson provides an early instance of the myth of supernatural Norwegian mountain music that became increasingly frequent in nineteenth-century sources, notably Grieg's *Den Bergtekne*, which is discussed in greater detail in Chapter 2. Later, Jean-Benjamin de la Borde published twenty-one Norwegian melodies, including sixteen *slåtter* (peasant dances), in his *Essai sur la musique ancienne et moderne* ('Essay on Ancient and Modern Music', 1780), the melodies provided by Johan

---

[66] Hutchinson, 'Cultural Nationalism', 128.
[67] Herresthal, *Med spark i gulvet*, 34.
[68] Ibid., 35.
[69] Grinde, *A History of Norwegian Music*, 63–6; Herresthal, *Med spark i gulvet*, 98.

Ernst Hartmann, a German-Danish musician based in Copenhagen.[70] The Abbé Georg Joseph Vogler wrote two sets of variations on a popular song entitled 'Stusle Sundagskvelden' ('The Lonely Sunday Evening') in 1794 and 1806. Significantly, given Norway's political status at the time, the *Udvalgte danskeviser fra middelårene* ('Selected Danish Songs from the Middle Ages') edited by Rasmus Nyerup and Knud Lyhne Rahbek (1812–14) included thirty Norwegian melodies without identifying their source. In many senses, identifying a distinctive national song was no less pressing for Denmark in the nineteenth century than for Norway. It was not until the 1840s, however, that serious interest began to be paid towards the collection of Norwegian folk music within Norway itself.

The belief that it was through folk music that a national spirit could be awakened found one of its most persuasive advocates in the writings of Henrik Wergeland.[71] Wergeland's address at Eidsvoll in 1834, 'Til Forfædrenes Minde' ('To the Memory of the Ancestors'), had called for a reunion of the old medieval kingdom and a new Norwegian nation state as 'two broken parts of the same ring'. The intervening Dano-Norwegian period Wergeland dismissed as 'impure soldering'.[72] According to Herresthal, Wergeland believed that Norwegian cultural and political independence 'could only be won once the nation had found its way back to the rural culture'; consequently, in Wergeland's mind, 'a simple folk tune was of greater beauty and importance than all the world's art music'.[73] Wergeland's call for a 'return to the folk' was therefore coloured, as were similar demands elsewhere in Europe, by a sense of anti-colonialism. In this sense, Wergeland's critique reflects Øystein Østerud's notion of nineteenth-century Norwegian nationalism as a form of resistance to a foreign dominant power, or counter-culture. In a letter to Frederika Bremer dated 4 May 1840, Wergeland wrote: 'At this moment (it is market), a *halling* sounds from the street from a wandering musician in hide trousers and white jacket. This unique, wild stirring music is our national poetry.'[74]

That the figure of a solo fiddler, playing a *halling* upon the street, should stand for Wergeland as a symbol of wild Norwegian music, was not coincidental. A second crucial figure in the popularisation of this folk counter-culture, and a significant influence on Grieg, was the Bergen-born violin

---

[70] Grinde, *A History of Norwegian Music*, 106.
[71] Herresthal, *Med spark i gulvet*, 36 ff.
[72] Sørensen, 'Development', 26.
[73] 'bare kunne gjenvinnes ved at nasjonen fant veien tilbake til bygdekulturen . . . var den enkle folketone av større skjønnhet og betydning enn all verdens kunstmusikk.' Herresthal, *Med spark i gulvet*, 39.
[74] 'I dette Øjeblik (det er Marked) toner en Halling fra Gaden fra en omvandrede Spillemand i Skindbuxer og hvid Kufte. Denne eiendommelige, vilde rørende Musik er vor Nationalpoesi.' Quoted in ibid., 100.

virtuoso Ole Bull. Bull's career embodies many of the paradoxes within the dialectical model of nationalism advanced by Hutchinson and others.[75] He had taken an elemental course in music theory in Christiania in 1829, and hoped to study general bass with the violinist Ernst in Paris in 1831, following the trend established by other Norwegian musicians who sought their professional classical training abroad. Ironically, it was during his time in Paris in the early 1830s, accompanied by a Hardanger fiddle (*hardingfele*) and a collection of the melodies of the Hardanger fiddler Torgeir Augundsson (better known as Myllarguten, 'the Miller's Boy'), that Bull's enthusiasm for Norwegian nationalism first gained momentum. Bull himself played the *hardingfele* in a Paris concert as early as 1833. His return to Norway marks his first significant encounter with Norwegian folk music through the playing of Myllarguten, though he did not actually meet Myllarguten until 1838.[76] For Herresthal, it was through his encounter with Myllarguten that Bull 'met the proto-Norwegian in music that Wergeland had a passion for'.[77] As a historical musical figure, Bull reflects many of the tensions and oppositions within the idea of a Norwegian musical identity. His career as a virtuoso classical violinist placed him very much within a cosmopolitan context as a touring international professional. From this perspective his interest in Norwegian folk music was simply another form of exoticism, as Dahlhaus's analysis of nineteenth-century nationalisms suggests. But his enthusiasm for French revolutionary politics and his direct support of folk musicians such as Myllarguten also had a catalysing influence on folklorism in Norway itself, where Bull was increasingly seen as a national hero. *Morgenbladet*, in a review dated 27 July 1849 of Bull's latest Bergen concert, which followed Myllarguten's first appearance in Christiania on 15 January, praised Bull's 'homely sounds, which are just as individual to our Norway as the yodel's harmonies for the Tyrol', aligning Norwegian folk music with a similar alpine repertoire to that evoked by the *ranz des vaches* in *Fjeldeventyret*. 'When Mjølnarguten [*sic*], the Lieutenant boys, Luråsen and many others play their peasant dances', *Morgenbladet* enthused, 'when one hears these homely sounds, which so warmly attract, or when one is in a meadow hut listening to the unaffected song of the Halling or Valders girl, who strikes chords upon their *langeleik*, then one believes the sounds are ours'.[78]

---

[75] For a comprehensive critical overview of Bull's career, with brief commentaries on his works, see Einar Haugen and Camilla Cai, *Ole Bull: Norway's Romantic Musician and Cosmopolitan Patriot* (Madison: University of Wisconsin Press, 1993), originally published as *Ole Bull: romantisk musiker og kosmopolitisk nordmann* (Oslo: Universitetsforlaget, 1992).

[76] For this information I am indebted to Harald Herresthal, whose own biography of Bull is forthcoming.

[77] 'Gjennom [Myllarguten] møtte han noe av det urnorske i musikken som Wergeland hadde svermet for.' Herresthal, *Med spark i gulvet*, 40.

[78] 'disse hjemlige Toner, de ere dog ligeså eiendommelige for vort Norge som Joddelens Harmonier for Tyrol. . . . Når Mjølnarguten, Løytnantdrengene, Luråsen og mange flere spiller sine Slåtte, da har

Bull's popularisation of Norwegian folk music, both at home and abroad, may have been a necessary precondition for, and not simply the outcome of, more academic or antiquarian interest in Norwegian folk music. But it also reflected a more general trend towards the revival of folk cultures including music, language, dancing and national costume, which was again heavily influenced by continental cultural practices even while it insisted on notions of authentic Norwegianness. Inga Ranheim notes that Lars Roverud, the author of the 1815 essay 'A Look at the Condition of Music in Norway', was awarded a state grant of 300 specie dalers in 1841 to teach the masses to sing properly. But in 1848 Ludvig Mathias Lindeman was granted a stipend from an official academic authority, Det akademiske Kollegium, 'to bring to light these despised and unappreciated Psalm tones from the branches of the mountains'.[79] Hence, Ranheim suggests, 'between Roverud and Lindeman – between 1841 and 1848 – a dramatic shift had therefore taken place in the official view of Norwegian folk culture, and folklorism certainly surprised no-one: it is national Romanticism which had flowed in over Norway'.[80] Lindeman had already contributed to the first substantial collection of Norwegian folk tunes to be published in Norway, Jørgen Moe's *Samling af Sange, Folkeviser og Stev i norske Almuedialekter* ('Collection of Songs, Folk Tunes and *Stev*[81] in Common Norwegian Dialect', 1840), before publishing his own first major anthology, *Norske Fjeldmelodier harmonisk bearbeidede for Pianoforte* ('Norwegian Mountain Melodies Harmonically Worked for the Pianoforte') the following year. Lindeman had also contributed a series of melodies, printed without harmonisation, to Magnus Brostrup Landstad's *Norske Folkeballader* ('Norwegian Folk Ballads', 1853), some of which had been originally collected by a woman, Olea Crøger, whose folklorist research was largely unacknowledged until the twentieth century. Grieg would later raid Landstad's collection for the text of his song *Den Bergtekne*. Lindeman's major collection, *Ældre og nyere Norske Fjeldmelodier* ('Older and Newer Norwegian Mountain Melodies'), initially containing 540 melodies, was published in a series of twelve volumes between 1853 and 1863; a subsequent volume containing a further fifty-two melodies appeared in

man disse hjemlige Toner, som så hjertelig tiltale, eller når man i Sæterhytten lytter til den ukunstlede Sang fra Halling- og Valdersjenten, som ved sin Langleik slår dertil Akorder, da synes dig Tonerne er vore.' Ibid., 91. In Norse mythology, Mjölnir ('Crusher') was Thorr's hammer (whose strike caused lightning); *Morgenbladet*'s (mis)spelling of Myllargut's name may be intended as a pun. The *langeleik* is a type of zither that has been identified as one of the oldest indigenous Norwegian folk instruments.
[79] 'for at drage frem for Lyset disse saa foragtede og miskjendte Psalmetoner fra Fjeldegrene'. Inga Ranheim, 'Folkedans og disciplinering', in Sørensen, *Nasjonal identitet*, 73–89.
[80] 'Mellom Roverud og Lindeman – mellom 1841 og 1848 – hadde det altså skjedd eit dramatisk skifte i det offisielle synet på norsk folkekultur, og folkloringa overraskar vel ingen: Det er nasjonalromantikken som har fløymt innover Noreg.' Ibid., 74.
[81] The *stev* are single-verse texts in fixed metrical patterns sung to traditional melodies; see Grinde, *A History of Norwegian Music*, 78–84.

1867, and a completely revised edition in 1874.[82] Many of the melodies
were notated during a series of government-funded trips to Valders (1848),
Telemark, Hardanger and Hallingdal (1851). Lindeman was awarded a state
grant to collect folk songs from 1859 until his death: he was therefore the first
Norwegian musician, before Grieg and Svendsen, to receive an annual state
award to support his artistic activities. But, as Herresthal observes, 'during
this period, Ludvig Mathias Lindeman did not need to travel out to the
rural districts to collect folk tunes. He could simply leave the organ gallery
in Our Saviour's Church and walk down to Stortorvet or to Youngstorvet.'[83]
The process of rural-urban migration was such that folk music from outlying
provincial districts was increasingly heard in urban Norwegian contexts.
Hence, the institutional support that enabled Lindeman to travel to collect
and publish folk tunes was not the only way in which Norwegian folk music
was becoming urbanised.

Lindeman's collection served several purposes. His government-spon-
sored collecting trips to southern and western Norway reflected (and
reinforced) a common belief that it was in those parts of the country (as
opposed to the relatively more urbanised south-east around Christiania, or
the far north) where the oldest and hence most 'authentic' Norwegian folk
music could be found.[84] This regionalism is a common nationalist strategy.
Finnish folklorists advanced similar arguments, for example, as they collected folk tales in the far-eastern region of Karelia in the mid-nineteenth
century, just as Spanish folklorists often privileged the southern province
of Andalucia.[85] The perception that it was the rural regions of Telemark and
Hallingdal in particular that embodied Norwegian musical and linguistic
purity was part of a process of gradual political and cultural decentralisa-
tion away from Christiania. But the purpose of Lindeman's collection was
also partly antiquarian. The belief that folk music was dying out and needed

[82] An extended second edition, with melodies 593–636, was published by Peter Lindeman in 1907,
followed by a third edition with melodies 637–64, edited by Øystein Gaukstad and O. M. Sandvik,
in 1963. A fourth edition in a single volume, with five additional melodies, was published in 1983
(Oslo: Norsk Musikforlag), edited by Øystein Gaukstad. These continual revisions and additions
underline the sense in which Lindeman's collection has remained a living, *organic* reference source for
Norwegian folk music.

[83] 'I dette tidsrummet behøvde Ludvig Matthias Lindeman ikke å reise utpå bygdene for å samle inn
folketoner. Han kunne bare forlate orgelgalleriet i Vor Frelsers kirke og spasere bort på Stortorvet
eller til Youngstorvet.' Herresthal, *Med spark i gulvet*, 102.

[84] Folk music in the central and eastern regions, around Christiania, Gudbrandsdal and the Swedish
border, was dominated by more recent dance forms (confusingly known as *gammeldans* or 'old dance')
such as the 'pols', 'Rheinlander' and the 'vals', which were (polemically) not regarded as 'Norwegian'
in the same way as the dance forms in the south-west. A sharp distinction between the two traditions
remains in the contemporary Norwegian folk repertoire.

[85] On Karelianism in Finnish culture, see Hannes Sihvo, 'Karelia: A Source of Finnish National
History', *National History and Identity: Approaches to the Writing of National History in the North-East Baltic
Region, Nineteenth and Twentieth Centuries*, ed. Michael Branch. Studia Fennica Ethnologica 6 (Helsinki:
Finnish Literature Society, 1999), 181–201.

to be preserved, previously articulated by the writer of 'Some Words on National Music', for example, was common. This pessimistic world view was presumably informed as much by processes of urbanisation and emigration as by any real sense that folk music (principally meaning the music of a rural working class) was actually in decline. Lindeman's anthology therefore functioned as a kind of repository, an aural museum whose collection constituted part of a national historiography. In this sense, *Ældre og nyere Norske Fjeldmelodier* was also a scholarly project, the first beginnings of academic study into the formation and characteristics of Norwegian folk song, although it was arguably not until later that a systematic ethnomusicological approach began to be developed (see Chapter 4). But, above all perhaps, the success of Lindeman's collection was its popular appeal. As Herresthal observes, there was a growing market for easy-to-play arrangements of folk tunes, for consumption in the urban middle-class homes of Christiania and Bergen. Lindeman's work was therefore addressed to various different audiences simultaneously: folklorists, antiquarians, academics, professional musicians and amateur pianists and singers.

As the largest single collection of Norwegian folk music, Lindeman's anthology became the primary reference source for later Norwegian musicians, including Halfdan Kjerulf and Grieg. But, as Herresthal notes, 'in opposition to Ole Bull, who believed that the Norwegian art "stood ready and waiting upon the mountains", Lindeman believed that folk music needed an artistic reworking before it could become the foundation for a national art'.[86] Exactly how far such artistic reworking or arrangement should go became an increasingly contentious issue in the nationalism debate, and not merely for musicians. For the more radical proponents, first Wergeland and, later, writers such as Aasmund Olavsson Vinje (one of the principal movers behind the advancement of *landsmål*), any hint of 'classicisation' compromised the music's Norwegianness. From their isolationist perspective, it was folk music alone in its 'raw' state that could form the authentic foundation for a national school. But, if this repertory was dormant, or in decline, as many commentators appeared to believe, it was only through some kind of revival that it could be brought into the national consciousness. For other more moderate participants in this debate, including Halfdan Kjerulf, such a revival could only be brought about in dialogue with mainstream classical trends, through which, they believed, the musical taste of the Norwegian public could best be educated. And Kjerulf perhaps sensed, as Grieg may have done later, that the notion of Norwegian folk music as an exclusive

---

[86] 'I motsætning til Ole Bull, som hevdet at den norske kunst «står fix og færdig på Fjeldet», mente Lindeman at folkemusikken trengte en kunsterisk bearbeidelse for å kunne danne grunnlaget for en nasjonal kunst.' Herresthal, *Med spark i gulvet*, 150.

category was an artificial one in any case.[87]

It is the tensions and contradictions between these isolationist and more assimilationist positions in nineteenth-century Norwegian music, and between conservative and progressive impulses (in either direction), that define the historical context in which Grieg's folk-music arrangements were critically received. They also raise deeper questions about the nature and aesthetic status of such musical constructions of nationalism. Dahlhaus's brief comparative analysis of Grieg's first dance from his *25 norske Folkeviser og Danser*, with one of the numbers ('L'Almée') from Bizet's opera *Djamileh*[88] (Exx. 1.3 and 1.4), places many of the issues which polarised the nationalism debate in the latter half of the century in a broader framework. As we have seen, for Dahlhaus, nineteenth-century musical nationalisms were ultimately concerned with a sense of exoticism or distance. In *Fjeldeventyret*, the evocation of local colour was therefore dependent more on a sense of difference than on specific detail. Hence, according to Dahlhaus,

> It is no easy matter to see a definite distinction between the combination of double bourdon, Lydian fourth, and chromatic colouration in the Jumping Dance of Grieg's purportedly Scandinavian *Nordic Dances and Folk Tunes* Op. 17 (1870), and the similar stereotype combination used as an orientalism in the dance 'L'Almée' from Bizet's *Djamileh*. In neither case can the local colour be localised in purely musical terms without a scenic or linguistic tag. Regardless of the milieu being depicted, exoticism and folklorism almost invariably make do with the same technical devices: pentatonicism, the Dorian [raised] sixth and Mixolydian [flattened] seventh, the raised second and augmented fourth, non-functional chromatic colouration, and finally bass drones, ostinatos, and pedal points as central axes.[89]

According to Dahlhaus's analysis, local colour is subordinate to a broader sense of foreignness. 'The key issue is not the original ethnic substance of these phenomena', Dahlhaus maintains, 'so much as the fact that they differ from European art music, and the function they serve as deviations from the European norm.'[90] At one level this reading seems valid, even when we consider the works' different performing venues and the respective audiences to which they were likely to have been addressed. Such 'deviations from the norm', Dahlhaus argues, were conventionally understood. Bizet's 'L'Almée' was part of a larger-scale stage work in which such exotic elements were a

---

[87] Ibid., 149–58.
[88] Bizet composed his work in 1871, but the opera was not premiered until October of the following year, when it received a lukewarm reception.
[89] Carl Dahlhaus, *Nineteenth-Century Music*, trans. J. Bradford Robinson (Berkeley: University of California Press, 1989), 306.
[90] Ibid., 306.

Example 1.3. Grieg: Springdans, op. 17/1

Example 1.4. Bizet: *Djamileh:* L'Almée

well-established topic, as for 'Aagots Fjeldsang' in *Fjeldeventyret*. Herresthal suggests that Grieg's op. 17 collection, like his first book of *Lyric Pieces*, op. 12, was composed partially for pedagogical use at the music academy which Grieg founded with a senior colleague, Otto Winter Hjelm, in Christiania in 1866. Winter Hjelm was a keen supporter of the idea that folk music should form the basis of a national school, though he believed that it was only through large-scale works ('de store Former') that Norwegian music could win international recognition.[91] Grieg's collection must presumably have been intended primarily for popular consumption, by a middle-class market of amateur pianists whose bourgeois origins would have been not so different from the audience for Bizet's *opéra comique*, even as it contributed to the ongoing debate about the status of Norwegian musical style.

The structural and aesthetic tensions in Grieg's collection are nevertheless of a slightly different nature from those in Bizet's opera, not least because the supposedly 'foreign' elements in op. 17 are precisely those, drawn from Norwegian folk music, with which its audience are being asked to identify.[92] Hence local context or milieu is more important than Dahlhaus's analysis initially suggests. All of the melodies in Grieg's op. 17 set (dedicated to Ole Bull) are taken from Lindeman's *Ældre og nyere Norske Fjeldmelodier*.[93] Following Lindeman's anthology, where the melody appears as no. 464, the first dance in Grieg's collection is identified as a *Springlått* (a fast triple-time 'leaping dance') from the village of Gol in Hallingdal: the title and place of origin serve as Dahlhaus's 'scenic or linguistic tag'. Grieg's treatment of the folk tune reveals some interesting parallels with and differences from Lindeman's arrangement (Ex. 1.5).[94] The majority of the tunes in Lindeman's anthology are set for piano in a straightforward, accessible style, with few stretches of register or complex part-writing (some numbers include brief postludes, upbeats or attempts at canonic imitation). Chromaticism is usually limited to cadential approach chords, so that the general impression is of a diatonic context in which modal variance (where present) is interpreted as part of a functional harmonic progression. This is certainly the case with Lindeman's setting of the *Springlått*. The dance begins in simple two-part style. The chromatic modal inflection in the opening bar (f♯) is retrospectively heard as a secondary dominant interval in the third bar. Lindeman provides a sense

---

[91] Herresthal, *Med spark i gulvet*, 185–93. Winter Hjelm himself arranged a number of Norwegian folk melodies especially for use by young pianists.

[92] On the complex subjectivities in nineteenth-century operatic evocations of the exotic, see Ralph P. Locke, 'Constructing the Oriental "Other": Saint-Saëns's *Samson et Dalila*', *Cambridge Opera Journal* 3 (1991), 261–302, or Susan McClary, *Georges Bizet: Carmen* (Cambridge: Cambridge University Press, 1992).

[93] A complete comparative list can be found in Findeisen, *Instrumentale Folklorestilisierung*.

[94] Note that Grieg alters the order of the two quavers in the third beat of the first bar. Whether this is an intentional detail or simply a misreading is unclear from the relevant documentary evidence.

Example 1.5. Lindeman: Springlaat

of harmonic-goal direction in the second system simply via the use of an interrupted cadence in bars 6–7, delaying the arrival of the tonic cadence until the final bar. There are no dynamic markings, and the *springar* (leaping dance) rhythm is indicated by the use of accents on the second beat of the bar. The overriding effect is one of familiarisation, so that the folk melody is rendered in as classically strict a manner as possible. The fundamental stylistic emphasis of Lindeman's arrangement is therefore very different from the deliberate emphasis on otherness or local colour that characterises the exoticism in both Bizet's *opéra comique* and *Fjeldeventyret*.

Even within its limited parameters, Grieg's setting is more daring. His arrangement is a varied strophic structure, so that there is a stronger sense of cumulative large-scale shape throughout. The opening two-bar introduction, bare fifths for left hand alone, is bolder and rhythmically more striking than Lindeman's version. The left hand remains in this fixed ostinato pattern for the whole of the first strophe, up until bar 14, so as to concentrate attention firmly on the melodic contour of the tune. In the second strophe, Grieg brings the accompaniment into a more active role, and the implied 2/4 metre in the left hand is heard against an unstable 3/4 in the right. The embryonic harmonic movement of bars 14–16 induces the striking linear treatment of bars 17–21, which finally succeeds in shifting the left hand from its pedal. Though the narrowly avoided parallel fifths in bars 17–20 point to an underlying spirit of brutalism, the momentum generated creates a more functionally cadential circle-of-fifths movement (IV^6–II^7–V^7–I) in bars 21–4. The sudden sense of harmonic rhythm means that the in-built metrical conflict between 2/4 and 3/4 in the previous bars is intensified just as the music seems to be driving towards its first real point of harmonic arrival. The other primary feature of the strophe is the first dynamic change from the *mezzo forte* of the opening. Though the *crescendo* is balanced by a *diminuendo* (to *piano*) in bars 23–4, the dynamic shading alone adds to the sense of cumulative design that proves to be the dance's most important formal characteristic.

The third strophe's principal innovation, aside from its *pianissimo* 'echo' dynamic, is the chromaticisation of the left hand descent in bars 28–35. Norwegian pianist Einar Steen-Nøkleberg describes the distinctive left-hand quaver figuration as resembling a *langeleik*.[95] The chromatic diminution in bars 28–35 is less redolent of the harmonic world of *Tristan*, with its decorated-dominant chromatic substitution chords, than of a contrapuntal academicism that could ultimately be attributed to Grieg's training at the Leipzig conservatoire. The effect is arguably more Bachian than Wagnerian. At the same time, however, the sheer linear momentum of the chromatic line creates a sense of physical propulsion. The fourth and final strophe correspondingly acts as the dynamic and registral climax of the dance. The change of dynamic and texture in bar 36 is the most extreme 'jolt' in the whole dance, but is heard as a syntactically consonant gesture given the prevailingly 'primitivist' orientation of much of the preceding music. Though the unprecedented rests in the left hand's ostinato accompaniment begin to provide some sense of metrical co-ordination, the metrical conflicts of the dance are not resolved satisfactorily until the final bar, which also acts as a point of registral and dynamic synthesis. The whole dance can therefore be understood as an end-oriented structure that is premised as much in physical as thematic or harmonic terms, a very different effect from that achieved by Lindeman's arrangement.

Perhaps a more useful and generically relevant comparison than Bizet's stage work with Grieg's op. 17 collection could be found among Chopin's mazurkas. Chopin's music provides an alternative non-Norwegian model for Grieg's folk-song arrangements, with which, as a professionally trained concert pianist, Grieg would surely have been aware. The C major mazurka, op. 24/2, is a good example: Chopin's strikingly white-note style is similar to that adopted by Grieg in the *springar*, op. 17/1, analysed above. Modally Chopin's mazurka tends more towards an Aeolian collection rather than the Lydian inflections in Grieg's op. 17/1, but the prevailing effect is similar. The magical harmonic slip which initiates the middle section of Chopin's mazurka (in D♭), and the enharmonic shift (a♭ = g♯ over V/vi) which leads back into the reprise of the A section, is more sudden and abrupt than anything in

---

[95] Einar Steen-Nøkleberg, *On Stage with Grieg: Interpreting His Piano Music*, trans. William H. Halvorson (Bloomington and Indianapolis: Indiana University Press, 1997), 155.

Grieg's setting, though they perhaps share a common spirit of brutalism (Ex. 1.6). Even if Grieg's sense of large-scale form often seems more four-square or overly symmetrical than Chopin's subtle play of open and closed harmonic phrases, further elements of Griegian syntax are foreshadowed in other mazurkas. The descending chromatic polyphonic lines in the famous F minor mazurka, op. 68/4, for example, resemble Grieg's practice, not so much in the op. 17 collection as in the later op. 66 set discussed in Chapter 2. In op. 24/2, Chopin even provides a Griegian liquidating passage to close the dance: the *sotto voce* clouding of alternating perfect fifths in the left hand anticipates the intervallic texture of one of Grieg's most radical exercises in musical syntax, 'Klokkeklang' ('Bell Ringing') from the *Lyric Pieces*, op. 54.

In her discussion of Chopin's mazurkas, Barbara Milewski observes that 'while direct contact with a rural musical practice doubtlessly made an impression on the young Chopin, it was not singularly defining for his particular evocation of a Polish musical landscape'.[96] Rather, she argues, 'the essential folkishness that listeners heard in Chopin's mazurkas was a fictional, mythopoetic folk, animated by stock rustic musical tropes and placed against the backdrop of a national genre as it was reconceived by Chopin'.[97] As much of the previous discussion has indicated, similar observations could be made, with reasonable justification, for Grieg's folk-song arrangements. Unlike Lindeman, Grieg did not undertake extensive collecting trips into the Norwegian countryside. Furthermore, as we have seen, his folk-song arrangements emerged against the complex background of an imagined Norwegian folk, whose roots paradoxically lay in a cosmopolitan European folklorism as much as within Norway itself. Hence, the 'essential' folkishness of Chopin's mazurkas becomes an 'essentialised' one in Grieg's op. 17. But Milewski's conclusion, that 'in the end, Chopin, like so many of his European compatriots, was not interested in recovering rural truths, but in bringing Poles of the urban upper classes a little bit closer to a highly constructed and desirable idea of themselves',[98] is less straightforwardly applicable to Grieg. The likely audience for Grieg's op. 17 collection, for instance, was drawn from Christiania's middle class, rather than the upper-class salons of Paris. Following chapters will suggest that Grieg's attitude to 'rural truths', a problematic category in any real historical sense, is more ambivalent than Milewski claims is the case for Chopin. Indeed, one of the recurring themes of this book is way in which the search for such perceived 'rural truths' becomes part of the structural tension in Grieg's work. Such 'truths' are less concerned in Grieg's music with actual details of ethnic authenticity

---

[96] Barbara Milewski, 'Chopin's Mazurkas and the Myth of the Folk', *19th-Century Music* 23/2 (1999), 113–35, here 134.
[97] Ibid., 121.
[98] Ibid., 135.

Example 1.6. Chopin: Mazurka in C, op. 24/1. Opening, transition and coda

(a) opening

(b) transition to D♭ major

(c) coda

than with a particular 'way of speaking' or tone of musical voice.

Brief comparison of other numbers from Grieg's op. 17 set confirms the impression of a level of structuralist thinking that is absent from Lindeman's anthology. Tune no. 402 from Lindeman's collection, the 'Jølstring' (dance from Jølster) is a particularly good example, as Peer Findeisen's analysis has demonstrated, since comparable settings exist by both Grieg and Halfdan Kjerulf (Ex. 1.7).[99] The 'Jølstring' is unusual in that the tune falls into two very distinct halves: an opening *halling* in D minor; and a triple-time second section in D major, in the style of a *kulokk* or *laling* (a nonsense song sung to the syllable 'la').[100] This strong bipartite form produces a slightly less neatly contained setting from Lindeman than for tune no. 464. Perhaps the most striking detail is the harmonic shift to the relative major towards the end of the first half, which prepares the change of mode at the start of the second section. Otherwise, the emphasis is very much on simplicity of register, accompanimental figuration and diatonic harmony, as was the case with the *Springlått*.

Kjerulf's *25 Udvalgte Norske Folkedandse* ('25 Selected Norwegian Folk Dances') were published in 1861. Though mostly based on tunes from the collections of Lindeman and Berggreen, as Kjerulf acknowledged in his foreword, his set also included two melodies transcribed from the Hardanger-fiddle player Hovar Gibjøen (Håvar Giböen), who was to reappear in Grieg's *Slåtter* (see Chapter 4).[101] Kjerulf's arrangement of the 'Jølstring' is in many senses comparable to Lindeman's, though the greater range of articulation and dynamic markings immediately suggests a slightly more ambitious scale of musical invention. Kjerulf's setting is particularly close to Lindeman's at the start of the second section (which Kjerulf marks 'scherzando'), where the shift to the major mode is prepared by use of the relative major in the preceding bars. But Kjerulf's setting is also more detailed. The use of register in the left hand is much greater than in Lindeman's setting, for example, and reflects the greater range of articulation and dynamics noted above. The idea of modal mixture seems more fully integrated into the conception of Kjerulf's arrangement. The enharmonic play between d♭ and c♯ in bars 8–11, for example, reflects the modal instability of both the passage in question, and, more broadly, the whole setting. Similarly, the b♭s in the left hand in bars 21–8 provide elements of the minor mode from the first half so that the tune's modal mixture is not resolved properly until the final two bars.

---

[99] Findeisen, *Instrumentale Folklorestilisierung*, 169–71.

[100] Nils Grinde, *A History of Norwegian Music*, 74–5.

[101] In his critical edition of Kjerulf's piano music, Nils Grinde suggests that it was the violinist Christian Suchow who provided the transcriptions which Kjerulf worked from. See Halfdan Kjerulf, *Samlede verker*, III: *Samlede klaverstykker*, ed. Nils Grinde (Oslo: Musikk-Huset, 1980), 240. There is also correspondence (from 1860) between Kjerulf and Carl Schart, who in 1865 published the first notated collection of Hardanger-fiddle music.

Example 1.7a. L. M. Lindeman: *Jolstring*

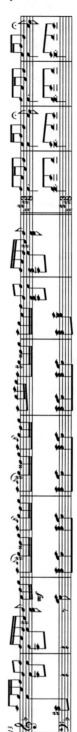
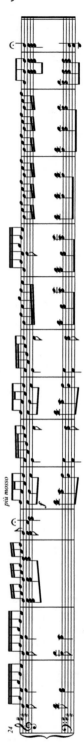

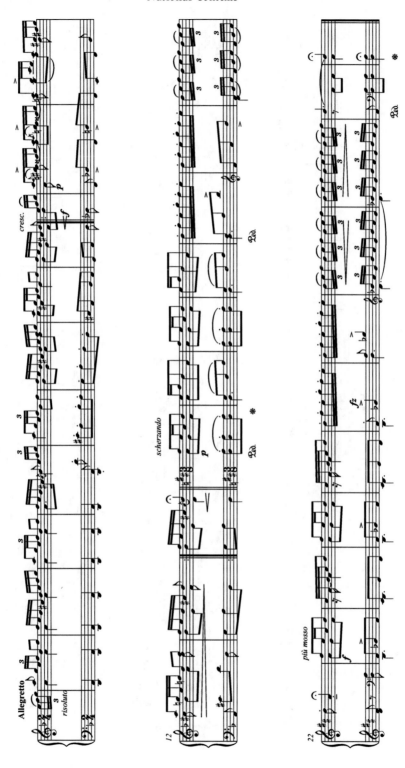

Example 1.7b. Halfdan Kjerulf: *Jølstring*

Example 1.7c. Grieg: *Jølstring*, op. 17/5

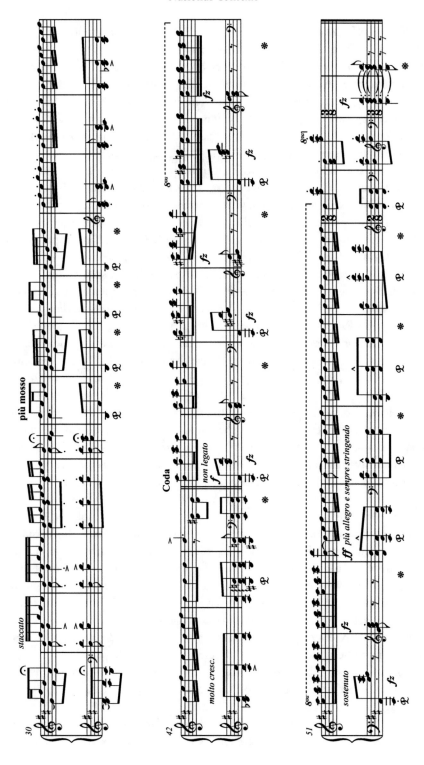

If Kjerulf's arrangement is concerned with modal instability as one of its primary formal parameters, then Grieg's setting is motivated above all by its use of register. An introductory four-bar gesture, unique to Grieg's arrangement and built from the triplet tag which kick-starts the *halling*, immediately creates a sense of registral and dynamic space. In the following chapter, this kind of texture will be identified as a landscape topic; Grieg's setting therefore opens with an idea that is both pictorial (associative) and structural (abstract) in function. The harmonisation of the *halling* in the first section is dominated by a series of descending chromatic parts, similar to the third strophe in the *springar*, whose sense of linear momentum is offset by strong offbeat *sforzando* accents. Grieg brings register to the fore once again in the second phrase, opening up a whole new registral space (the bass end of the keyboard) and then transferring the simple left-hand accompaniment figure through four different registral levels. This effect is emphasised as the figure is displaced into a fifth, higher tessitura (with crossed hands) when the phrase is repeated in bars 18–21. Whereas both Lindeman and Kjerulf negotiate the transition from the first section of the tune (the *halling*) to the second (the *kulokk* or *laling*) neatly, with a simple tonic chord, in Grieg's setting the transition is dramatised so that it becomes one of the focal points of the number. The approach to the pause bar is intensified by the dynamic level (*fortissimo*, and then *sempre più forte e pesante*), the textural thickening in the left hand, and by the deliberate slowing up (through the addition of two extra bars plus the augmentation of the pause itself). Grieg's harmonisation supports these other parameters: the pause is held on a dissonant ii$^4_2$ chord (rather than a simple tonic harmony), whose immediate resolution is delayed arguably until the end of the setting. The transition therefore becomes a moment of structural crisis, rather than simply a formal pivot.

The start of the triple-time section not only brings a change of musical climate (of mode, dynamic level and register), but also implies a shift of narrative or some kind of programmatic progression. After the crisis of the preceding bars the music sounds infeasibly calm or unreal, the lack of continuity creating a temporary sense of displacement or misalignment. It is as though the music inhabits a dream world, a temporal state commensurate with the mountain environment of 'Aagots Fjeldsang' in its sense of distance from normative modes of perception or behaviour. This is achieved in spite of remnants of previous material, such as modal mixture in the accompaniment. The sense of hesitancy (nostalgia or retrospection) with which the section begins is swiftly replaced by a sense of forward propulsion (assisted by the *più mosso* direction in bar 35, and the harmonic reinterpretation in bar 43 so that the end of the tune leads directly into the coda). In the extended final section, the *kulokk/laling* motive (a circular triplet figure) becomes transformed into a series of celebratory fanfare figures that lead to an exciting stringendo conclusion. Given the formal trajectory of the rest of the setting, the coda suggests a number of interpretative possibilities: the liberation or apotheosis of a heroic folk subject, for example, or alternatively the abandonment of a synthetic neo-Norwegian folk idiom in favour of more cosmopolitan bravura virtuosity. Whichever reading seems best, the coda also serves to summarise the setting's various registral elements, providing resolution (or, at least, tonic saturation) in several different tessituras before the leaps of the final bars. Unlike Lindeman's and Kjerulf's settings, therefore, Grieg's arrangement of the *jølstring* is powerfully goal-directed. The sense of structural progression, from crisis through hesitancy to transcendence, is strong, even as the setting arguably intensifies, rather than resolves, the tensions between its folk material and art-music treatment.

Taken together, these two numbers from op. 17 – the 'Jølstring' and the 'Springdans' – offer a paradigmatic way of reading Grieg's folk-song arrangements that will be pursued in the remaining chapters. But they also reveal the tensions, both historical and stylistic, that underpinned the formation of a Norwegian cultural identity in the nineteenth century. In common with other forms of national self-determination, Norwegian cultural nationalism was above all an *imagined* discourse, through its association of community with shared ethnicity, language, history, music, folk customs and topography. As we have seen, the whole notion of an independent Norwegian folk culture was in some ways a constructed one, defined against a perception of mainstream continental European traditions. In that sense, Norwegian cultural nationalism was *retrospective*: its celebration of peasant culture looked backwards towards a (geographically and historically) remote agricultural society that, it was believed, offered evidence of shared ethnic or cultural origins. Like all nationalisms, Norwegian cultural nationalism was therefore *exclusive*, reliant upon a sense of difference, or even isolation, in order to support its definition of commonality. Hence the promotion of the dialect language, folk music and landscape as authentic expressions of Norwegian identity. But, following John Hutchinson's model, Norwegian cultural nationalism can also be seen as *emancipatory*. According to Hutchinson, 'cultural nationalism has everywhere generated a flowering of the historical sciences and the arts as intellectuals have established cultural forums in which to challenge ossified political and cultural elites and to inspire a rising educated generation to campaign to "recreate" the idea of the nation as a living principle in the lives of people'.[102] This tendency towards social improvement and renewal in Norway was simultaneously a form of resistance to Danish (and later Swedish) political and cultural domination, in which music played a significant part. Like other

---

[102] Hutchinson, 'Cultural Nationalism', 124.

peripheralised discourses in the nineteenth-century, therefore, the goal of political and cultural independence ensured that Norwegian nationalism also had a heroic character. In the construction of a national historiography, figures such as Ole Bull, Henrik Wergeland, Bjørnstjerne Bjørnson and Grieg could be seen (not always retrospectively) as pioneers, assuming a 'national voice' on behalf of the Norwegian nation. But Grieg's folk-song arrangements suggest that the assumptions on which such definitions of nationhood are based are unstable and constantly shifting. As we shall see, it is the constant interplay between contradictory impulses – the progressive versus the retrospective, or the isolationist versus the assimilationist – that defines the creative character of Grieg's folk-song arrangements and their relationship with Norwegian cultural nationalism. In speaking of Grieg and the 'invention' of Norwegian folk music, therefore, we need not subscribe uncritically to superficial narratives of authenticity or ethnic origin, but refer more deeply to patterns of musical behaviour or a compositional state of mind.

CHAPTER TWO

Landscape as Ideology:
Nature, Nostalgia and Grieg's 'Culture of Sound'

Grieg's music is rich in evocations of nature and of open space. Mountain echoes, herding calls or distantly heard folk melodies saturate his work, and are among the most characteristic features of his music. Such musical representations of nature or landscape can be understood within the context of the Romantic *Naturklang*. Analysis of the 'Jølstring', op. 17/5, in the previous chapter argued that landscape in Grieg's music sets up dualities of authenticity and musical purity that were especially relevant given contemporary debates about Norwegian identity. As we have already seen, the construction of a Norwegian musical style during the nineteenth century was a function of broader processes of cultural and political self-determination in which folklorism played a central role. Such processes were closely linked with representations of the Norwegian landscape in art, music and literature. At the start of the century, the Norwegian countryside was commonly perceived as being of little economic or social value, a wasteland that was emblematic in turn of Norwegian geographical and political isolation. By the end of the century, however, the Norwegian landscape became increasingly celebrated as a site of cultural and ethnic difference or uniqueness (*eiendommelighed*), characteristics that, for Grieg and others such as the author Arne Garborg, supported demands for an independent Norwegian nation state. As Patricia G. Bernan has noted, for example, the idealised figure of the Norwegian rural economy, the peasant farmer, became disassociated from the historical reality of hard manual labour, 'and relocated into a discourse of eternal renewal and immersion in the earth'.[1] Various categories recur in Grieg's musical representations of landscape, from the use of pictorial devices such as wedding marches to provide conventionalised local colour, to the exploration of more abstract

---

[1] 'Edvard Munch's Peasants and the Invention of Norwegian Culture', in *Nordic Experiences: Exploration of Scandinavian Cultures*. Contributions to the Study of World Literature 71, ed. Berit I. Brown (London and Westport: Greenwood, 1997), 213–33, here 222.

'environmental elements' such as bell sounds and mountain echoes, which serve to create a sense of musical depth and distance. But landscape and nature can also be understood in more abstract ways, as particular means of organising musical time and space, and it is ultimately towards an understanding of this structural representation of landscape in Grieg's work that the present chapter is directed. Landscape in Grieg's music, this chapter will argue, is as discursive as other forms of musical representation.

Considering the historical diversity of its forms, representations and meanings, it is not surprising that landscape is an ambivalent phenomenon that resists single definition. Above all, landscape in the Western tradition is not natural, something created by nature without human intervention, but a series of environments, characters (moods or feelings), views or perspectives that are artificially constructed and perceived.[2] Hence, landscape can be imagined or conceived as a form of invention. As Edward S. Casey has observed:

> Places, like the landscapes they collectively compose, are bound up with representation, just as representation in turn calls for places as the bounded particulars of any given landscape domain. The truth is that *representation is not a contingent matter, something merely secondary; it is integral to the perception of landscape itself – indeed, part of its being and essential to its manifestation*.[3]

Landscape therefore presupposes both a process of composition (the creation of frames of reference or forms of spatial organisation) and the presence and active participation of a viewer (their sense of perspective). Furthermore, as Casey suggests, landscape is not merely concerned with spatial perception, but also possesses a temporal dimension. Like other static visual fields, landscape is experienced through time, just as it is experienced in space. In both cases, however, such perception depends upon the establishment of fixed boundaries or reference points, within which the landscape is represented and perceived but ultimately cannot be contained. As Casey explains:

> Just as a given landscape cannot be contained in a finite part of space, so its full perception cannot be confined to an instant of time. By its radical circumstance, landscape exceeds both kinds of unit, the indecomposable and uncontainable excess of the natural world over chronometric and spatiometric delimitations.[4]

This tension, between the infinite and the enclosed, is fundamental to the

---

[2] On the deceptive 'naturalness' of landscape, see Stephen Daniels, 'Marxism, Culture, and the Duplicity of Landscape', in *New Models in Geography: The Political-Economy Perspective*, ed. Richard Peet and Nigel Thrift (London: Unwin Hyman, 1989), 196–220.
[3] Edward S. Casey. *Representing Place: Landscape, Painting and Maps* (Minneapolis: University of Minnesota Press, 2002), xv.
[4] Ibid., 8–9.

nineteenth-century Romantic perception of landscape in particular.[5] Indeed, the inability to resolve this tension accounts for the melancholy quality of landscape in the nineteenth-century imagination. But this tension is also a formal process, linked to the technique of observation itself.[6] Other writers have drawn attention to the 'grammar and syntax' of landscape as a structure or form of organisation. John Barrell, for example, writing of John Clare's landscape poetry, suggests that

> A descriptive poem does not simply present us with an image, but, through the energy and disposition of its verbs especially, it can imitate the way in which the poet has perceived relationships between the objects he describes and between those objects and himself. A poem, therefore, which describes a landscape as a composition, does so particularly by imitating – through syntax, grammar, and the order of words – the process of composition which the poet performs.[7]

In Grieg's music, landscape similarly is not merely concerned with pictorial evocation, but is a more broadly environmental discourse, a representation of the sense of being within a particular time and space. It therefore becomes a central component of what W. Dean Sutcliffe has called Grieg's 'ideology or culture of sound', an interpretative complex that integrates attitude or intention, historical context and reception.[8] In common with the music of other contemporary Northern composers such as Sibelius and Carl Nielsen, landscape is often expressed as a static, contemplative musical object within the internal structural discourse of Grieg's work. It is defined by its sense of difference from normative musical behaviour. Julian Johnson has described this process more broadly as a conventionalised means of representing landscape in late Romantic music:

> Nature music, in its apparent self-containment and avoidance of linear motion, seems to suspend time. In this it seems to offer an analogy for our experience of spaciousness in which there is little or no movement. Space without perceived directed movement appears timeless. The perception of time, correspondingly, requires boundaries and limits against which things move, which is why mountain landscapes were so often associated with images of the eternal.[9]

[5] See Charles Rosen's discussion, 'Mountains and Song Cycles', in his *The Romantic Generation* (London: Harper Collins, 1996), especially 131–2.
[6] For a rich and insightful analysis of the ways in which the act of observation changed in the first half of the nineteenth century, see Jonathan Crary, *Techniques of the Observer: On Vision and Modernity in the Nineteenth Century* (Cambridge, Mass.: MIT Press, 1990).
[7] John Barrell, *The Idea of Landscape and the Sense of Place 1730–1840: An Approach to the Poetry of John Clare* (Cambridge: Cambridge University Press, 1972), 17.
[8] Sutcliffe, 'Grieg's Fifth', 165.
[9] Julian Johnson, *Webern and the Transformation of Nature* (Cambridge: Cambridge University Press,

Landscape in music therefore appears to play on a powerful contradiction, between its temporal nature (its perception in time), and the way in which it appears to collapse ordered or linear notions of time into a potentially illimitable sense of space. As this chapter will attempt to demonstrate, Grieg's music richly draws on, and is shaped by, this tradition of musical representation. Grieg's musical landscapes are also associated with feelings of nostalgia, nihilism and enchantment, familiar late Romantic topics that gain particular currency in his work. Close study of Grieg's *19 norske Folkeviser*, and the song-cycle *Haugtussa* (considered in Chapter 3), suggests that landscape also serves a more abstract, structural purpose. This chapter traces various trajectories through the representation of landscape in Grieg's music. Beginning with visual modes of representation, we consider briefly the context in which pictorial images of the Norwegian landscape were created in the nineteenth century. Grieg's music responds powerfully to this visual tradition. But landscape and nature also emerge in Grieg's work as signals of nostalgia, a subjectivity that initially seems distant from the idea of Norwegian political independence. Finally, we shall consider the way in which landscape informs the grammar and syntax of Grieg's music: Grieg's obsession with bell sounds in particular offers an example of the way in which associative factors and structural details coincide and become defining elements of Grieg's musical landscapes.

Landscape as pictorial representation

Changing trends in the pictorial representation of the Norwegian landscape in the nineteenth century were significant, not only for Grieg's music, but also for the wider dissemination of Norwegian culture in the European imagination. Among the most influential of these trends was a series of *tableaux vivants* staged at the Christiania Theatre between 28 and 30 March 1849. The project was the brainchild of an informal group of artists, writers and musicians (the Kunstnerforening), which was committed to the promotion of Norwegian culture.[10] Music for the presentation was provided, among others, by Ole Bull, whose melody entitled *Sæterbesøget* ('The Visit to the Mountain Pasture') later became one of his hit tunes. Texts by Andreas Munch, Jørgen Moe, Johan Sebastian Welhaven dealt with a variety of nationalist subjects including idealised descriptions of Norwegian nature, the midsummer night and traditional folk customs. The driving force behind the presentations were the painters Adolph Tidemand and Hans Gude, who provided series of striking visual images that functioned not as a backdrop

1999), 232.
[10] See Herresthal, *Med spark i gulvet*, 80–90; Herresthal provides a detailed description of the *tableaux* including a synopsis of the individual numbers and contemporary accounts of the performance.

but as a series of focal points that highlighted the centrality of landscape in the performance. At first it seems ironic that the visual component in the *tableaux* was the work of artists not permanently resident in Norway.[11] Both Tidemand and Gude were based in Düsseldorf, but had left temporarily following the political chaos of 1848. Such input from a continental European milieu evidently acted as a catalyst. As a theatrical genre, the *tableau vivant* had enjoyed particular popularity in Germany in the 1830s and 1840s,[12] and in effect it provided a context or framework for the 'romanticisation' of the Norwegian landscape.

Music played a central role in this process of contextualisation, through which the Norwegian landscape became aestheticised. In July 1849, following success of the *tableaux vivants*, composer Halfdan Kjerulf travelled with Gude to the western Norwegian mountains, ostensibly to record scenes of folk life for use in future projects.[13] The trip prompted Kjerulf's first attempt to notate and arrange folk music for piano, including a piece entitled *Hallingslaat* which Kjerulf subtitled ambivalently 'something which is yet not something' (Ex. 2.1).[14] As in earlier evocations of Norwegian folk song such as Thrane's *Fjeldeventyret*, the folk melody is placed within a more cosmopolitan musical discourse. The piece begins with a ruminative improvisatory prelude, after which follows a nocturne-like melody (marked 'Andante cantabile') with a simple theme-and-accompaniment texture that eventually gives way to a series of evocative horn calls (bars 21–4). The *halling* itself is announced after a chain of solo cries, marked 'ad lib.', and presents an immediate textural contrast, dominated by pedal drones and open fifths that serve as a pastoral symbol or folk topic. The tune consists of four-bar units recycled with minimal alteration, whose sheer repetitiveness is opposed to the periodic structure of the nocturne music. Since the dance is entirely enclosed within statements of the prelude-nocturne, its exotic quality is effectively framed or contextualised by a more familiar or assimilable musical style. Kjerulf's disarming subtitle similarly draws our attention to the *halling*'s unreal, magical character. Significantly given Grieg's later musical representations of the Norwegian landscape in which images of enchantment play a prominent role, the *halling* is both picturesque and eerie, ultimately supernatural in its appearance.

---

[11] This pattern had already been established by earlier Norwegian painters such as Johan Christian Dahl, who was based in Dresden. See Neil Kent, *The Triumph of Light and Nature: Nordic Art, 1740–1940* (London: Thames and Hudson, 1987), 63–72.

[12] On the association of music and the *tableau vivant* with representations of the romantic landscape in Germany, see Thomas S. Grey, 'Tableaux Vivants: Landscape, History Painting, and the Visual Imagination in Mendelssohn's Orchestral Music', *19th-Century Music* 21/1 (Summer 1997), 38–76.

[13] See Jan Askeland, *Adolph Tidemand og hans tid* (Oslo: Aschehoug, 1991).

[14] 'Noget som endnu ikke er noget.' The piece was published for the first time in the critical edition of Kjerulf's piano works ed. Grinde, 234–5.

Example 2.1. Kjerulf: Halling

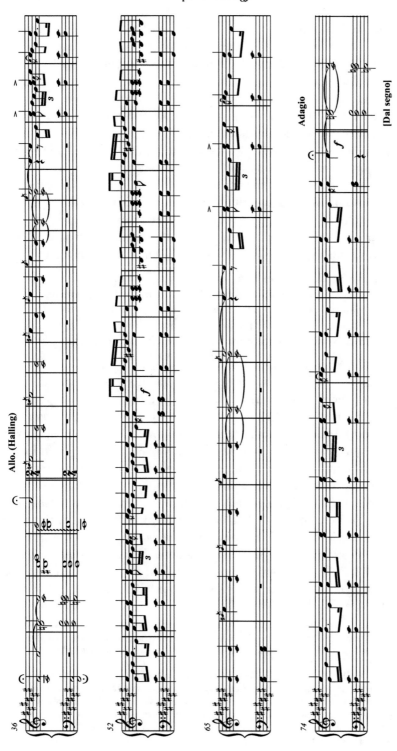

The combination of folk music with pictorial representations of the Norwegian landscape is apparent also in Christian Tønsberg's *Norske National-dragter* ('Norwegian National Costumes', 1852). Tønsberg's lavishly produced volume consists of thirty-three specially commissioned illustrations of regional costumes with accompanying commentary on local topography, climate and folk traditions in Norwegian, English and German. The book was presumably intended as a colourful souvenir for the growing foreign tourist market, as well as for domestic consumption.[15] But, like Lindeman's collection, Tønsberg's book also served as both an ethnographic project, cataloguing and analysing the variations in local folk life, and as an assertion of a Norwegian national identity. Significantly, as Astrid Oxaal has noted, in the illustrations it is the depiction of the Norwegian landscape that is often the primary focus of attention, rather than the costumes themselves.[16] Tønsberg's introduction reveals the ideological agenda underpinning the book:

> Our folk costumes have lost and continue to lose with every passing year more and more of their characteristic uniqueness, and the time is unfortunately not far off when our picturesque national costumes will have passed into oblivion. It is therefore necessary to use the time to preserve at least the memory of what remains.[17]

A similar fear, that Norway's regional folk traditions faced extinction in the face of advancing modern trends such as industrialisation or emigration, had presumably motivated the inclusion of six folk tunes notated and arranged for piano by Ole Bull at the end of the volume. Bull's arrangements, a 'Halling from Hallingdal' and 5 'Norske Fjeldmelodier' ('Norwegian Mountain Melodies'), include some of the earliest attempts to transcribe Hardanger-fiddle music. Like the accompaniments in Lindeman's collection, Bull's piano writing is mostly straightforwardly diatonic and intended to appeal to amateur players. Two exceptions, the 'Halling from Nummedal' and a 'Springar from Bø Parish in Thelemark', however, are more complex and dissonant, and anticipate the angular rhythmic style adopted by Grieg in his *Slåtter* (Exx. 2.2 and 2.3). The pervasive use of a sharpened fourth, modal mixture and extreme dynamic contrast in the *springar* in particular are radically different

---

[15] Tønsberg's later publications included a similar illustrated volume based on Tidemand's work, *Norske Folkelivsbilleder, efter Maleries og Tegninger af A. Tidemand* (Christiania: Christian Tønsberg, 1854) and a travel guide, *Norge. Illustreret Reisehaandbog. Med Prospekter og Karter* (Christiania: Christian Tønsberg, 1874).

[16] Astrid Oxaal, 'Folkedragt som uniform', in Sørensen, *Nasjonal identitet*, 91–112.

[17] 'Vore Folkedragter har tabt og taber fremdeles med hvert Aar mere og mere af sine karakteristiske Eiendommeligheder, og den Tid er desværre neppe fjern, da vore maleriske National kostumer ville være gaaende i Forglemmelse. Det gjelder saaledes at benytte Tiden for at bevare i det mindste Mindet om hvad der er tilbage.' Christian Tønsberg, *Norske Nationaldragter* (Christiania: Christian Tønsberg, 1852), forord.

Ex. 2.2. Ole Bull, Tougdands: Haugtusslaatten (Halling fra Nummedal)

from anything found in Lindeman's anthology, where dynamics are seldom indicated and modal inflections are commonly reinterpreted by simple diatonic progressions. In that sense, Bull's arrangements in Tønsberg's book fulfilled both a retrospective and prospective function, preserving folk traditions that were believed to be in terminal decline, while laying the foundations for a new independent Norwegian musical style. Like the whole of Tønsberg's project, Bull's transcriptions were intended to appeal as much to foreign readers as to Norwegians themselves.

Two of the focal themes in the 1849 *tableaux vivants* and Tønsberg's *Norske Nationaldragter*, the trip to the *sæter* (mountain pasture) and the western Norwegian folk wedding, became favourite topics in representations of Norwegian cultural identity in the second half of the nineteenth century. The *sæter*, which became the title of a *syngspill* (comic opera) by Reissiger and Claus Pavel Riis (1850) and a waltz cycle by Johan Svendsen, as well as the subject of several paintings and sketches by Tidemand, enjoyed particular popularity. For example, the commentary accompanying plates 5–6 ('Thelemark') in Tønsberg's book, with its combination of pastoral idyll and fairy-tale nature mysticism, reads like a sketch for a *tableau vivant*:

> *Sæter*-life here, as in all our mountain regions, is common, and often on Saturday or Sunday evenings in summer so many young men gather on the *sæter* that they decide to fetch a musician from far away for a dance. When the musician arrives, he sits down on a rock and plays his Hardanger fiddle, while the energetic young boys and girls swing themselves around the *sæter* in a lively dance. The bush stands and listens sadly to the suddenly melancholy, suddenly high-spirited music, and often playful kids and lambs hop among the rows of dancers as if to show that they too can dance.
>
> But it is not only the flock that takes part in the simple mountain folk's innocent fun upon the *sæter*. Even the *huldre*, that fairytale creature who dwells in the mountains and forests in countless tales across the land, sometimes mingles in the young people's dance. Everyone wants to dance with the strange attractive girl in the blue skirt and white headscarf, as long as they do not notice the hateful cow's tail that hangs under the skirt.[18]

[18] 'Sæterlivet er her som i alle vore Fjeldbygder almindeligt, og ofte samles om Sommeren paa Löverdags eller Söndagsaftener saamange unge Mennesker paa Sæteren, at man beslutter at hente en Spillemand langveisfra for at dandse. Naar Spillemanden er kommen, sætter han sig gjerne paa en Steen og spiller paa sin Hardangerfele, medens de raske Gutter og Jente i livlig Dands svinge sig paa Sætervolden. Buskapen staaer da omkring tungsindig lyttende til den snart melancholske, snart omgivne Musik, og ikke sjælden hænder det at muntre Kid og Lam komme hoppende ind imellem de Dandsendes Rækker, som vilder de vise, at ogsaa de kunne dandse.

Det er imidlertid ikke blot Qvæget, der tagen Deel i de enfoldige Fjeldfolks uskyldige Lystighed paa Sæterne. Selve Huldren, dette eventyrlige Væsen, der efter utallige Sagn rund om i Landet

Example 2.3. Ole Bull.

Springar fra Bøe Præstegjeld i Thelemarken (opening)

The kitsch elements in such nineteenth-century representations of the Norwegian landscape partly reflect a process of urbanisation, defined by tourism and other forms of popular consumption, analysed in detail by Herresthal.[19] The cover picture from Christian Teilman's *Paraphrase over Sæterjentens Söndag* ('The *Seter*-girl's Sunday'), an easy piano piece for middle-class amateurs based on Ole Bull's famous theme, is typical of later examples of the genre (Fig. 2.1). A young maiden in local folk costume is seated on a rock overlooking a dramatic western Norwegian fjord landscape. In the

findes i Bjergene og Skovene, skal stundom blande sig i Ungdommens Dands. Alle ville de da gjerne dandse med den vakkre fremmede Pige i blaat Skjört og med hvidt Skaut, saalænge de ikke opdage den hæslige Kohale, der hænger ned under Skjörtet.' Tønsberg, *Norske Nationaldragter*, commentary accompanying figs. 5 and 6.

[19] Herresthal, *Med spark i gulvet*. See particularly the chapter 'Folkemusikken i bykulturen' ('Folk Music in Urban Culture'), 98–109.

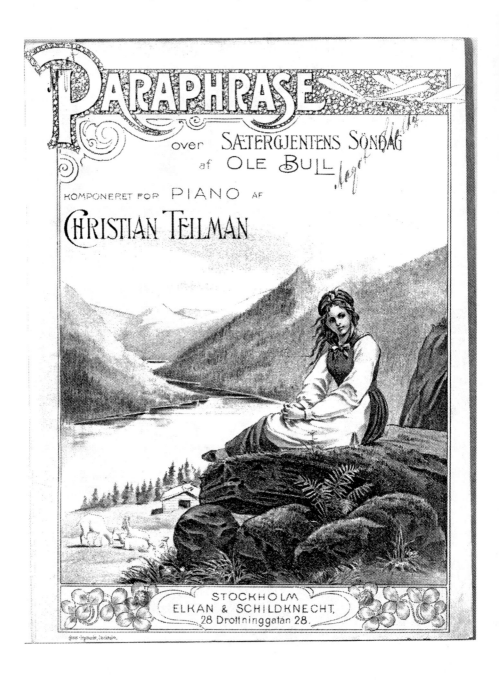

Fig. 2.1. Cover image, Christian Teilman: *Paraphrase over Sæterjentens Söndag*.
Courtesy, Bergen Offentlige Bibliotek

middle ground are familiar objects from Norwegian folk life, including a group of goats and a turf-roofed wooden cabin or *sæter* hut, and the glassy waters of the fjord curve away into the distance amid dramatic mountain peaks. As in the illustrations in Tønsberg's book upon which Teilman's cover picture is closely based, it is arguably the landscape, rather than the figure in the foreground, that ultimately captures our attention. But as Peer Findeisen observes, landscape also functioned as part of a post-colonial discourse in nineteenth-century Norway. 'The national-Romantically coloured Sæter-idyll relied not only upon a new bucolic idealisation of the Rousseauian wilderness, but also upon the urban–rural conflict as a manifestation of the social divisions grounded in pro- and anti-Danish tendencies.'[20] Hence, the kitsch aspect existed alongside a deeper, more essentialised notion of the Norwegian landscape, and it is this atavistic sense of place that many of Grieg's pieces evoked.

Like the *sæter*, the folk wedding offered an opportunity to combine generic themes from the Romantic landscape with figures and ritual traditions from local Norwegian folk life. Tidemand's and Gude's most famous painting, *Brudefærden i Hardanger* ('The Bridal Procession in Hardanger'), was the centrepiece of the 1849 *tableaux vivants*, following Bull's *Sæterbesøg* and a setting by Halfdan Kjerulf of Andreas Munch's poem *Brudefærden* ('The Bridal Procession'). Motives used in the picture are similar to those found in the illustrations for Tønsberg's book: a wedding party rows across a fjord towards a distant bank on which can be seen a medieval stave church. As was the case in the *sæter* pictures, the boat is almost completely overshadowed by the scale of the surrounding mountain scenery, the fjord leading towards a distant glimpse of the Folgefonn glacier in the background. Two figures provide a focal point in the foreground: a *Freischütz*-like rifleman who fires bullets into the air, and a lone fiddler accompanying the bridal procession. This collection of images, with its suggestion of church bells and distant mountain perspectives, is in many ways typical of the Swiss Alpine Romanticism that enjoyed particular popularity on the continent in the first half of the nineteenth century. Only small details such as the design of the stave church or the identity of the fiddler (Ole Bull was the model in some versions of the painting) provide elements of more specific local colour. In this sense, the painting supports Dahlhaus's analysis of nineteenth-century musical nationalism, in that its actual sense of place is ultimately subordinate to its broader generic features. Indeed, for continental audiences, the picture's imagery might have seemed almost tired or over-familiar. The spectacle of

[20] 'Dem nationalromantisch eingefärbten Sæteridyll liegt bei weitern nicht nur einer neuerliche bukolische Idealisierung der Rousseauschen Wildnis, sondern der Stadt-Land-Konflikt als Erscheinungsform der Gesellschaftsspaltung in pro- und antidänische Strömungen zugrunde.' Findeisen, *Instrumentale Folklorestilisierung*, 251.

the wedding, as symbol of a new Norwegian folk nationalism, was parodied for example in the first act of Ibsen's *Peer Gynt* (1864) for which Grieg later provided incidental music. But this sense of over-familiarity does not seem to have affected contemporary Norwegian audiences. In a review of the *tableaux vivants* dated 30 March 1849, the newspaper *Morgenbladet* declared: 'the North's earnest soul revealed itself here through poetic views, tones and forms, and struck a mighty blow in every disposition for which the national is not just an empty sound'.[21]

Considering the cultural weight associated with such imagery, it is possible to recontextualise Grieg's creative response to the folk wedding. There are several wedding melodies in the op. 17 collection based on tunes taken from Lindeman's anthology, including a 'Brurelåt' ('Wedding Tune') and 'Reiseslåt' ('Recessional March') from Gol in Hallingdal and a 'Brurelåt' from Vang in Valdres. Furthermore, a series of three wedding marches dominates the first half of the *Slåtter*. 'Gibøens Bruremarsj' ('Gibøen's Wedding March') opens the set, and a 'Bruremarsj fra Telemark' comes third, while the contrasting eighth number, 'Bruremarsj (etter Myllarguten)' ('Myllarguten's Wedding March') is perhaps the emotional high-point of the collection. Wedding marches also appear among the *Lyric Pieces*, not least 'Bryllupsdag på Troldhaugen' ('Wedding Day at Troldhaugen'), op. 65/6 (written to celebrate Grieg's own silver wedding anniversary).[22] Generic characteristics of the wedding march can be found in other pieces, such as the festive 'Hjemad' ('Homeward') that concludes the op. 62 set. Herresthal also suggests that 'there is a clear connection between Adoph Tidemand's picture series "Brudeslåtten", Bjørnson's folk tale of the same name and "Brudefølget drar forbi" ['The bridal procession passes by'] from Grieg's *Folkelivsbilder* ['Scenes from Folk Life'], op. 19'.[23] Unlike the *Slåtter* or the tunes in op. 17, the *Folkelivsbilder* are not based on actual folk tunes. Rather, as Herresthal argues, the impetus seems to have been a visual or pictorial one. The second number, for example, is notable for its processional form, beginning with hushed accompanimental figuration and gradually building up to a point of dynamic and registral saturation at its centre, before winding down to a *pianissimo* conclusion. More innovative perhaps is the poignancy of the moment of distant remembrance in the centre of the third number,

[21] 'Nordens alvorsfulde Ånd åbenbarede sig her gjennem digteriske Anskuelser, Toner og Gestalter; og slog mægtigt an i ethvert Gemyt, for hvilket det Nationale ei er blot en tom Klang.' Quoted in Herresthal, *Med spark i gulvet*, 90.

[22] See Benestad and Schjelderup Ebbe, *Edvard Grieg*, 329. The piece was originally titled 'Gratulanterne Kommer' ('The well-wishers are coming'): two pages from the manuscript of this version were reproduced the year after Grieg's death in Gerhard Schjelderup and Walter Niemann, *Edvard Grieg: Biographie und Würdigung seiner Werke* (Leipzig: Peters, 1908), between pp. 112 and 113.

[23] 'Det er en klar sammenheng mellom Adoph Tidemand's billedserie "Brudeslåtten", Bjørnsons bondefortelling med samme titel og "Brudefølget drar forbi" fra Griegs *Folkelivsbilder* Op. 19.' Herresthal, *Med spark i gulvet*, 79.

'Fra Karnevalet' ('From the Carnival'), where fragments of the wedding procession are briefly heard in the unrelated key of F major. This deliberate 'cross-cutting' is a spatial technique, not just a cyclic return, that anticipates Debussy's suggestion of distantly heard festival music in 'La Sérénade interrompue' from the *Première livre de préludes*. It also suggests that it is the sudden sense of temporal displacement, the momentary suspension of normal musical time, that is an important element in Grieg's representation of landscape, and not simply the stylised evocation of a particular local tradition. Hence, the folk wedding as a topic in Grieg's music points to deeper qualities that define his sense of musical landscape: notions of distance, space and time, and the primacy of bell sounds in particular, that identify landscape as a special category in his work.

Landscape, space and temporality: Grieg's 'culture of sound'

In a letter to Gottfred Matthison-Hansen, dated 10 April 1869, Grieg remarked: 'Bjørnson has written a pretty sketch of me in today's *Norsk Folkeblad*, which you should read. In it he says that I am a landscape painter – how fitting, for my life's dream is to set the North's nature in sound.'[24] Grieg's diaries and correspondence reveal many instances of his first-hand response to the Norwegian landscape, often in terms that recall earlier pictorial representations such as the 1849 *tableaux vivants*. In a letter to August Winding, dated 28 June 1896, for example, Grieg wrote:

> I am now 53 years old and have just learnt that one should go to Hardanger before midsummer, if one wants to see its poetry in all its greatness and charm. Then the waterfalls' immense symphony can be heard, the glaciers shimmer, the air is filled with an aroma, the nights are light, and the whole existance is like a fairy-tale. Just imagine, we didn't go to bed in the evenings. We sat out in the light night one evening after another, drinking in the beautiful air and the light dawning fjord, which then lay in its deep calm.[25]

Other descriptions are similarly ecstatic and, for Grieg, the Norwegian landscape often appears to have performed an epiphanal function. At times, this was combined with a heightened sense of patriotism, so that

[24] 'Bjørnson har idag i "Norsk Folkeblad" skrevet en smuk Skizze af mig, som Du skulde læse. Han siger deri, at jeg er landskabsmaler – hvor træffende, thi mit Livs Drøm er at kunne give Nordens Natur i Toner.' *Brev*, I, 142.
[25] 'Jeg er nu bleven 53 År og har først iår lært, at man skal rejse i Hardanger før St. Hans, om man vil se dets Poesi i al sin forende Storhed og Ynde. Da har Fosserne sine vældige Symfonier at lade høre, da skinner Isbræerne, da er Luften mettet med Aroma, da er Nætterne lys, hele Tilværelsen derinde som et Æventyr. Tænk Dig, vi var ikke at få tilsengs om Kvælden. Vi blev siddende den lyse Nat udover det ene Døgn efter det andet, drikkende ind den skjønne Luft og den lyse dæmrende Fjord, som den lå i sin dybe Fred.' *Brev*, II, 279.

topography became elided with the image of the nation. To Otto Aubert, for instance, he confided that 'no yearning pulls me like that towards home's mountain nature',[26] and to Johan Andreas Budtz Christie he wrote: 'Yes, the mountains, the mountains! I feel for them as though they were human characters. God knows, there is something called love for the Fatherland, which is more than just a phrase.'[27] This sense of the landscape as a human character or presence is another recurring theme in Grieg's writing. In an oft-quoted letter to Jonas Lie, he wrote: 'my western mountains draw me continually back with an irresistable force. It is as though they still have so much to tell me.'[28] Here there is a strong sense of disembodiment, as though the landscape adopts its own tone of voice so that we could imagine nature 'speaking through' Grieg's music. Another letter to Christie, written from Amsterdam, records: 'I hope to be at home again in the spring and gladden myself with the thought of seeing my dear, dear Norway again, wandering in the mountains and concealing myself in Nature's never-failing embrace.'[29] But on other occasions landscape seems not to have served simply as a retreat or a human presence so much as a physical, creative and emotional cure. To the younger Norwegian composer Iver Holter he wrote:

> Should we meet in Jotunheim this month? The day after tomorrow I'll march up to Turtegrøsæter in the vicinity of the Skagastøltinder – via the ascent from Fortun in Sogn – to get my nerves steeled for the winter. Will you come along, or shall I meet you elsewhere? Ich bin zu allen Schandthaten fähig. You have fished, swum and sailed down in that Norwegian civilisation enough. Now let Nature have you for a while. You need an inoculation of mountain stuff into your work.[30]

Hence, for Grieg the western Norwegian mountains also represented a form of *Körperkultur*, a celebration of healthy physicality whose beneficial effects were directly related to creative well-being (and, by implication,

---

[26] 'Ingen Længsel drager mig som den mod Hjemmets Fjeldnatur.' Letter dated 25 January 1891, *Brev*, I, 19.

[27] 'Ja, de Fjelde, de Fjelde! Jeg føler for dem, som om de var menneskelige Væsener! Gud ske Lov, at det er Noget, som hedder Fædrelandskjærlighed, det er dog Noget mere end en Frase.' Letter dated 27 January 1880, ibid., 137.

[28] 'Mine vestlandske Fjeldtrakter drager mig bestandig tilbage med uimodståelig Magt. Det er, som om de endnu havde så meget, meget at sige mig.' Letter dated 18 October 1888, ibid., 502.

[29] 'Jeg håber i Foråret at være hjemme igjen og glæder mig allerede ved Tanken om at se mit kjære, kjære Norge igjen, vandre i Fjeldene og gjemme mig bort i Naturens aldrig skuffende Favn.' Letter dated 28 December 1883, quoted in ibid., 140.

[30] 'Skulde vi træffes i Jotunheimen i denne Måned? Jeg drager iovermorgen til Turtegrøsæter i Nærheden af Skagastølstinderne – Opgang fra Fortun i Sogn – forat skaffe mi Stålnærver til Vinteren. Vil Du komme did, eller skal jeg møde Dig et andet Sted? Ich bin zu allen Schandthaten fähig. Du har nu fisket, badet og sejlet nok dernede i den norske Civilatation. Lad nu Naturen få Dig en Stund. Du trænger også en Indpodning af Fjeldstoffer til Din Virksomhed.' Letter dated 11 August 1890, quoted in ibid., 415.

were opposed to the supposedly unhealthy effects of urban civilisation).

Grieg's emphasis on the physicality of the western Norwegian landscape and its perceived healthiness reflects a broader cultural shift in Norway in the second half of the nineteeth century. While artists and writers had already eulogised the west's rugged mountain scenery as picturesque or sublime, it was increasingly seen as emblematic of Norwegian cultural difference and political independence. Among such hardened attitudes to the rural environment, a series of youth organisations (*ungdomslaga*) were established across Norway to promote a greater spirit of patriotism through increased self-esteem, physical health and a sense of local community. Significantly, their work included a revival (or in many cases the reinvention) of folk customs, including folk dancing and the dialect language, as well as outdoor activities such as fell walking.[31] Such movements were not exclusively Norwegian: Germany, Austria and other coutries across northern Europe also saw the creation of a large number of youth groups and *Wanderverein* in the second half of the century, dedicated to the promotion of physical health, whose ideological basis was often nationalistic in origin. Even if Grieg did not feel entirely committed to such political agendas, it is not difficult to read elements of this *Körperkultur* in many of his folk-song arrangements or folk-inspired pieces. In a letter to Johan Halvorsen from Copenhagen, he wrote:

> Though I am abroad, my thoughts are all about Norway and Norwegians, about all our youthful combativeness up there. Yes, it is like the music of harsh triads compared with all the soft sugary seventh chords down here. Up there the conflict concerns spiritual existence, but down here it is just a matter of trivialities.[32]

Grieg's archetypal Norwegian 'music of harsh triads' can be heard most forcefully in the *Slåtter*, and works such as the 'Gangar' from the *Lyric Pieces*, op. 54, or 'Morgo ska du få gifte deg' ('Tomorrow you shall marry her') from the *19 norske Folkeviser*, op. 66/10. In such pieces, the evocation of a folk idiom is combined with a strikingly diatonic (or triadic) harmonic language and highly rhythmic and repetive melodic textures, to generate music where the sense of physical momentum outweighs other parameters.

One of Grieg's most extreme examples of this energetic physicalised music is the 'Gangar' from the op. 54 set of *Lyric Pieces*. A *gangar* is a moderately

---

[31] See Inga Ranheim, 'Folkedans og disiplinering', in Sørensen, *Nasjonal identitet*, 73–89. The various independent *ungdomslaga* were rationalised into a centralised association, Noregs ungdomslag, on 12 July 1896, and membership reached around 50,000 by the 1920s (76).

[32] 'Mine Tanker kredser trods al Udlændighed bare om Norge og Nordmænd, om al vor unge Stridbarhed deroppe. Ja, den er som Musik af hårde Treklang sammenlignet med alle de blødsøde Septim-akkorder hernede. Deroppe gjælder Kampen åndelig Ekistents. Hernede Pavens Skjæg.' Letter dated 3 February 1900, quoted in *Brev*, I, 364.

Example 2.4. Grieg: 'Gangar', op. 54/2

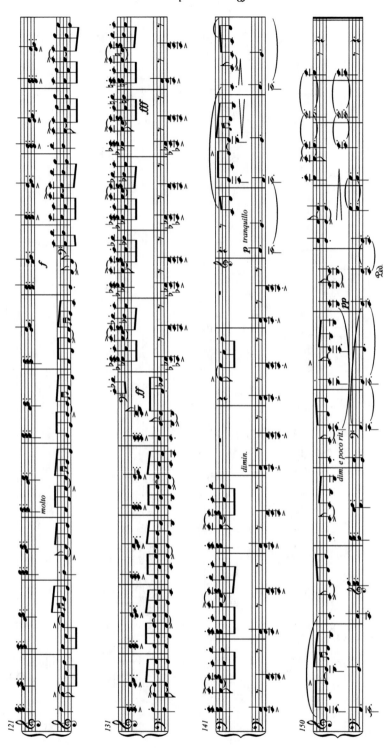

Example 2.5. Grieg: 'Klokkeklang', op. 54/6. Opening, climax (middle section) and coda.

(a) Opening (bb. 1 to 18)

(b) Climax (bb. 37 to 61)

(c) Coda (b. 77 to end)

paced walking-dance in duple metre, but in op. 54/2 structural emphasis is placed on register and dynamic accumulation, rather than on motivic development. Indeed, in the long sequential passages which dominate the middle section of the dance, motivic material is almost entirely liquidated (Ex. 2.4). Chromatic elements from the opening page which initially supported functional diatonic harmony (principally f♯, g♯ and c♯ over secondary dominant progressions) are strikingly absent, and the music is almost exclusively based on white-note collections. The single exception to this pattern is the cadential (flat-side) chromatic swerve in bars 68–72, but even here chromatic diversion is swiftly followed by the return of the white-note collection as the remaining black notes are 'drummed out' by the music's heightened dynamic level and the left hand's swinging fifths.[33] This process of harmonic 'cleansing' is reinforced by a short epilogue marked *tranquillo* (bars 80–4), before the whole process is repeated from the start of the second phrase.

The 'Gangar' can be understood as landscape music not simply because of the way in which it responds to a particular pictorial representation of Norwegian folk life (as was the case with 'Brudefølget drar forbi' from the *Folkelivsbilder*, for example), but also by drawing up precise formal boundaries within which it operates according to a set of more abstract musical rules. In this sense, the 'Gangar' is a musical equivalent of the process of spatial and temporal organisation described by Edward Casey. These rules involve patterns of registral behaviour (the opening and filling-in of particular tessituras), harmonic-intervallic syntax (the primacy of 'harsh triads' and white notes over dissonant chromatic pitch elements) and dynamic shape. The design of the sequential passages in particular is essentially a spatial one. Their purpose is to unfold register, and there is a sense that, without the chromatic interjection at bars 68 and 135, they could continue unfolding register indefinitely until out of human auditory range, an example perhaps of what Casey understands as landscape's resistance to containment within a fixed space. But their purpose is also temporal: the repetitiveness of the rhythmic figuration and the restricted pitch content creates a partial suspension of regular musical time, and encourages the listener's pyschological conversion of time into space through the mapping out of highly regular musical units. The dance only seems to move forward in certain parameters (register, dynamics), while other normally privileged aspects (pitch content, harmonic rhythm) stand still. The epilogue functions as a framing device, enforcing a temporary sense of closure on material whose momentum otherwise seems unstoppable. Ultimately, the dance can

---

[33] An analogous process is developed in the final bars of Sibelius's Third Symphony (1907), where a block of triadic C major music resolves the symphony's large-scale structural harmonic tension by 'drumming out' a single chromatic pitch element, f♯.

be understood as the expression of powerful structural divisions, between material which is dynamic and generative and other elements which remain static.

The final number in the op. 54 set, 'Klokkeklang', is even more radical than the 'Gangar' in its pursuit of an abstract structuralist agenda. W. Dean Sutcliffe has shown how the piece sets up a fundamental tension between an intervallic language based on the vertical primacy of the perfect fifth, which dominates almost all of the musical foreground in the work, and the expectation of functional diatonic behaviour. Landscape again figures prominently as an important element in the work's design. As the title suggests, at one level the piece can be heard as a study in bell sonorities, a sound world premised on the realisation of a single acoustical object (or *Klang*). In this sense, the work presents a kind of 'photographic' realism. On another level, however, the music resists such pictorial evocation. As Sutcliffe suggests, 'the apparent inflexibility of [the music's] presentation and lack of contextualising support, such as the emergence of a point of melodic focus or cadential articulation, seem to leave no room to accommodate either the player or the listener'.[34] One particular moment in the work crystallises the tension between the figurative and structural elements in 'Klokkeklang' (Ex. 2.5). The start of the coda in bar 77 is significant because it marks the first break in the pattern of ostinato fifths that has hitherto underpinned the work. The sudden change to a hymn-like chordal texture could be heard as representing the sound of a church organ, serving to 'sacralise' the sense of place evoked by the preceding musical material. But, as Sutcliffe's analysis demonstrates, the chord in bar 77 also serves other more purely structural purposes, by recontextualising the e–b dyad from the earlier climax of the work in bar 49, resolving a diatonically dissonant pitch element that had been left hanging unresolved at the apex of the work's arch-form. Furthermore, the coda summarises other aspects of the work's structure by a process of gap-filling to articulate a complete C major scale in the left hand, bars 77–81, and by compressing the work's overall dynamic and registral shape into the space of barely eight bars. Sutcliffe suggests that the prominence of the perfect fifth in the musical argument of 'Klokkeklang' can be heard as an attempt to achieve a 'more elemental expression of national identity'. But, he argues, this sense of identity is less reliant on the evocation of actual folk music, as in op. 17, than on an act of essentialisation. 'The distillation of national idiom into open fifths even lends a certain pagan quality that fights against the pictorial and programmatic associations of the title.'[35] This process of abstraction and refinement is fundamental to Grieg's landscape music. It suggests that, in Grieg's music, the pictorial associations and structural

[34] Sutcliffe, 'Grieg's Fifth', 165.
[35] Ibid., 179–80.

functions of landscape co-exist uneasily, but that the tension between these different modes of perception is one of the primary dynamics in his work. In effect it becomes a creative dissonance. It also suggests that landscape can be understood as a site of intense auditory awareness in Grieg's work, as a state in which normative patterns of linear temporal behaviour in music are momentarily suspended. The extended white-note sequential passages in the 'Gangar' suggest an infinite reproducability that resists diatonic closure, and the ostinato in 'Klokkeklang' creates a wholly new sense of ordered musical space. And it is arguably the denial of personal subjectivity and the longing for transcendence that this systematic organisation and division of musical space creates that is the most powerful expression of Grieg's landscape vision.

'Taken into the mountains': enchantment, distance and nostalgia

Landscape often seems to have provided an environmental context or framework for Grieg's experience of folk song. On particular occasions, such direct 'environmental' encounters with folk music are associated with a sense of enchantment, of being drawn into a privileged inner sound world similar to that revealed in 'Klokkeklang'. In a letter to the Danish composer Niels Ravnkilde on 17 October 1887, for example, Grieg described a recent walking trip he had taken to the Jotunheim mountains in western Norway:

> It is a long time since you've heard from me, but my life has been so quiet over the last year that there is nothing great to report. I have lived at my 'Troldhaug' throughout the winter and most of the summer, except for a tour in our western mountains, Jotunheim, with passion, where for a fortnight every summer, together with my fine friend Frants Beyer, I bathe in the timelessness. Yes, here one stands face to face with greatness: it is Shakespeare, Beethoven, and whatever genius you could desire in pure form! I would not swap this for a dozen Gewandhaus concerts![36]

Here, nature stands as a metaphor for Grieg's own sense of creative isolation. His stress on the 'pure' greatness of the Norwegian landscape over and beyond the work of canonic figures such as Beethoven and Shakespeare arguably articulates his own sense of peripheralisation. In other words, landscape becomes a means of asserting Grieg's own artistic independence, even if,

---

[36] 'Det er nok lang Tid siden Du hørte fra mig, men, mit Liv er i det sidste År henrundet så stille, at derom ikke er Stort at berette. Jeg har boet på min "Troldhaug" hele vinteren og det meste af Sommeren, faregnet en Tur i vore vestlandske Højfjeld, Jotunhjem, mit Sværmeri, hvor jeg hver Sommer i 14 Dags Tid med min prægtige Ven Frants beyer bader mig i Oprindelighed. Ja, her står man Ansigt til Ansigt med det Store: det er Shakespeare, Beethoven og hvad Du vil af Sligt i ren Ekstrakt! Jeg bytter ikke dette for et Dusin Gewandhauskoncerter!' *Brev*, II, 224.

as his reference to the Gewandhaus implies, it also demands a renunciation of one of the most privileged institutions associated with the mainstream Austro-German symphonic tradition. But it also represents a heightened sense of aural awareness or sensitivity to sound. Grieg proceeds to describe one particular experience from the trip, a chance meeting with two herding girls high on the mountain pasture:

> I must tell you about one marvellous, clear sunny August day amid the Skagastøl range. We wanted to climb over a mountain called 'Friken', but couldn't obtain a guide, partly because it was Sunday, and partly because the men were away reindeer herding. Then two pretty farm girls appeared on the mountain pasture, an older girl and a fine young blonde girl, called Susanne. They offered to lead us over the mountain. With laughter and singing we set off, and on the top we sat and enjoyed whatever our rucksacks could offer. Cognac and glacier-water raised the mood to ethereal heights. But the most beautiful part had yet to come, for Susanne had with her a small, national instrument, a goat horn, which only has three notes; and when the girls had bid us farewell on the top, because they had to return to milk the cows, and as Frants and I stood absorbed over the beautiful scene as we watched them wander along the mountain edge, blonde, slender and erect, with the blue horizon as background – suddenly they stopped, Susanne set the goat's horn to her mouth – I will never forget the sight of their shape against the sky – and we heard a gentle, melancholy sound, as if from the mountains around us:

> When that final G had died away, we looked at each other, and stood in tears! For we had felt the same![37]

Grieg dwells especially on the sound of the goat horn heard from a distance so that it assumes a nostalgic, disembodied quality. Grieg transcribed the

[37] 'Jeg må fortælle Dig om en herlig, solklar Augustdag midt mellem "Skagastøltinderne". Vi skulde stige over et Fjeld, som hedder "Friken", men kunde ingen Fører få, dels fordi det var Søndag og dels fordi Mændene var på Rensdyrskytteri. Så var der to snilde Budejer på Sæteren, en ældre og en yngre blong prægtige Jente, som hed Susanne. Disse tilbød sig da at følge os over Fjeldet. Under Sang og Jubel bar det nu opover og på Højden satte vi os ned og levede højt med hvad Randslerne kunde byde. Konjac og Brævand lod Stemningen stige til en formelig ætherisk Højde. Med de Skjønneste havde vi endnu tilbage, thi Susanne havde et lidet nationalt Instrument med sig, et Bukkehorn, som blot ejer *tre* Toner, og da Jenterne havde sagt os Farvel deroppe på Toppen, fordi de nu måtte ned igjen og malke Kjørene, og da Frants og jeg just stod fortabt over det skjønne Syn at se dem vandre henad Fjeldets Rand, lys, let og rank, med den blå Horisont som Baggrund, da med Et – Jenterne stod stille – satte Susanne Bukkehorn for Munden – jeg glemmer aldrig Stillingen, Formernes Udtryk imod Luften: Da tonede det mildt vemodigt, som ud af Fjeldnaturen omkring os: [music example]. Da det sidste G var henklinget, så vi på hinanden – og stod i Tårer! Thi vi havde følt det Samme!' Ibid., 225.

melody and quoted it eight years later in a song entitled 'Ku-Lok' ('Herding Call') originally intended for his song cycle *Haugtussa*, a setting of poetry in the western Norwegian dialect language *nynorsk* by Arne Garborg, discussed in more detail in Chapter 3. At the end of his letter, Grieg reflected:

> And so you see how it was that a Norwegian musician was bewitched. It is wonderful – but whether it is actually something one would wish for is another thing altogether. For to be overwhelmed to the point of annihilation by the majesty of Nature is a dangerous business, and I realise that there is something within my character that leads that way, and yet it cannot be otherwise unless you prefer to pull on kid gloves and settle in one of Europe's capital cities, as the majority of our great men wonderfully understand it.[38]

The idea of enchantment or bewitchment, of abduction by supernatural powers or literally of being 'taken into the mountains', is a recurrent theme in Nordic mythology, not least among the tales collected by folklorists such as Asbjørnsen and Moe. Enchantment is also fundamental to much of Grieg's landscape music. The sense of suspended temporality in the middle sections of the 'Gangar', or the radical spatial geometry of 'Klokkeklang', can be heard as forms of musical enchantment: the 'pagan quality' identified by Sutcliffe that conflicts with the music's purely pictorial mode of evocation.

Grieg's setting of a poem from Magnus Brostrup Landstad's collection of *Norske Folkeviser*, *Den Bergtekne*, offers a parallel example of musical enchantment. The folk text, in the dialect language, narrates the story of a lone man wandering in the mountains who is bewitched by the daughter of the mountains (*jutuldottri*), before being abandoned alone in a state of madness, unable to find his way out of the forest. Grieg's setting responds to this idea of enchantment on several musical levels. The setting is a varied strophic structure that begins with an instrumental play-over of the refrain (Ex. 2.6), preceded by a two-bar introduction that articulates a deceptive cadence, opening with a bold G minor chord (marked *fp*) that resolves to V/ E (fading to a mysterious *pianissimo*). The sense of harmonic disorientation created by this opening cadential gesture is reinforced by the placement of pauses over each bar, so that the music also lacks a sense of regular pulse until the start of the refrain in bar 3. Julian Johnson argues that the use of such mediant modulations is so frequent in nineteenth-century music that it would be wrong to identify this gesture alone as a landscape signifier.

---

[38] 'Ser Du, sådan går det til, at en norsk Musiker blir bjergtagen. Dejligt er det, – men om det er Noget at ønske sig, er an anden Sag. Thi at overvældes indtil Tilintetgjørelse af det Store i Naturen er en farlig Sag og jeg ved, at der er Noget i min Sjæl, der lider ved dette, men, det kan ikke være anderledes, – når man da ikke foretrækker at trække Glacéhandsker på sig og sætte sig ned i en af Europas Hovedstæder, således som de Fleste af vore store Mænd vidunderligvis forstår det.' Ibid.

Example 2.6. Grieg: *Den Bergtekne. Opening (playover) and climax.*

Climax (bb. 93 to110)

Nevertheless, he maintains that it is significant that the device came to be associated with notions of transcendence or (as here) of the uncanny, of the shift from the earthly world to an ethereal other realm. Hence, 'the mediant modulation is not merely a conventional sign or symbol for the idea of transcendence; rather, it does quite literally transcend the gravitational field of the key system it leaves behind'.[39] The chromaticism inherent in the opening bars of *Den Bergtekne* subsequently inflect the presentation of the principal theme, which is harmonised by a descending chromatic bass line that constantly avoids cadential closure. The implications of this deceptive opening gesture are felt on a broader structural level. The music includes two large-scale harmonic swerves. The first takes place at the end of the opening strophe (bars 34–42), so that instead of cadencing in the tonic (E minor), the music veers towards V/G minor (a key centre associated with the chord that 'deceptively' opened the refrain). This is simultaneously the point at which the narrator's retelling of the process of bewitchment begins. Though the music returns towards E minor at the end of the second strophe, the expected return of the refrain is undermined by a German sixth chord (bars 74–5), a second harmonic swerve motivated by the persistence of a single pitch element (b♭) from the work's opening bar. The third strophe is a lilting folk dance in C major that describes the narrator's state of hallucination as he is enchanted by the mountain spirit, complete with falsetto top g (bar 97) creating a heightened sense of intoxication. The music reaches an ecstatic climax on the 'unreal' key of D♭ (bar 101) before collapsing in a state of cold reality back onto a stern *G minor* sonority (bars 106–7) that leads into the return of the refrain with which song concludes. It is only here, finally, that the song achieves tonal closure.

There are various formal and structural tensions within *Den Bergtekne* which remain unresolved by the song's conclusion. The position of the narrator, for example, remains ambiguous: the tale is narrated in the past tense, yet the music suggests that events are replayed in 'real time', creating a cinematic sense of displacement between musical structure and textual narrative (a familiar distancing device in nineteenth-century song). Similarly, the precise alignment of the two crucial harmonic climaxes in bars 101 and 106–7 is not completely synchronised with the text. The moment of disillusionment textually begins at bar 101 ('men ingin så heve eg!', 'yet I have no-one!'), but is followed by a brief glimpse of the 'enchanted' C major music from the third strophe, while the moment of disillusionment musically is only reached five bars later as the song returns to its initial G minor sonority in a crushing *fortissimo*.

As in 'Klokkeklang', the role of landscape in *Den Bergtekne* is to create an

---

[39] Johnson, *Webern and the Transformation of Nature*, 55.

underlying desire for the resolution of seemingly irreconcilable oppositions, in this case of narrative and harmonic key area. The yearning for closure is a fundamentally *nostalgic* musical vision, since in *Den Bergtekne* it ultimately results in a sense of loss, hollowness or incompleteness. Svetlana Boym has identified this quality in her analysis of the structure of nostalgia as a historical topic. For Boym,

> Nostalgia (from *nostos* – return home, and *algia* – longing) is a longing for a home that no longer exists or has never existed. Nostalgia is a sentiment of loss and displacement, but it is also a romance with one's own fantasy. Nostalgic love can only survive in a long-distance relationship. A cinematic image of nostalgia is a double exposure, or a superimposition of two images – of home and abroad, past and present, dream and everyday life. The moment we try and force it into a single image, it breaks the frame or burns the surface.[40]

Nostalgia therefore relies on a double temporal vision, the simultaneous existence of past and present. Landscape arguably works in a similar way: it is something that is historically shaped or constructed yet is perceived in an active present, so that it exists in two timeframes at once. This is partly responsible for the sense of displacement which, as Boym suggests, is characteristic of nostalgia. But landscape, like nostalgia, is also concerned with issues of subjective authority or control. Boym argues that 'unlike melancholia, which confines itself to the planes of individual consciousness, nostalgia is about the relationship between individual biography and the biography of groups or nations, between personal and collective memory'.[41] Landscape is similarly something both collectively and personally defined: it relies on a series of generically defined conventions or traditions, but is constructed and perceived individually. Hence, in musical representations of landscape such as *Den Bergtekne* it becomes unclear whose voice speaks, whether it is the voice of the composer, a narrative character, or a more collective identity (history, nature or tradition). Grieg himself appears to have sensed as much. In a letter to his biographer Gerhard Schjelderup, dated 18 September 1903, he wrote:

> I knew that you had a keen eye out for *Den Bergtagne* [sic]. Between the Sørfjord's mountains in winter mood, when I wrote that and much else of the best I have done (for example the String Quartet), I got hold of Landstad's *Folkeviser*. I sought more of the same stuff as that which I had used in *Den Bergtagne*. I would have included choir and large orchestra. But I couldn't find the text I sought and so it became simply these fragments. It was the years

[40] Boym, *The Future of Nostalgia*, p. xiii.
[41] Ibid., p. xvi.

> 77–78. That was an important period in my life, rich in incidents
> and mental shocks. I sought peace and clarity and self-absorption,
> and found all this in splendid Hardanger. The place became so
> dear to me that I built myself a little working hut and returned
> regularly each summer for 4–5 years. But finally I realised that it
> was as if the mountains had nothing more to tell me. It was foolish
> of me to watch them and I realised it was high time to leave.[42]

Having been bewitched by the landscape and become immersed in self-absorption, Grieg's letter suggests, he is ultimately abandoned and left in silence, unable to find a way forward. Hence, it is tempting to hear *Den Bergtekne* as an allegory of musical creativity, a loss of inspiration or control as much as an act of creative will or organisation.

This nostalgic sense of loss or displacement is especially prevalent in Grieg's settings of *lokks* (herding calls), similar to the melody heard on the fellside in his letter to Niels Ravnkilde of 1887. Such *lokks* are often characterised by a feeling of decentredness that is as much temporal as spatial. Boym argues that, although nostalgia is associated with a sense of space, it is simultaneously a 'yearning for a different time – the time of our childhood, the slower rhythms of our dreams'. Hence, nostalgia becomes an act of resistance, a 'rebellion against the modern idea of time, the time of history and progress. The nostalgic desires to obliterate history and turn it into private or collective mythology, to revisit time like space, refusing to surrender to the irreversibility of time that plagues the human condition.'[43] Grieg's attempt to 'mythologise time' can be heard in two of the *Lyric Pieces* in particular: 'Gjetergut' ('Shepherd's Boy'), the first of the op. 54 collection, and 'Aften på Höyfjellet' ('Evening in the Mountains') from op. 68. These two pieces exemplify different kinds of nostalgia identified by Boym: *restorative* nostalgia, which 'ends up reconstructing emblems and rituals of home and homeland in an attempt to conquer and spatialise time', and *reflective* nostalgia, which 'cherishes shattered fragments of memory and temporalises space'.[44]

'Gjetergut' is concerned more with ritual reconstruction than with reflection. The piece opens with the stylised sound of a folk pipe suspended

---

[42] 'Jeg vidste nok, at De havde Blikket åbent for "Den Bergtagne". Mellem Sørfjordens Fjelde i Vinterstemning, da jeg skrev dette og meget Andet af det Bedste, jeg har gjort (f. Ek. Strygekvartetten) fik jeg også Fat i Landstads Folkeviser. Jeg søgte mere Stof af samme Surdejg som det, jeg har brugt i "Den Bjergtagne". Jeg vilde da have medtaget Kor og større Orkester. Men jeg fandt ikke den Tekst, jeg søgt og så blev det da bare dette Brudstykke. Det var i Årene 77–8. Det var et betydningsfuld Afsnit i mit Liv, rigt på Begivenheder og sjælelige Rystelser. Jeg søgte Ro og Klarhed og Selvfordybelse og fandt alt dette i det herlige Hardanger. Stedet blev mig så kjært, at det jeg byggede mig en liden Arbejdshytte og i 4–5 År hver Sommer stadig vendt tilbage. Men endelig forekom det meg, som om Fjeldene Intet mer havde at fortælle mig. Jeg blev dum af at se på dem og fandt at det var på højeste Tid at forsvinde.' *Brev*, I, 613.

[43] Boym, *The Future of Nostalgia*, p. xv.

[44] Ibid., 49.

above a seemingly motionless bass (Ex. 2.7). The figure of a shepherd boy playing on a willow flute is both an archetypal pastoral topic and a more localised Norwegian folk image: willow flutes were cut from bark in spring, when the tree sap is rising, so that they became fertility symbols.[45] In Grieg's piece, the willow flute becomes homoeroticised. The chromatic inflections of the melodic line (particularly the augmented second between $c\sharp^2$ and $b\flat^1$), the sighing appoggiaturas and lack of clear cadential articulation result in a constant suspension of harmonic closure, creating a longing for stability which was identified as a conventional signifier of desire in late-nineteenth-century music after its paradigmatic use in Wagner's *Tristan und Isolde* (a piece to which both 'Gjetergut' and 'Aften på Höyfjellet' refer).[46] As the piece develops, this eroticisation becomes a process of chromatic saturation, intensified via rising sequential repetition until the music reaches a sudden diatonic moment of release (*fortissimo*, bar 28). From this dynamic and harmonic high-point, the music descends to the lowest reaches of the piano register in a series of parallel fifths (the texture of the left hand in the opening bar) until it reaches the dominant in a hushed *pianissississimo*, a rare moment of clarity after the chromaticism of the preceding page. In the reprise (Tempo I), the willow flute melody is intertwined canonically around itself in the inner parts. After a final harmonic crisis, in which the left hand's parallel fifths of bars 30–5 are vertically superimposed on top of each other,[47] the chromaticism of the opening page is liquidated in a series of descending chromatic lines until only a single oscillating intervallic fragment remains: the brooding $a\flat$–d tritone of bars 55–6. Grieg dedicated the op. 54 collection to his friend, the Dutch composer Julius Röntgen. Writing to Grieg to express his thanks on 20 December 1891, Röntgen wrote that the pieces would be 'a special souvenir from last summer and a reminder of those unforgettable days in the Jotunheim mountains'. He added:

> there is a bit of yourself and of the Norwegian nation in each of them, and I think I can actually follow your thoughts in them. The mood of the first piece, for example, is without a doubt that of Turtagrö. It conveys a feeling of utter loneliness. The piece in

[45] On the tradition and repertoire of the willow flute in Norway, see Ola Kai Ledang, 'Magic, Means and Meaning: An Insider's View of Bark Flutes in Norway', *Selected Reports in Ethnomusicology* 8 (1990), 105–24, and Grinde, *A History of Norwegian Music*, 88–9.

[46] For a colourful summary of chromaticism and the erotic in fin-de-siècle music, see Lawrence Kramer, *Music as Cultural Practice, 1800–1900*, California Studies in Nineteenth-Century Music 8 (Berkeley: University of California Press, 1990), 147–8: 'the musical realisation of desire depends on a cluster of distinctive effects: melodic motion by semitones, ambiguous or indefinite harmonies, a texture dense with appoggiaturas, many of which "resolve" to unstable referential sonorities . . . The [lust] trope occurs where two illocutionary forces overlap, one suggesting the fulfilment of desire, the other suggesting a deferral of fulfilment . . . this typically involves a passage that reaches a climactic melodic cadence at the same time as it defaults on a full harmonic cadence.'

[47] Sutcliffe, 'Grieg's Fifth', 179.

Example 2.7. Grieg: 'Gjetergutt', op. 54/1

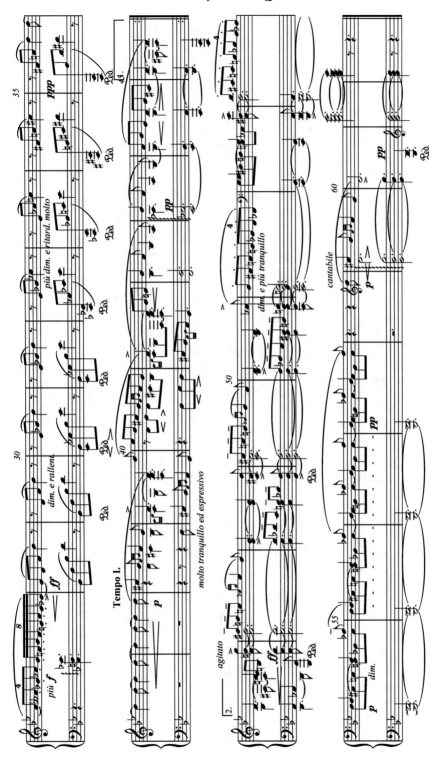

Example 2.8. Grieg: 'Aften på höjfjellet', op. 68/4

C major ['Gangar'] is very amusing. Here I see you again as you were when you took such great delight in the peasant playing his fiddle, and when one looks around one sees the mountains and inhales that wonderfully crisp air. 'Bell Ringing'! — a veritable apotheosis of fifths! — is really quite crazy; something like this is only an expression of moods, and for those who don't have a sense for that sort of thing it obviously will be unintelligible.[48]

'The Shepherd's Boy' articulates a ritualised process of eroticisation, release and liquidation in which landscape mostly figures as a background presence. The only exception to this background role is the moment of diatonic clarity or release in the transition in bars 28–35, where the music suddenly opens up a new sense of harmonic and registral space. In 'Aften på Höyfjellet', landscape is in some senses more clearly foregrounded. Structurally, the piece is in two strophes. After an austere eight-bar introduction, consisting of a single held note in the right hand and a descending walking bass in the left, the first strophe consists of a single slowly unfolding musical call or *lokk*. This line is principally concerned with filling out registral space, first the octave b¹–b, and later ascending to f♯² from which the music descends in a series of winding chromatic cells (bars 27–30) (Ex. 2.8). Elements of acoustic realism are provided by a series of echo repetitions, initially growing in intensity (bars 15–16 and 23–7) and then fading away into an increasingly remote distance (bars 35–46), which evoke a sense of open mountain spaces. Like the 'Alte Weise' from the third act of Wagner's *Tristan*, the lack of harmonic or textural support for the *lokk* in the opening strophe also creates a sense of intangibility. As in 'Gjetergut', the melody is characterised by a sense of longing or yearning for release through cadential closure and contextualisation. Similarly, any normal progressive sense of musical time is temporarily suspended, so that the melody sounds as though it is heard in a dreamworld. The mood is the same as that described by Grieg in his letter to Ravnkilde in 1887 after hearing the *bukkehorn* melody in the western Norwegian mountains. The prevailing emphasis is on distance and a sense of loss.

The second strophe provides a harmonic context for the melody unfolded in the first half of the work, and promises some kind of resolution. But the effect of this harmonisation is ultimately tragic (or rather disinterested and objective) rather than affirmatory. The lack of clear dominant–tonic articulation creates a sense of incompleteness, despite the *lokk*'s textural support. Diatonic cadential resolution is denied at several key points: first of all, after the agitato climax in bars 62–5, and then following the chromatic descent in bars 66–72 (where the lack of a raised leading note indicates that local voice leading has prevailed over functional harmonic relationships).

---

[48] Quoted in Benestad and Schjelderup-Ebbe, *Edvard Grieg*, 317.

Even the coda creates a sense of closure principally through registral and dynamic means rather than by strong cadential articulation. This suggests perhaps that the work's tensions are only genuinely resolved by the start of the following number, 'Bådnlåt' ('Cradle Song'), which begins in a comforting hymn-like E major. Though the middle section of the 'Bådnlåt' also unfolds a series of magical nature sonorities and distant horn calls (bars 22–7), they are of a more domesticated and contained kind than the wild loneliness of 'Aften på Höyfjellet'. Nature in this piece initially invites what Boym calls reflective nostalgia, but any sense of collective memory is ultimately lost, as the end of Den Bergtekne, denied by the music's impersonal objectivity. This tension between competing visions of landscape and nature in much of Grieg's music, not least the 19 norske Folkeviser, gains a sharp, modernist quality. As the following section will argue, landscape is not simply tied to its associative qualities (though they continue to play an important role), but becomes an integral part of the music's 'writerliness'. It gains an abstracted quality, as in the 'Gangar' and 'Klokkekang' from op. 54, that reinforces a more geometric sense of musical time and space.

The bells at Ola Lake: memory, modernism and the 19 norske Folkeviser, op. 66

Writing of 'Aften på Höyfjellet' in a letter dated 15 February 1899 to his close friend and walking companion from the Skagastøl trip in 1887, Frants Beyer, Grieg described how 'the thought of the high mountains one evening is found in a new volume of piano pieces. I do not know whether I shall call it "Kulok" or "Evening in the Mountains". I think you will love it and hope to be able to send it to you one day.'[49] In the copy that Grieg sent to Beyer for his silver wedding anniversary (1902), the piece carries the title 'Kulok', and Grieg added that music 'can be thought of as an evening mood at Skogadalsbøen'.[50] Skogadal was a significant location since it was the place where, together with Beyer in August 1891, Grieg had heard and notated a cradle song from the singing of a young herding girl called Gjendine Slålien, which later became the inspiration for the 19 norske Folkeviser. Slålien lived for over a hundred years until her death in 1983, and she maintained a written correspondence with Frants Beyer following their first meeting, some of which is preserved in the archives of the Norwegian folk-music collector Arne Bjørndal in Bergen.[51] Slålien later wrote to Bjørndal (with a

[49] 'Tanken på Højfjeldet en Aftenstund findes i et nyt Hefte Klaverstykker. Jeg ved ikke om jeg skal kalde det «Kulok» eller «Aften på høyfjellet». Jeg tror Du vil holde af det og håber at kunne skrive det af til Dig en Dag.' Quoted in Grieg, *Brev til Frants Beyer, 1872–1907*, ed. Finn Benestad and Bjarne Kortsen (Oslo: Universitetsforlaget, 1993), 235.

[50] 'Kan tenkes som en Kveldstemning på Skogadalsbøen.' Ibid.

[51] There are at least fifteen extant letters between Beyer and Slålien preserved in a folder marked 'Edvard Grieg' in the Arne Bjørndal Samling, dating from 21 May 1894 to 26 July 1918. The folder

possibly failing memory) that 'the first time I met Grieg and his comrades was in 1890 [*sic*], after which I saw them whenever they were in Jotunheim. He often asked me whether I would sit and learn music properly and was not more restrained in my youth, but I have often regretted that I did not follow his advice.'[52] Slålien recalled how she used to sing her school songs for Grieg, who 'hummed and wrote' them down.[53]

In a letter to Slålien dated 29 September 1904, Frants Beyer wrote 'Grieg and I talk of "The child lies in the cradle" [the melody Grieg had notated in 1891], and we shall never forget that pretty evening at Skogadalsbøen'.[54] Grieg made four preliminary arrangements of the melody between 1892 and 1893, before eventually publishing it as the final number in his op. 66 set. The remaining melodies in the anthology were notated by Beyer on walking trips in the mountains between July and September 1896. Beyer was an amateur composer who maintained a keen interest in Norwegian folk music. He was a member of the adjudicatory panel for the competition at the inaugural meeting of the west Norwegian Hardanger-fiddle association (Vestmannalaget) in Bergen, 1896, while Grieg sat in the audience. Beyer's transcriptions on four manuscript pages are preserved in the Grieg collection in Bergen Offentlige Bibliotek and provide a fascinating insight into Grieg's compositional process in the op. 66 collection.[55] Grieg first began the harmonisations while staying at a hunting cabin called Trondbu owned by Beyer's brother-in-law, Börre Giertsen, on the Hardangervidda plateau. Work on op. 66 continued at Fossli, a tourist hotel near the Vöring waterfall, and in Bergen, from where Grieg wrote in an enthusiastic letter to Johan Halvorsen on 15 September, 'I have amused myself these past few days by harmonising a load of splendid folk tunes which Frants [Beyer] has collected in Jotunheim. Unbelievable, what treasures we possess! You are the man to go round the country systematically and stage a raid on the state's behalf.'[56] The set was finally completed in Leipzig in January 1897.[57]

also contains two songs, headed 'En vise' ('A tune') and 'Karl og Emma', notated by Beyer, which are undated (*c.* 1895?).

[52] Slålien's letters to Arne Bjørndal, preserved in the Arne Bjørndal Samling, are largely undated and in unclear order, but most likely date from the 1950s. 'Jo förste gang jeg mødte Grieg og hans Kamerater var i 1890 og siden så traf jeg dem når de var i Jotunheim, han spurgte mig ofte om jeg ikkje vilde sit og lære musik og var ikkje så Behersk i min ungdom men jeg har ofte angref at jeg ikkje fulgte hans tråd.'

[53] Undated letter, Arne Bjørndal samling.

[54] 'Grieg og jeg taler om "Barnet ligger i Vuggen ned" og vi glemmer aldrig den vakkre Kvelden på Skogadalsbøen.' Quoted in Arne Bjørndal, 'Edvard Grieg og folkemusikken', orig. 1951, reprinted in *Grieg og folkemusikken – en artikkelsamling* (Oslo: Landslaget Musikk i Skolen, 1992), 9–29, here 25.

[55] The relevant pages have been published online by Bergen Offentlige Bibliotek at http://www.bergen.folkebibl.no/grieg-samlingen/grieg_samlingen_intro.html.

[56] 'Jeg har i disse Dage moret mig med at harmonisere en Ladning herlige Folkeviser, som Frants har optegnet i Jotunheim. Utroligt, hvad Skatter vi ejer! Du var Manden til, systematisk at drage Landet rundt og foretage en Razzia på Statens Vegne', *Brev*, I, 355.

[57] Benestad and Schjelderup-Ebbe, *Edvard Grieg*, 334 ff. See also the critical commentary in the

After publication, Grieg wrote to the Norwegian composer and pianist, Agathe Backer Grøndahl,

> What should especially interest the Norwegians about the collection is that none of the melodies has ever been published before. They were transcribed during the past two years as they were sung by milkmaids and cattlemen in the Jotunheim mountains. They are characterised by the deepest melancholy, interrupted only now and then by a passing ray of light.[58]

Grieg's claim, however, was not entirely accurate. The fourteenth number, 'I Ola-Dalom, i Ola-Kjønn' ('In Ola Valley, in Ola Lake'), which has since become the most famous melody in the set, had previously been published in an arrangement for mixed chorus in the second volume of Andreas Peter Bergreen's anthology, *Folkesange og Melodier* (Copenhagen, 1842). Though the melody and text vary substantially from that recorded in Beyer's notation, they are recognisably the same tune. Different melodies to some of the same texts in the op. 66 anthology had also appeared previously. Grieg himself had composed a powerfully intense setting of 'Det er den største Dårlighet' ('It is the greatest folly', op. 66/2) in his *Album for Mannssang* ('Album for Male Chorus'), op. 30. Similarly, a setting of 'En Konge hersket i Østerland' ('A king reigned in the east', op. 66/3) had appeared in Lindeman's *Ældre og nyere norske Fjeldmelodier* (no. 113) with twenty-six verses of text, and a version of 'Jeg går i tusen tanker' ('I wander deep in thought', op. 66/18) had been published in *Danmarks Melodibog* (1895).[59]

Even if Grieg had slightly misjudged the primacy of the melodies in the op. 66 set in terms of their appearance in publication, his description of them as characterised by 'the deepest melancholy, interrupted only now and then by a passing ray of light', hints at the anthology's innovative character. The op. 66 set, to a greater degree even than 'Gjetergut' or 'Aften på Höyfjellet', exemplifies Boym's definition of reflective nostalgia, the inverted process which 'cherishes shattered fragments of memory and temporalises space'. Musical representations of landscape are far more integrated into the structural conception of the set than in Grieg's earlier collection of folk-

---

Edvard Grieg Edition, vol. III. The autograph manuscript was copied in Vienna and Leipzig between 5 December 1896 and 28 January 1897. Titles of individual numbers were originally listed in Norwegian with German translations added later. The place of origin of each tune was added in the top right-hand corner, but later crossed out (though whether by Grieg is uncertain). No fingering was originally indicated, but it was added to the first edition by Adolf Ruthardt. The manuscript does, however, include some autograph pedalling indications.

[58] 'Hvad der særlig skulde interessere Norske ved denne Samling er, at samtlige Melodier hidtil har været utrykt. De er optegnet i Jotunheim efter Budeiers og Fækarers Sang i Løbet af de sidste to År. Hovedtrækket i dem er den dybeste Melankoli, kun hist og her afbrudt af et forbigående Lysstreif.' Letter dated 28 May 1897, *Brev*, I, 232.

[59] These correspondences, with copies of the appropriate music, are noted in a folder in the Bergen Offentlige Bibliotek, compiled by Karen Falck Johanssen, former curator of the Grieg Samling.

song arrangements, the *25 norske Folkeviser og Danser*. Register, in particular, is a primary structural component. Significantly, the opening song in the op. 66 collection is a *kulokk*, a herding call that 'lures' or entices the listener into the mystical mountain realm of the collection (Ex. 2.9). It functions as a magical gateway or threshold. Similar *lokks* recur as the sixth and eight numbers in the collection, carefully placed between larger, more expansive settings so that they function partly as the background to the whole collection, a natural 'window' into an alpine sound world, through or against which the other melodies are heard. The initial *kulokk* itself, in Beyer's transcription, is marked '(Roligt)' ('peacefully'), and consists of little more than a three-note melodic cell, d^2–e^2–$f\sharp^2$, embellished in a series of turn and mordent figures and framed by an introductory call characteristic of such semi-pitched cries on the pasture.[60] Beyer indicates words for the introductory call ('Rosko, kom no!'), and the nonsense syllables known as *lalling* ('la-li-la') for the main part of the melody. The final two bars are marked 'roligt', and scored in 2/4, though elsewhere Beyer's transcription shows some sign of uncertainty as to the tune's exact metrical structure. Over the sixth and seventh bars, however, Beyer writes the direction 'halvt talende, kjælende' ('half-spoken, affectionately'). Grieg's scoring of the sonorous D major chord with which the song begins, in the piano's richest register with a prominent horn-like perfect fifth in the bass, defines the harmonic and registral domain of the whole collection. The effect is almost entirely static, emphasised by the pentatonicism of the call in the right hand and the echo dynamics (indicated in Beyer's transcription). Indeed, in his transcription Beyer placed pauses over the first two bars and indicated a silent third bar before the main part of the tune begins, so that the sense of timelessness is even more marked than in Grieg's arrangement. This sense of stillness, of the suspension of regular musical time, is one of the characteristics of a *Naturklang* in Carl Dahlhaus's definition. For Dahlhaus, the special status of such sonorities or *Klangfläche* (sound-sheets) as a conventionalised nineteenth-century landscape topic is understood as much from a historical perspective as an internal structural one, and is defined against a mainstream symphonic musical discourse:

> A musical depiction of nature is almost always defined negatively, by being excluded from the imperative of organic development which, at least in the mainstream of compositional history, dominated the thematic and motivic structure of nineteenth-century music as well as its harmonic schemes The *Klangfläche* conveys a landscape because it is exempted both from the principle of teleological progression and from the rule of musical texture which nineteenth-century musical theorists referred to, by no means simply metaphorically, as 'thematic-motivic manipula-

---

[60] See Grinde, *A History of Norwegian Music*, 75–6.

Example 2.9. Grieg: 'Kulokk', op. 66/1

tion', taking Beethoven's development sections as their *locus clas-sicus*. As Hegel would have put it, musical landscapes arise less from direct tone-painting than from 'definite negation' of the character of musical form as a process.[61]

Dahlhaus suggests that such *Klangflächen* are further characterised by a sense of 'internal motion', derived either from layered rhythmic patterns (such as the stratified ostinato textures that open many Bruckner symphonies), or from the creation of an unresolved harmonic dissonance. Without such internal motion, the *Naturklang* simply sounds 'dull and lifeless'. In the absence of active ostinato figuration, the sense of internal motion at the start of op. 66 is provided by register and by a subtle harmonic tension between pentatonic and diatonic collections. The registral space unfolded by the opening bars is gradually filled in, and then expanded, by the music that follows: the whole of the central part of the *kulokk* consists of a decorated large-scale bass movement from d^1–D. This descent is prefigured by the octave transfer a^2–a^1 in the right hand in bars 1–2. The other structural element in the opening bar is the distinctive sighing appoggiatura with which the piece begins. This b–a cell, with its pentatonic colouring, saturates the setting, occurring in the inner parts in bars 4 and 6, for example, and prominently in the melody itself in bars 10–11 where it is almost immediately echoed in the tenor.[62] Even the plagal cadence with which the *kulokk* concludes can be understood as a distillation of the whole setting, the b–a cell prominent in the tenor part once again. The return of the introduction is especially poignant because it is elided within the chain of seventh chords that liquidates the harmonic climax of the song (the *forte* III chord in bar 14) and articulates closure. The heightened expressive and syntactical status of these chords resolves the tension between diatonic and pentatonic collections that underpins the song. Landscape operates at several different levels in the setting. As a pictorial device, it can be heard in the pastoral associations of the opening *Naturklang*. But, as this analysis has suggested, the implications of this sonority for the development of the remainder of the setting are more structural than pictorial in character. The setting furthermore implies a strong formal and expressive trajectory for the remainder of the collection: a gradual withdrawal into a remote distance or vanishing point, created by the tune's descending melodic character and prevailing dynamic shape (a long *diminuendo* with a single rise to *forte* in bars 12–14). In this sense, the *kulokk* sounds as though it is receding towards a silent horizon, vanishing out

[61] Dahlhaus, *Nineteenth-Century Music*, 307. Dahlhaus cites two examples from Wagner: the Forest Murmurs and the song of the woodbird from *Siegfried*, and the sound of the hunting calls in the distance at the start of Act 2 of *Tristan und Isolde*.

[62] Note the way in which b^1 is left hanging at the end of bar 16 in the right hand. In this instance, it is 'resolved' in the following bar, but it also leads via registral displacement to the super-expressive $c\sharp^1$ in the alto.

of audible range just as the anthology has barely begun.

Grieg's setting of the fourth number, 'Siri Dale-Visen' ('The Siri Dale Song') (Ex. 2.10) is similarly intense and compressed. The folk song in Beyer's transcription consists of a single strophe with a regular structure (four four-bar phrases), elaborated in Grieg's arrangement only by the addition of a two-bar introduction and a four-bar coda that echoes the final notes of the fourth phrase. Registrally and texturally, the piece is remarkably restricted: it would be very easy to hear the setting as the piano reduction of a four-part choral setting. Despite its apparent simplicity, Grieg's setting is characterised by a very strong linear sense of cumulative harmonic, tonal and dynamic design. After the unaccompanied left-hand introduction, the austere modal harmonisation of the opening phrase (rooted on G with a flattened sixth and modally unstable seventh degree) is intensified until it reaches its harmonic climax in bar 17, a chromatically altered dominant substitution chord and the most dissonant sound in the piece. The setting concludes with a powerful chain of descending parallel seventh chords, similar to those in the final bars of the *kulokk*, which liquidate the harmonic tension of bar 17 and lead towards the final cadence. 'Siri Dale-Visen' therefore traces a tonal curve from modal to diatonic stability via a process of systematic chromaticisation, an expressive structural effect reinforced by its dynamic shape. The music rises from *piano* through two sets of hairpins to the *forte* in bar 17, coincident with the greatest point of chromatic tension, and falling to *piano* again in the final bar.

For Dahlhaus, this formal trajectory can be heard as the abstract expression of a syntactical conflict that reflects the historical state of the musical material. Dahlhaus suggests that, if the opening bars still permit a functional diatonic interpretation, 'the parallel chords in the accompaniment gradually form a structural element in their own right as the simple G minor melody increasingly comes into conflict with chromatic harmony'. Functional diatonic harmony is therefore opposed to, or distinct from, modal music and non-functional linear chromatic textures. The pivotal moment in Dahlhaus's analysis, which crystallises the music's sense of stylistic and historical progression, is the structure of the liquidating passage in the final fourth phrase:

> Grieg has notated the passage [bars 15–18] so as to maintain a
> semblance of functional tonality, but this merely proves to be a
> façade behind which can be seen a harmonic mechanism bursting
> the bonds of tonality. Melodic pitches so straightforward as to
> have ineradicable tonal implications are forced into bizarre
> nonfunctional roles in the harmony. This collision between
> harmonic alteration, a by-word for late-nineteenth-century
> modernity, and folk melody, an element of archaic provenance,

Example 2.10. Grieg: 'Siri Dale-Visen', op. 66/4

gives rise to techniques, such as bitonality and chord streams, that anticipate modern music of our own century. Hence, it is no exaggeration to see a historical dialectic between them.[63]

The significance of this 'bizarre nonfunctional' harmonisation in the final phrase can be appreciated by comparing bars 15–22 with a recomposition of the passage that maintains the original voice-leading as far as possible but substitutes a more conventionally diatonic progression for the chromatic harmony in the lower parts (Ex. 2.11).[64] One of the defining features of

Example 2.11. Grieg: 'Siri Dale-Visen', final strophe recomposed

Grieg's setting is the symmetrical chromatic rise and fall of the bass line. Not only does the descent in bars 17–22 extend the final four-bar phrase of the song so as to emphasise closure, the resultant contour of the bass-line could also be heard as an echo of the contour of the original melody itself. The harmonic climax in bar 17 is significant, according to the reharmonisation, because Grieg avoids striking a dominant chord at just the moment, at the corresponding point in bar 9, where such a chord had been unproblematic. The enharmonic spelling of the bass of the chord in bar 17^2 is critical: c♯ would have naturally led to an unequivocal $\hat{5}$, but d♭ instead falls to c♮, and initiates the semitonal descent that leads back, non-functionally, to the tonic root. For Dahlhaus, Grieg's setting is ultimately significant for the way in which it enacts, and problematises, a process of stylistic and historical change. The music encodes a particular evolutionary reading of the Western musical tradition, namely the shift from an archaic folk-music source, through classical (functional) diatonic practice, to the non-diatonic voice-leading linearity of early-twentieth-century modernism. This can be heard in turn to support Dahlhaus's ontological definition of the musical work, as developed in the opening chapters of his *Foundations of Music History*, as an aesthetic object whose materials and configuration reveal the state of the historical context in which they emerged. The syntactical conflict

---

[63] Dahlhaus, *Nineteenth-Century Music*, 310.

[64] My recomposition is in no way intended as an 'improvement' upon Grieg's original. Indeed, the barely concealed parallel fifths in the tenor and bass parts in bar 17, and the somewhat redundant use of a dominant seventh in inversion in the second half of bar 16, lead to a considerably weakened effect.

identified by Dahlhaus, between the simple modality of the folk tune and the apparent complexity of its chromatic treatment, is emblematic of the broader crisis of tonal syntax in modernist musical practice at the close of the nineteenth century. The setting becomes a 'linguistic battleground', to borrow Sutcliffe's phrase,[65] between opposing musical tendencies that the final bars cannot resolve conclusively. But we can also hear the conflict that underpins the setting as an expression of the tension between Grieg's musical cultures, the mainstream Austro-German tradition of which he was essentially a product, and the Norwegian folk tradition to which he felt strongly attracted but ultimately did not belong. In a letter to Röntgen dated 22 August 1896, Grieg wrote:

> Life is just as strange as folk songs; one doesn't know whether they were conceived in major or minor . . . I spent the afternoon in my room where I harmonised the many folk melodies which Frants had sent me. It was truly festive . . . some of them are incredibly beautiful. In any case, I have set some hair-raising chord combinations on paper. But by way of excuse, let me say that they weren't created at the piano but in my head. When one has Vöring Falls nearby, one feels more daring than down in the valley.[66]

Grieg's commentary inverts the traditional historical model of peripheral and mainstream development in nineteenth-century music. According to Dahlhaus, Grieg's treatment of harmony is 'advanced' because it resembles mainstream Austro-German practice; hence, those techniques 'such as bitonality and chord streams, that anticipate the modern music of our own century' point to the fundamentally assimilationist nature of Grieg's music. Grieg, however, seems to suggest precisely the opposite, that it is the sense of distance or remoteness from the mainstream that is responsible for the more radical or advanced aspects of his musical style.

Like the opening *kulokk*, however, the formal trajectory of 'Siri Dale-Visen' is also concerned with a process of withdrawal. This suggests perhaps that Grieg's act of self-exile from mainstream musical circles, whether involuntary or not, also involves a sense of loss. Further support for this reading could be found in the text that Beyer provided with the melody in his transcription. The narrative in 'Siri Dale-Visen' is essentially one of lost love and passing youth:

> I was but barely seventeen
> When I fell in love
> Which will never leave my memory
> For as long as I shall live.
> While others enjoy themselves in their youth,

---

[65] Sutcliffe, 'Grieg's Fifth'.
[66] Quoted in Benestad and Schjelderup-Ebbe, *Edvard Grieg*, 335.

101

> I must grieve in sorrow
> And shed many tears.[67]

Grieg's setting responds powerfully to this narrative idea: the process of chromaticisation, coupled with the prevailing mood of withdrawal, could be heard as eloquent metaphors for the loss of innocence lamented in the text. But the text is also concerned with different states of temporality: of memory, present awakening and future expectation. Hence, it could also be read, like the text of *Den Bergtekne*, as an allegory of creativity. Grieg's setting therefore becomes self-reflexive, creating a level of irony in which images of memory, distance and isolation serve as symbols for a loss of individual voice.

Benestad and Schjelderup-Ebbe suggest that 'Grieg had no intention in Opus 66 of creating a work that would be suitable for the concert hall',[68] a comment which at first seems curious given the music's obvious harmonic richness and 'picturesque' folk colouring. But their assessment perhaps points to a sense in which the structural rigour of Grieg's set, and the lack of contextualisation or softening in its presentation, must have seemed to stretch the genre of the Romantic folk miniature to breaking point, a problem which was even more severe for the *Slåtter*. The same is arguably true also for 'Klokkeklang' and other numbers in the op. 54 *Lyric Pieces*. Sutcliffe argues that 'the exotic has no point of contact, with reasonable stylistic expectations. In other words, this is a raw form of musical expression, out of scale within a nineteenth-century genre we are likely to be rather sniffy about nowadays.'[69] In that sense, among others, op. 66 challenges one of the principal critical streams in Grieg's historical reception. This tendency to 'break out' from conventional frames of reference, or to resist containment, is particularly apparent in the fourteenth number, 'I Ola-Dalom, i Ola-Kjønn' (Ex. 2.12). Op. 66/14 invites at least four different levels of analysis. The first level proposes that the work can be heard as a vivid pictorial illustration of Norwegian folk life, different in tone perhaps, but essentially the same in function to 'Brudefølget drar forbi' from the *Folkelivsbilder*. Elements of the familiar folk wedding march topic can be imagined in the setting's evocation of bell sonorities. It was perhaps this picturesque quality that attracted Delius to the tune, which formed the basis for his 'On Hearing the First Cuckoo in Spring' (1913–14), though Delius's setting eschews bell sounds.[70] A second,

---

[67] 'Jeg var vel neppe sytten Aar, / da jeg fik Kjæreste, / som aldrig mig af Minde gaar, / saalænge jeg er til. / Naar andre de forlyste sig i sine unge Aar, / jeg maa i Sorgen græmme mig/ og fælde mangen Taar.' Undated note in Bergen Offentlige Bibliotek.

[68] Benestad and Schjelderup-Ebbe, *Edvard Grieg*, 337.

[69] Sutcliffe, 'Grieg's Fifth', 165.

[70] In his *Study of Grieg's Harmonic Style with Special Reference to His Contributions to Musical Impressionism* (Oslo: Johan Grundt Tanum, 1953, Norsk Musikgranskning), Dag Schjelderup-Ebbe wrote (98): 'Delius borrows from Grieg the idea of giving the theme a complex harmonic treatment. But while the particularly successful result in Grieg's case is due to his subtle restraint and discrimination in the

Example 2.12. Grieg: 'I Ola-Dalom, i Ola-Kjønn', op. 66/14

deeper level of analysis follows Dahlhaus's commentary on 'Siri Dale-Visen'. Like op. 66/4, 'I Ola-Dalom, i Ola-Kjønn' exploits the tension between different forms of harmonic and textural organisation. Grieg's setting is on a larger scale than that in 'Siri Dale-Visen' or the opening *kulokk*, and consists of three varied strophes, plus an introduction, transition passages and coda. The melody itself consists of four variations upon a simple two-bar pattern, so that the piece articulates a highly circular repetitive structure, a formal character commonly associated with folk dance forms in nineteenth-century music. In the first strophe the melody is in the treble part, harmonised in the tonic, A major, and is preceded by a swinging two-bar introduction whose ostinato pedal fifths function both as a powerful generic folk signifier and as the representation of a bell sound. Harmonically, the first strophe leans very much towards the flat-side of the tonic: the music initially rocks gently between I and IV^7, and the use of a tonic seventh chord, and the affective dynamic drop, creates a poignant sense of harmonic colour in bar 7. The subsequent dynamic rise to *mezzo forte* at the cadential end of tune highlights the striking use of non-diatonic harmony in bar 9, resolved via an elided I^7–IV^7–V–I cadence in bars 10–11. The harmonic function of the first transition sequence is to modulate away from the tonic to the relative minor, and the voice-leading in the bass traces a falling third (A–F♯), an inversion of the melodic range of the folk tune itself. The upper neighbour note in bars 13–14 (a^1), is left hanging, so that the first strophe is ultimately left unresolved. This pattern, of repetition–intensification–(transition)–release, defines the formal shape of the whole piece.

In the second strophe, Grieg transfers the melody into an inner part in the left hand (equivalent to the upper cello register) to create a sense of textural contrast. The new harmonisation, in the relative minor, involves no actual adjustment in the original notes of melody but, like the shift in tessitura, darkens the music's overall tone. Grieg hence responds to the modal mixture, or rather the ambiguous non-diatonic quality, of the original tune. The strophe begins with a registral transfer in the right hand, a^1–a^2. The harmony is initially directed by a more linear sense of purpose and the left hand continues the pattern of descent from end of first strophe. However, the music begins to circle around vi:V^6_5 and IV^6_5 (corresponding to the intensification in the preceding strophe), until reaching a point of crisis at the cadence in bar 24. Here, the tune is temporarily submerged as the right hand floods over into an extended transition sequence (or release). Bars 24–34 are characterised by a remarkable process of harmonic recontextualisation: the swaying appoggiaturas in the right hand are slowly

choice of means, Delius employs an extremely complicated, impressionistic chromaticism, which, in the opinion of this writer, seems overloaded and which also in its restless obliterating of key feeling, is out of style with the nature of the tune itself.'

reinterpreted over a series of drifting left-hand chords that gradually returns towards the tonic via the subdominant, ultimately reinforcing the flat-side tendencies of the opening phrase.

In the third strophe, chromatic elements of the preceding music remain in the inner parts despite the regained sense of tonic stability. The music begins a process of large-scale resolution, resolving previously disruptive chromatic elements symmetrically in reverse: e♭^{1}, bar 38, resolves the d♯s in bars 35–6. As the tune approaches its final point of cadential intensification again in bar 42, f♮s resolve the e♯s (from bars 13 and 21), and there is a final passing reference to the g♮ from the first strophe (bar 7). In the coda, the music is led up to its highest register, the final four bars spanning the widest vertical space in the piece. The setting therefore articulates a complete rounded binary structure in which dissonant elements are symmetrically resolved in a manner that corresponds to conventional diatonic practice. Yet the materials upon which the structure depends are not in themselves entirely diatonic (the lack of clear dominant articulation, for example), so that closure is articulated as much by registral and dynamic parameters as by harmonic means alone.

Further hermeneutic readings of the piece move beyond this purely structuralist level of analysis. Beyer's transcription includes a transcription of the song's text, similar to that printed by Berggreen in his earlier arrangement of 1841. Beyer furthermore sent Grieg an uncorroborated version of the story associated with the song. An undated note by Beyer in Bergen Offentlige Bibliotek reads as follows:

> 'In Ola Valley, in Ola Lake' from Gudrund Skattebo, Skattebo farm, East Slidre, notated by Frants Beyer[.] High up in East Slidre, in a little valley with precipitous mountain sides in the vicinity of the Jotunheim, lies a lake known as 'Ola Lake'. Here there lies a mountain farm, the Ola Farm. A woman called Eli lived there one summer with her son. One day the boy drowned in Ola Lake, without anyone knowing what had become of him. They searched everywhere for him, without success. So they believed that he had been taken into the mountain, bewitched ['bergteken']. They brought the church bells up to the Ola Farm, and began to ring and ring, ring and ring – ring and ring. Finally the church bells sang:
>
> > 'In Ola Valley, in Ola Lake
> > There Eli lost her boy,
> > They searched in the valley, they rung in the lake,
> > But Eli never found her boy.'
> (see Edv. Grieg, op. 66, no. 14)[71]

---

[71] 'I Ola-Dalom, i Ola-kinn/fra/Gudrund Skattebo/Skattebo Gaard, Östre Slidre/optegnet af Frants Beyer/Höit oppe i Östre Slidre, i en liden Dal med bratte Fjeldsidder, i Nierheden af Jotunheimen,

Beyer's note is striking, not least as an informal field record of the moment when he transcribed the melody. The folk tale connected with the song draws on several topics which appear to have attracted Grieg: the western Norwegian mountains, bewitchment or enchantment, a journey into the underworld (the boy believed to have been 'taken into the mountains'), the magical ritualistic sound of bells ringing, and, above all, images of memory and loss. Though Grieg omitted the words in his setting, these topics invite a narrative reading of the piece in which Grieg's arrangement re-enacts the events told by the song's original text. Hence, the music begins with an illustration of diatonic innocence (a cradle song?), so that the lullaby character of the subdominant inflection in the first strophe seems all the more poignant. The second strophe seems increasingly troubled, through the affective darkening of the minor mode and encroaching chromaticism, until it reaches a point of crisis: the boy's drowning in Ola Lake graphically represented by the 'submersion' of the tune in bar 24. Death is followed by transfiguration, and as the song returns at the start of the third strophe, the music is filled with a powerful sense of retrospection and nostalgia, reminiscences of previous happier times still coloured by remnants of chromatic mourning. The piece closes in a mood of benediction, the ethereal tremolo in the right hand in the final measures shimmering like a halo above the fading left hand ostinato (which functions throughout as both a bell sound and a *Naturklang*).

However, the images of enchantment, memory and loss also invite an environmental reading of the setting, which focuses on the work's sonic-temporal qualities suggested by the continual ringing of bells described in Beyer's account. Like 'Klokkeklang', 'I Ola-Dalom''s sound and design are motivated principally by the exploration of a single acoustical object: the whole setting is saturated by the sound of bells. This is evident most clearly from the left hand's swinging ostinato fifths in the first strophe, but it also inflects other sounds within the piece, especially the chromatic chords, bars 24–33, which can be heard as more complex representations of the spectrum produced by bell sounds. It is easy to point to similar 'bell pieces' in late-nineteenth-century piano music. Debussy's 'La cathédrale engloutie' from the *Première livre de préludes* is perhaps the most obviously comparable

ligger et Vand, som kaldes "Ola-Vatne". Ved dette ligger et Sæter "Ola-Sæteren". Der boede en Sommer en Kone, som hente Eli, med sin Sön. En Dag druknede Gutten i Ola-vatne, uden at Nogen kjendte til, hvor han var bleven af. Man ledte allersteder efter ham, forgjæves. Saa troede man at han var taget ind i Berget: "Bergteken". Man fik da Bugdens Kirkeklokker bragt op til Ola-Sæteren, og saa begyndte man at ringe og ringe, ringe og ringe – ringe og ringe. Til sidst sang Klokke-Klangen:
I Ola-Dalom, i Ola-Kinn
Der tapte ho Eli bort Guten sin,
Dei döra I Dalom, dei ringde i Kinn,
Men aldrig fann Eli att Guten sin.'
(See: Edv. Grieg, op. 66, No. 14)

example, with its evocation of submerged bell sonorities, but Liszt's remarkable 'Evening Bells' from *Weihnachtsbaum* (1874–6) unfolds a radical non-diatonic texture that is as quietly shocking as that of 'Klokkeklang'. However, both Liszt's and Debussy's bell pieces are ultimately more static and much less goal-directed than 'I Ola-Dalom'. Their pictorial mode of evocation does not cut against other structural tensions in the music, unlike op. 66/14. Similarly, Delius's treatment of the folk tune in the rhapsodic structure of his 'On Hearing the First Cuckoo in Spring' shifts the burden of formal expectation onto a constant circular recycling of the melody through a kaleidoscopic range of harmonic contexts.[72] Long-range formal parameters play little part in this kind of reiterative structure.

One of the reasons for the fundamental formal difference between other bell pieces, Delius's setting and Grieg's work is apparent once we return to the text of 'I Ola-Dalom'. Grieg's setting depicts not the events themselves, the boy's drowning and death and the villagers' futile search for his body, but the memory of events in the past. As Alain Corbin has written, 'the Romantics – Schiller, Chateaubriand, and Lamartine among them – had grasped the intense power of the bell to evoke, to impart a feeling of time passing, foster reminiscence, recover things forgotten, and to consolidate an individual's identification with a primordial auditory site'.[73] Bells are conventionally associated with a sense of loss, of things faded, and with remembrance. From the moment of their striking, their sound is audibly in decay. But Grieg's setting also takes on a darker meaning. The continual, obsessive ringing of bells depicted in the music induces a nihilistic state or a sense of the infinite, a longing for closure or death. This process of regression or distancing is most powerful in the central transition sequence, which audibly seems to withdraw from the real world into a dream-like state. But it also affects the closing bars, which are no longer heard as a benediction, but a final shivering inaudibility. The setting's sense of goal-direction is therefore also an attempt to resolve a deep temporal tension in the music, like 'Siri Dale-Visen', between present awareness and the remembrance of past events. Like Boym's reflective nostalgia, 'I Ola-Dalom' cherishes its fragmentary recollection of the past, but simultaneously provides a strong sense of linear direction forwards towards a distant vanishing point.

Grieg's setting of op. 66/14 is a vivid pictorial evocation of the Norwegian landscape with its bell sounds and mountain echoes, an assertion of

---

[72] For a concise and thoughtful comparison of Delius's and Grieg's settings, see Trevor Hold, 'Grieg, Delius, Grainger and a Norwegian Cuckoo', *Tempo* 203 (January 1998), 11–19, especially 14–17. Hold describes Delius's work as a meditation upon both the folk tune and Grieg's harmonisation, and identifies a 'cuckoo cell' in the cadential figuration of bars 11–12 in Grieg's setting, which may have served as one of the catalysts for Delius's piece.

[73] *Village Bells: Sound and Meaning in the Nineteenth-Century French Countryside*, trans. Martin Thom (New York: Columbia, 1998), p. x.

Norwegian musical identity and an intense musical contemplation of a single acoustical object. The piece ultimately reveals a deep anxiety concerning creative process and our human relationship with the natural world. In this sense, 'I Ola-Dalom, i Ola-Kjønn', like the other numbers in op. 66, breaks out of the generic boundaries established by the familiar image of Grieg as miniaturist. And ironically, given Grieg's peripheralised pattern of historical reception, the sense of uncertainty that underlies his setting strikes a strangely urgent note.

Landscape in Grieg's music serves a number of functions. As a spatial phenomenon, it is associated with a series of pictorial images drawn from Norwegian nature and folk life whose cultural meaning was partly determined by their role in the definition of an independent Norwegian identity in the second half of the nineteenth century. But as a temporal phenomenon, landscape is also concerned with the recovery (or reconstruction) of past events, a sense of historical memory and a sense of expectation. This of course supports the idea of the nation as both preordained and modern: a guiding principle of nineteenth-century nationalism identified by Anthony Smith and others (see Chapter 1). But the temporal structure of landscape also points towards its formal character. Landscape is no longer concerned solely with pictorial evocation but becomes a more abstract mode of musical discourse, one grounded in Grieg's music with a particular grammar and syntax. Dahlhaus writes that 'the nineteenth century's fondness for linking musical landscapes with exoticisms and folklorisms seems to be rooted in the material of the music itself rather than being explainable aesthetically with reference to the category of the picturesque'.[74] Hence, what Dahlhaus persists in describing as 'musical landscape painting' is largely a generic category, defined purely in opposition to a normative mainstream musical practice. Analysis of Grieg's music, from *Den Bergtekne* and 'Klokkeklang' to 'I Ola-Dalom', however, suggests that landscape plays a more significant role in his works than a purely 'exotic' or 'colouristic' element, and that the 'category of the picturesque' is more complex than Dahlhaus suggests. It is arguably the multi-layered structure of landscape, the sense of temporal suspension while being simultaneously guided towards a distant horizon or musical goal, which defines the function of landscape in Grieg's work. Coupled with the sense of nostalgia identified by Boym, and its objective or depersonalised quality, landscape becomes one of the primary structural elements in Grieg's music, and, as we shall see in the following chapter, a central theme in one of his most complex works, the song cycle *Haugtussa*.

---

[74] Dahlhaus, *Nineteenth-Century Music*, 309.

CHAPTER THREE

Grieg, Landscape and the *Haugtussa* Project

The previous two chapters have argued that landscape is both an abstract and representational function of Grieg's music. Landscape can be constructed through purely musical means, such as particular harmonic progressions and the prolongation of diatonically dissonant sonorities (*Klangfläche*) to create the impression of temporal suspension, a musical effect which suggests depth and perspective, or it can be evoked through the innovative use of conventional musical signifiers such as herding calls and echo effects to suggest space and distance. Landscape is also a strong element in the contemporary critical reception of Grieg's work. For example, a biography by the Norwegian composer Gerhard Schjelderup published in Leipzig in 1908, a year after Grieg's death, opens with a panoramic celebration of the Norwegian natural world:

> In the east, endless forests and deep blue glittering lakes, – in the west, from the stormy North Sea's wild jagged coastline – a desolate waste with a few pitiful fishermen's huts, the sea birds' nests clinging to the cliffs amid the crashing waves; – and then the numerous fantastically formed bays and islands, the charming and yet deeply solemn fjords, finally the lofty, immense mountain world! It hears the roar of the waves, which brings a message from the World Sea, from Niflheimr's icy realm resting in darkness, which only shines in the dazzling glare of the brief summertime. What mysterious animal life: at the coast, where millions of fish swarm in zest for life, on the lonely bird-cliffs in the magical light of the midnight sun, – in the deeps, where colossal monster shoals of herring and cod pursue each other into the distant ocean!
>
> These innumerable wonders of Nature must of course awaken the richest folk art, and thereby was the foundation for serious, profound art actually laid. The enchanting songs, which express the whole of nature in this legend-rich land, find their voice in a thousand ways, and thus the Norwegian national soul finds its most eloquent expression in music. *Edvard Grieg's* art was entirely rooted in this magical national spirit; and if he, like many

others, was obliged by unfavourable artistic circumstances to
spend time abroad, he was never more individual or greater than
when his mood was one of fervent longing for the far north.[1]

The function of such vivid proto-cinematic images in Grieg reception was
far from neutral. They often supported ideological readings of Grieg's music,
figured in terms of Norwegian independence or the Norwegian landscape,
which reflected the broader historical context in which his music was
heard. Schjelderup's description is an essay in Nordic exoticism, suitable
for consumption both within Norway and abroad. The emphasis is on the
uniqueness and difference of the Norwegian natural world, and on the organic
relationship between landscape, art and nature. Furthermore, Schjelderup
subscribes to a Hegelian model of national self-determination. Norwegian
music, according to Schjelderup, is born from the unconscious spirit of the
Norwegian people (where it finds its 'most eloquent expression'). Great art
is brought into being in the 'magical light of the midnight sun'. The whole
of nature is expressed in 'enchanting' songs, an image of bewitchment or
enticement that points to the supposedly mythic nature of this 'fairy-tale
land'. At its heart, however, lies a sense of inwardness and melancholy:
'No artist has loved his homeland more deeply than he, no artist abroad
has suffered more than he, and yet none has known how to shape this
yearning and suffering more deeply and touchingly than Grieg.'[2] Hence, for
Schjelderup, Grieg's music is characterised by a sense of hollowness and
loss. The search for national origins turns into a grail-like quest in which the
absence of an ultimate goal or endpoint is replaced by a continual sense of
evolution or coming into being.

[1] 'Im Osten unendliche Wälder und tiefblau glitzernde Seen, – im Westen die von dem stürmischen
Nordmeer wild zerrissene Küste, – eine trostlose Wüste mit wenigen elenden Fischerhütten, die
Seevogelnestern gleich sich mitten in Wellengebrause an die Felsen klammern; – dann weiter die
unzähligen phantastisch geformten Meerbusen und Inseln, die bald lieblichen, bald tief ernsten Fjorde,
endlich die erhabene, gewaltige Gebirgswelt! Er hört das Rauschen der Wellen, die Botschaft bringen
vom Weltmeer, von Niefelheims eisigen in Finsternis ruhenden Gefilden, die nur in der kurzen
Sommerzeit in überwältigendem Glanz erstrahlen. Welch' geheimnisvolles Tierleben: an der Küste,
wo Milliarden von Fische in Lebenslust sich tummeln, auf den einsamen Vogel-Felsen im magischen
Lichte der Mitternachtssonne, – in des Wassers Tiefen, wo gewaltige Ungetüme Schwärme von
Heringen und Dorschen bis in den fernen Ozean verfolgen!
  Diese ungezählten Wunder der Natur mußten natürlich reichste Volkskunst erwecken und damit war
der Boden geschaffen für ernste, tiefe Kunst überhaupt. Die bezaubernden Lieder, die in Norwegen –
diesem Märchenlande, die ganze Natur singt, konnten in ihren tausendfach wechselnden Stimmungen
nur Töne wiedergeben und so findet in der Musik die Norwegische Volksseele ihren beredtesten
Ausdruck. – Auch *Edvard Griegs* Kunst wurzelt voll und ganz in diesem zauberischen Heimatswesen
und wenn die trotzalledem ungünstigen Kunstverhältnisse Norwegens ihn, gleich vielen anderen,
oftmals zwangen in fremden Ländern zu weilen, so war er niemals eigenartiger und größer, als wenn
die heiße Sehnsucht nach dem fernen Norden in seinen Weisen lebendig wurde.' Schjelderup and
Niemann, *Edvard Grieg*, 1–2.
[2] 'Kein Künstler hat seine Heimat glühender geliebt als er, kein Künstler in der Fremde mehr gelitten
als er, keiner aber auch dies Sehnen und Leiden inniger und ergreifender zu gestalten gewußt als
Grieg!' Ibid., 2.

Such images of nature, landscape and national identity seem especially prevalent in German criticism. One of the most striking examples of this tendency is the work of Walter Niemann, perhaps the most influential German writer on Nordic music at the turn of the century. Niemann dedicated his survey of Nordic music, *Die Musik Skandinaviens*,[3] to Grieg, and contributed a lengthy discussion of Grieg's work to Schjelderup's biography.[4] The underlying principle of Niemann's criticism was unreservedly positive. For Niemann, Grieg was 'the greatest composer that Scandinavia has produced in the nineteenth century', a status that Niemann compared with the work of Henrik Ibsen and Bjørnstjerne Bjørnson (as his comparison suggests, Scandinavian literature enjoyed a higher international profile than Scandinavian music at the time). 'Like their poetry', Niemann maintained, Grieg's music 'expresses the spirit of the Norwegian folk itself.'[5] This leads to the central theme of Niemann's writing: the interrelationship between Norwegian nature, nationalism and Grieg's music. For Niemann, like Schjelderup, Grieg's music was essentially *Heimatkunst*, art born from the spirit of his homeland, which drew its inspiration 'directly from native folk music, adapting its essential characteristics to form a foundation for art music'. This, Niemann believed, was Grieg's 'most splendid achievement: to express his native nature and native folklore in sound'.[6] Niemann thereby accorded Grieg a special historical status, as pioneer and father figure of Norwegian music, implicitly aligning his work with the political ideal of Norwegian independence (a topical image, since that goal had only just been achieved in 1905). Hence, Grieg's 'deep understanding of Norwegian folk music, and his inspired incorporation of it, made him the regenerator, saviour and leader of the Norwegian school of composition'. Yet, at the same time, Niemann claimed that Grieg's music was 'not merely *Heimatkunst*, but also the product of a distinctive and rich personality which raises into the sphere of high artistry the native sounds treasured within his heart'.[7] Grieg's music,

---

[3] *Die Musik Skandinaviens: ein Führer durch die Volks- und Kunstmusik* (Leipzig: Breitkopf & Härtel, 1906).

[4] Schjelderup and Niemann, *Edvard Grieg*, 103–99.

[5] 'der größte Komponist, den Skandinavien im 19. Jahrhundert überhaupt hervorbrachte. Griegs kunst steht in einer Reihe mit derjenigen der größten norwegischen Dichter dieses Jahrhunderts, Björnson und Ibsen. Wie aus ihren Dichtungen, spricht auch aus seiner Musik die norwegische Volksseele selbst.' Niemann, *Die Musik Skandinaviens*, 74.

[6] 'Sie ist Heimatkunst, sofern sie sich von heimischer Volksmusik in allem unmittelbar anregen läßt, ihre wesentlichen Eigenheiten in die Kunstmusik übernimmt, ja, die eigne Kunstmusik auf ihren Grundlagen aufbaut. Nirgends gibt Grieg darum Herrlicheres, als da, wo er die heimatliche Natur, das heimatliche Volkstum in Tönen besingen kann.' Schjelderup and Niemann, *Edvard Grieg*, 103.

[7] 'Durch bewußte, mit genialer künstlerischer Begabung vorgenommene Einführung und Verschmelzung der norwegischen Volksmusik in die Kunstmusik wird er Regenerator, Retter und Haupt der norwegisch-nationalen Tonschule. Seine Kunst ist aber nicht nur Heimatkunst, sondern zugleich der Ausfluß einer ausgeprägten und reichen Persönlichkeit, die die Töne der Heimat, welche als teurestes Gut in seinem Herzen schlummert, umrauscht und in die Sphäre hohen Künstlertums hebt.' Niemann, *Die Musik Skandinaviens*, 74.

he believed, therefore aspired to a supposedly higher universal truth:

> It would be wrong to reproach him for only producing
> *Genrekunst*, choosing to remain within the fjord's narrow local
> dialects and declining to venture out upon the open sea. His art
> is of international significance, because it is the expression in
> miniature of a sharply etched personality, and because it shows
> in its purest form, through the prism of its own rich colours,
> the pure Nordic-Germanic spirit of music, with which we are
> increasingly losing touch. It expresses, with wonderful delicacy,
> the spiritual stirrings and emotions of mankind, and so it has
> *universal human* value and importance.[8]

The terms of Niemann's debate are worth considering. Niemann sought
to distance Grieg from the claim of being limited to *Genrekunst*, presumably sensitive to his lack of large-scale symphonic works (and the claim of
miniaturism that had dogged Grieg's career). But the 'universal human value
and importance' embodied by his work is that of the 'pure Nordic-Germanic spirit of music', hardly a neutral geographical or historical category.
Furthermore, while praising the music's expression of mankind's 'spiritual
stirrings', Niemann employed familiar aspects of Norwegian topography,
namely the western fjords, to illustrate Grieg's groundedness in his home
soil. Niemann saw no contradiction between these positions, between the
supposed universalism of Grieg's music and its powerful sense of *Heimat*:
rather the opposite, in fact, since the music's expression of its own local
identity was, for him as for Schjelderup, a sign of its authenticity or spiritual
truth. The relationship between Grieg and his homeland was therefore an
organic, natural one. Niemann concluded:

> So, through his art, Grieg accomplished the creation, from
> the spirit of Norwegian folk music, of a Norwegian school of
> composition of international rank. This had been the objective
> of his like-minded predecessors and contemporaries, but
> he outstripped them all in the folk colouration, authenticity
> and refinement of his art. The folk music of his homeland
> is transfigured and resurrected in his art music. Indeed, the
> instinctive, nourishing relationship between the composer and
> folk music has the effect that, rather than merely reworking
> popular airs or working within existing folk forms and

---

[8] 'Doch nichts Falscheres, als ihm vorwerfen, daß er nur Genrekunst gegeben, daß er im Fjord
engbegrenzten lokaldialekts stecken geblieben und nicht auf die hohe See hinausgelangt sei. Seine
Kunst hat internationale Bedeutung, weil sie die Äußerung einer auch, oder sogar grade im Kleinen
großen scharfgeprägten Persönlichkeit ist, weil sie im Prisma ihrer reichen Farbenwelt den reinen
nordisch-germanischen Geist der Tonkunst, welcher der unsrigen mehr und mehr abhanden kommt,
in seiner reinsten Form widerspiegelt, weil sie für alle seelischen Regungen und Empfindungen
des Menschen mit wundervollen Feinheit den rechten Ausdruck zu finden weiß, daher *allgemein
menschlichen* Wert und Bedeutung besitzt.' Schjelderup and Niemann, *Edvard Grieg*, 103.

categories, Grieg builds free, non-folk forms, unconsciously and unintentionally creating a musical folk language from the depths of his soul.[9]

For later writers on music and nationalism, especially Theodor W. Adorno, Niemann's alignment of folklorism, landscape and music was a deeply sinister one that was inextricably linked with extreme right-wing aesthetics. Indeed, it is easy to identify a racial subtext in Niemann's discussion, particularly given his emphasis on notions of purity and on the so-called 'Nordic-Germanic' spirit of music, a synthetic construction that looks forward particularly to the 1930s. As Tomi Mäkelä has argued, however, it is a mistake to judge Niemann's *Blut und Boden* aesthetics solely according to the political beliefs and practice of a later age, albeit one which fed upon precisely those images of race, homeland and cultural purity invoked by Niemann.[10] The *Heimat* movement at the start of the twentieth century was a broad phenomenon, based as much on a spirit of what Mäkelä calls a transcendental post-Romantic utopianism as on a rejection of contemporary urban culture.[11] Hence, it was not simply a reactionary conservatism, but an alternative counter-culture or state of being, whose closest modern counterparts could as easily be the Green environmental lobby as some of the ultra-right-wing nationalist movements on the fringe of current European politics.[12] Niemann's criticism could be read, in this light, as a celebration of regional diversity or difference, rather than purely an assertion of supposed racial superiority.

Certain aspects of Niemann's writing could therefore have appealed to Grieg, whose own political sympathies were broadly liberal-democratic, and he wrote to thank Niemann for the dedication of *Die Musik Skandinaviens*.[13]

---

[9] 'So wird Grieg in seiner Kunst fürs eigne Volk der Vollender dessen, was seine Vorgänger und gleichstrebenden Freunde auf den übrigen Geistesgebieten vorbereitet und erreicht hatten: der Schöpfer einer norwegischen Tonkunst aus dem Geiste norwegischer Volksmusik von internationalen Range. Aber er übertrifft sie alle an volkstümlicher Färbung, Echtheit und Feinheit seiner Kunst. Die Volksmusik der Heimat feiert in seiner Kunstmusik verklärte Auferstehung. Ja, die gegenseitige innerliche Ergänzung ist so vollkommen, die natürliche innerliche Verwandtschaft zwischen dem Tondichter und der Volksmusik so instinktiv, so eng und stark, daß Grieg da, wo er nicht nur Volksweisen frei bearbeitet oder in volkstümlichen Formen und Gattungen schafft, sondern auch dort, wo er freie, nicht volkstümliche Formen bebaut, unbewußt und unwillkürlich in allen Einzelheiten aus tiefster Seele heraus in Wendungen der musikalischen Volkssprache schafft.' Schjelderup and Niemann, *Edvard Grieg*, 103–4.

[10] Tomi Mäkelä, 'Natur und Heimat in der Sibelius-Rezeption. Walter Niemann, Theodor W. Adorno und die "postmoderne Moderne"', *Sibelius Forum II, Proceedings from the Third International Jean Sibelius Conference, Helsinki, December 7–10, 2000*, ed. Matti Huttunen, Kari Kilpeläinen and Veijo Murtomäki (Helsinki: Sibelius Academy, 2003), 365–82.

[11] Ibid., 369.

[12] See also Elizabeth Boa and Rachel Palfreyman, *Heimat, a German Dream: Regional Loyalties and National Identity in German Culture, 1890–1990* (Oxford: Oxford University Press, 2000), especially 'Introduction: Mapping the Terrain', 1–29.

[13] Letter dated 5 August 1906, reproduced in *Brev*, II, 529 (translated into Norwegian).

At the same time, however, Grieg sought to distance himself from some of the fundamental principles of much German criticism. In a letter to an American biographer, Henry Finck, written only a few years previously, Grieg had looked back retrospectively over his career and attempted to influence aspects of his own critical reception.[14] As Niemann was to do in *Die Musik Skandinaviens*, Grieg began by asserting his commitment to his Norwegian homeland: 'Norwegian folk life, Norwegian legends and history, and above all Norwegian nature, have been a great influence on my creativity ever since my youth.'[15] But Grieg was sensitive to the idea, propounded by many German critics, that he owed his greatness or originality purely to Norwegian folk music, claiming (with perhaps a selective memory):

> The opportunity to immerse myself in Norwegian folk song did not arise until later. When I wrote the piano pieces op. 3 and especially op. 6, where a national element occurs in several places, I knew next to nothing about our folk songs. The fact is of importance in view of German assertions that I am nothing more than a copying machine of Norwegian folk songs.[16]

For Grieg, the influence of folk songs was limited to a particular syntactical device, 'the treatment of the leading note, and particularly its descent to the lower fifth scale degree', a neat summary of the so-called 'Grieg motive' that famously opens the Piano Concerto. Even here, however, Grieg maintained that 'a similar progression can be found in the work of other composers',[17] so it could hardly be described as a definitive characteristic. Rather, Grieg defined the sense of national identity in his work as something more unconscious, natural or spiritual. In this sense, he drew surprisingly close to Niemann's description of *Heimatkunst* while simultaneously laying claim to a more cosmopolitan musical discourse in his songs :

> The history of culture shows us that every lasting art has been national. I stand like every other modern artist who wishes to achieve something, consciously or unconsciously, upon national soil, and feel myself, particularly when I am dealing with national poetry, obviously also national. But my songs have fewer

[14] The letter was dated Troldhaugen 17 July 1899 and written in German. It has been reproduced in several sources, including the volume *Artikler og taler*, ed. Øystein Gaukstad (Oslo: Gyldendal, 1957), 49–63. All further references are to this source (in my translation).

[15] 'Norwegisches Volksleben, norwegischen Sagen und Geschichte und vor Allem norwegische Natur übten seit meiner Jugend einen grossen Influss auf meinem Schaffen.' *Artikler og taler*, 49.

[16] 'Die Gelegenheit, mich in dem norwegischen Volkslied zu vertiefen, hatte ich aber erst später. Als ich die Klavierstücke Op. 3 und ganz besonders Op. 6 schrieb, wo ein nationales Element vielfach emportaucht, kannte ich unsere Volkslieder so viel wie gar nicht. Diese Thatsache ist, gewissen deutschen Behauptungen gegenüber, dass ich Nichts als eine Copiemaschine des norwegischen Volksliedes sei, von Wichtigkeit.' Ibid., 49.

[17] '. . . die Behandlung des Leittons und ganz besonders der Schritt desselben abwärts nach der Quinte. Eine solche Fortschreitung findet sich aber auch bei anderen Componisten.' Ibid., 50.

national tendencies than my other works, for the simple reason that I have often been inspired by Danish or German poets. In such songs *I* cannot discover any direct link to the Norwegian folk tune. I would go a step further with the following assertion: when the *Norwegian* poets do not describe nature, folk life and legends, but simply everyday human life, I have never thought about a national colouring. In fact, I have never consciously sought such colouring. It came of its own accord. I do not believe that a national colour can be successfully reflected. Where the national element is not in your *blood*, it has no more justification as 'creative' art than as 'photographic'.[18]

Nationalism for Grieg, like Niemann, was therefore an organic process, defined by metaphors of blood and soil, an authentically 'creative' spirit or genius rather than a merely 'photographic' object or product. Furthermore, nationalism was supposedly the expression of the artistic material (national poetry, folk tunes or nature), and not intentionally or consciously willed by the artist themselves. Where such national material was not present, Grieg maintained, his work could not reasonably be called national in character. Grieg's letter is a complex, multi-layered document, in which the sense of peripheralisation, of marginalisation from a perceived mainstream, is as strong as the sense of local identity. Grieg remarked acidly, 'when I speak with my own voice, which has nothing to do with folk tunes, the conservative German music critics have also found a term of abuse for it. It is called: "Norwegerei".'[19] In his letter to Niemann, Grieg expressed similar concerns about the perceived universalism of German art:

It really is about time that Norwegian art was at least met with understanding in Germany. And to say it plainly: especially my art in particular. How often in the German papers have I had to endure accusations against my works in the form of cheap banalities such as 'Norwegerei', 'He Norwegianises' etc. Such lack of understanding! No-one would ever permit themselves

---

[18] 'Die Culturgeschichte zeigt uns, dass jede Kunst, die am Leben bleibt, national gewesen ist. Ich stehe, wie jeder moderne Künstler, der etwas will, bewusst oder unbewusst, – auf nationalem Boden und empfinde, ganz besonders wo ich mit nationalen dichterischen Stoffen zu thun habe, selbstverständlich auch national. Meine Lieder sind aber oft weniger national angehaucht wie meine sonstigen Werke. Ganz einfach, weil mich vielfach dänische und deutsche Dichter inspirierten. In solchen Liedern kann *ich* wenigstens keine directen Beziehungen zum norwegischen Volkslied entdecken. Ich gehe aber einen Schritt weiter und behaupte: Wo die *norwegischen* Dichter nicht Natur, Volksleben oder Sagen, sondern lediglich allgemein menschlich-seelische Vorgänge schildern, ist mir niemals ein nationales Colorit in den Sinn gekommen. Im ganzen habe ich das Colorit nie gesucht. Es kam von selbst. Ich glaube überhaupt nicht, das sich eine nationale Farbe mit Erfolg reflectiren lässt. Wo das nationale Element nicht *im Blut* steckt, hat es auch keine Berechtigung als «schaffende», sondern nur als «photographische» Kunst.' Ibid., 51.

[19] 'Wenn ich meine eigene Sprache spreche, welche mit dem Volkslied Nichts zu thun hat, haben die conservativen deutschen Kritiker ein Scheltwort auch dafür gefunden. Es heisst: «Norwegerei.»' Ibid., 50.

to use as a term of abuse labels such as 'Germanness', 'Germanicism' about any German composer. And yet this is exactly how the German music critics are themselves distrustful and unsympathetical towards not only Norwegian, but all expressions of national identity in music outside Germany. How small-minded and one-sided this is! I hope that you in your book will speak out courageously and seriuosly against this unfortunate situation! You would thereby do a both good and *just* deed.[20]

As in Niemann's analysis, therefore, Grieg points to a tension between local and cosmopolitan modes of musical discourse in his work, elsewhere acknowledging a dialogue with German music (specifically with the voice leading of the 'eternal masters' Bach, Mozart and Wagner), but then resisting German claims of universalism as a form of marginalisation. Nationalism in music, Grieg suggested, was ultimately an attempt to uncover something deeper and more atavistic, a perspective that again is close to that of Niemann. Writing of the influence of folk music on his work, he returned to an organic model of musical inspiration:

> It is difficult for me to talk of harmonic innovation. The realm of harmony has always been my dreamworld and the relationship between my own harmonic way of feeling and Norwegian folk tunes was a mystery even to myself. I have found that in the dark depths of our folk tunes lies a wealth of unknown harmonic possibilities. In my arrangements of folk tunes op. 66 and elsewhere I have sought to give expression to my awareness of the hidden harmonies in our folk music. To this purpose, I have been especially attracted by the chromatic lines within the harmonic texture.[21]

As we have seen in Chapter 2, the purpose of such chromatic lines in the op. 66 collection is partly a structural one, to create a tension between forms

---

[20] 'Det er virkelig ikke for tidlig at norsk kunst også i Tyskland i det minste blirr møtt med forståelse. Og for å si det rett ut: ganske særlig *min* kunst. Hvor ofte har jeg ikke i tyske aviser måtte tåle anklagen mot mine verker i form av lettkjøpte banaliteter som: «Norwegerei», «Er norwegeret» etc. Hvor forståelsesløst! Ingen ville tillate seg å benytte som skjellsord betegnelser som «Deutschtum», «Deutscherei» om noen tyske komponist. Og dog er det faktisk slik at tyske musikkritikere stiller seg mistroisk og usympatisk ikke bare overfor norske, nei, overhodet overfor ale nasjonalitetsytringer i tonekunsten utenfor Tyskland. Hvor smålig og ensidig dette er! Jeg håper at De i Deres bok vil komme med et modig alvorsord om denne uheldige tilstand! De ville derved gjøre en både god og *rettferdig* gjerning.' Letter dated 5 August 1906, *Brev*, II, 529.

[21] 'Über harmonischen Neuerungen zu reden, fällt mir schwer. Das Reich der Harmonien war immer meine Traumwelt und das Verhältnis meiner harmonischen Empfindungsweise zu der norwegischen Volksweise war mir selbst ein Mysterium. Ich habe gefunden, das die dunkle Tiefe unserer Weisen in deren Reichtum an ungeahnten harmonischen Möglichkeiten ihren Grund hat. In meiner Bearbeitung der Volkslieder op. 68 [*sic*: 66] und auch sonst, habe ich versucht, meine Ahnung von den verborgenen Harmonien unseres Volkstones einen Ausdruck zu geben. Für diesen Zweck haben mich ganz besonders die chromatischen Tonfolgen im harmonischen Gewebe stark angezogen.' *Artikler og taler*, 51–2.

of diatonic and modal progression, for instance in 'Siri Dale-Visen'. But they also create a sense of objectivity or depersonalisation, in 'I Ola-Dalom, i Ola-Kjønn' for example, that is characteristic of much of Grieg's nature music. In other words, their function is not merely associative, the reflection of a supposedly national condition or colour, but also representational. Such voice-leading patterns help to construct landscape in Grieg's music. It is also significant that Grieg chooses to talk in terms of a harmonic 'dreamworld', since such notions of enchantment and bewitchment, both literal and figurative, are closely allied to representations and descriptions of Norwegian nature and landscape in paintings, folk tales and poetry. These images come to the foreground again in the song cycle *Haugtussa*, where Grieg's sense of *Heimatkunst* is perhaps at its most powerful.

Garborg, Grieg and the language debate

Haugtussa, Grieg's only genuine song cycle, cannot be fully understood without reference to its immediate historical environment. The context in which Grieg chose to set verses by Arne Garborg was a sensitive and politically charged one. The consensus politics of the *Embedsmannstat* ('civil-servant state') which had governed Norway from 1814 gave way in the mid-1880s to a more polarised discourse in which claims for cultural and political independence had gained much greater urgency.[22] As suggested in Chapter 1, this shift is part of a broader European trend in which nationalist movments gained a harder edge in the second half of the nineteenth century. Hence, the struggle for Norwegian independence, read as a historical narrative, can be understood in a wider international context and not as an isolated phenomenon. As in other regions during this period (such as Finland, for example), debates about national identity in Norway centred on language. For those on the left of the debate, the official language of government, known as *riksmål* (now *bokmål*), was increasingly seen as being too closely tied to Danish, and was therefore associated with the image of Norway as a colony rather than an independent state. This 'Dano-Norwegian' became a symbol of oppression and of centralised systems of control (focused on Christiania, which in turn looked to Sweden for its ultimate authority). In contrast, western and central Norwegian dialects were seen as embodying a purer, supposedly indigenous Norwegian identity. The earliest attempts to synthesise a variety of dialect forms into a standard language known as *landsmål* (now *nynorsk*), took place in the 1840s to 1850s, on the back of the first wave of Norwegian Romantic nationalism.[23] The first regional *landsmål*

---

[22] See, for example, Sørensen, 'Development', especially 21.
[23] Folklorist Ivar Aasen (1813–96) published a series of important books on *landsmål*, including *Det norske Folkesprogs Grammatik* (1845), the *Ordbog over det norske Folkesprog* (1850) and the *Prøver af Landsmålet*

organisations, intended to promote interest in the new standard language as well as the revival of folk customs and the ultimate goal of political independence, were founded in 1868.[24] The Norwegian parliament (the *Storting*) held its first *landsmål* debate on 20 May 1874, and in 1878 passed a law which stipulated that instruction in state schools should be as far as possible in the children's own speech.[25]

The language debate in Norway in the second half of the nineteenth century was not simply concerned with forms of expression but with deeper issues of national identity. In particular, it articulated a tension between rural and urban forms of nationalism, between isolationism and cosmopolitanism, and between centralised and decentralised models of political and cultural control. As Øystein Sørensen notes, for example, the political dominance of Venstre (a loose amalgamation of rural farming interests and those supporting the dialect language) after 1884 was charactised by 'a democratisation of the political system through extensions of the suffrage',[26] and represented a geographical shift in power away from the urbanised south-east (Christiania) towards the more rural regions of western and central Norway. *Landsmål* can therefore be regarded as a form of counter-culture, the expression of a Norwegian *Heimat* movement similar to those which developed in German and other parts of Europe towards the end of the nineteenth century. As Jostein Nerbøvik observes, *landsmål* served at least two functions: 'the one was pedagogical: it was to provide better means of communication for rural people across the country', while 'the other was ideological: it was to be a focal point for historical and national identity and continuity'.[27] Hence, the vision of community that it promoted was an organic one, in which the reinvention of national traditions (including *landsmål* itself) was a necessary prerequisite for the achievement of the modern goal of full cultural and political sovereignty. Nerbøvik notes that 'the return to the old farming society went hand in hand with the presentation of an alternative social-economic order'. The key thing, according to Nerbøvik, 'was that the farming culture should be restored in a new, adequate form. It should not be antiquarian or archaic, but authentic.'[28]

i Norge (1853), which sought to create a new standardised language from non-metropolitan dialects.
[24] Kjell Haugland, 'An Outline of Norwegian Cultural Nationalism in the Second Half of the Nineteenth Century', in *The Roots of Nationalism*, ed. Rosalind Mitchison. Studies in Northern Europe (Edinburgh: John Donald, 1980), 21–9, here 27. The two organisations were Vestmannalaget in Bergen and Det Norske Samlaget in Oslo.
[25] Frøyen, 'Kulturell og politisk nasjonalisme', 21; the ruling read: 'Undervisningen i Almueskolen saavidt muligt meddeles paa Børnenes eget Talesprog.'
[26] Sørensen, 'Development', 23.
[27] 'Det eine var folkepedagogisk; det skulle gje betre kommunikasjonstilhøve or bygdefolk landet over. Det andre var ideologisk; det skulle vere ein samneemnor for historisk og nasjonal identitet og kontinuitet.' Nerbøvik, 'Den norske kulturnasjonalismen', in Sørensen, *Nasjonal identitet*, 139–58, here 140.
[28] 'vendinga attende til den gamle bondesamfunnet gjekk hand i hand med presentasjonen av ei anna

The poet and novelist Arne Garborg was a keen supporter of *landsmål*, and became a prominent player in contemporary debates about Norwegian national identity. For Garborg, born in Jæren in south-western Norway, two kinds of Norwegian nationalism existed in an unequal relationship: the rural folk culture, which he regarded as 'oppressed', and the cosmopolitan urban elite, which he saw as 'colonisers'.[29] As Morten Haug Frøyen has argued, the language debate for Garborg was ultimately a means to an end rather than a goal in itself.[30] In an essay on *landsmål* from 1877 entitled *Den ny-norske Sprog- og Nationalitetsbevægelser* ('The New Norwegian Language and Nationality Movements'), Garborg defined his vision of the nation as an organic unity, which, on the foundation of its unique natural characteristics (*natureiendommeligheder*), 'sought to lead an independent spiritual life'.[31] Garborg therefore stressed that defining characteristics of *landsmål* must be originality and uniqueness. 'That language', he argued, 'will have *originality*, independent content, independent, distinct idiom, independent validity.'[32] Biological metaphors of organic growth once again lay at the heart of his argument. Compared to the colonial Dano-Norwegian, which was like an 'old plant' in the process of decay, *nynorsk* was a 'young, naturally healthy shoot of life'.[33]

Garborg saw no tension between the apparently contradictory impulses in his definition of an authentic Norwegian national identity, such as between the retrospective character of *landsmål* and the future prospect of Norwegian political independence. Like Niemann, he saw the process of national self-determination through regionalism as a universal historical principle:

> The formation of every popular individuality, each folk-unit, which steps out distinctly and clearly from the formlessness and mass existence of barbarism, is a historic victory. It is a victory for cosmopolitanism itself; for the true cosmopolitanism is based precisely upon the principle of nationality, namely upon the originality of folk individualities, upon the division of labour.[34]

og alternativ socialøkonomisk ordning . . . Eit hovedelement vat at bondekulturen måtte restaurest i ei ny, adekvat form. Han skulle ikkje vere antikvarisk eller arkaisk, men autentisk.' Ibid., 155.
[29] Bodil Steensen, 'Borgelig nasjonalisme og bygdenasjonalisme', in Sørensen, *Nasjonal identitet*, 159–69, here 161.
[30] Frøyen, 'Kulturell og politisk nasjonalisme', 30.
[31] 'søger at føre et selvstændigt aandeligt Liv'. Quoted in Sveinung Time, 'Språk og nasjonalitet hos Arne Garborg', in *Arne Garborgs kulturnasjonalisme*, KULT skriftserie no. 61 (Oslo: Noregs Forskningsråd, 1996), 107–95, here 155.
[32] 'Det Maal . . . maa have Oprindelighed, selvstændigt Indhold, selvstændigt, bestemt Idiom, selvstændig Gylidhed.' Garborg, *Den ny-norske Sprog- og Nationalitetsbevægelser*, quoted in Frøyen, 'Kulturell og politisk nasjonalisme', 31.
[33] 'medens Dansk-Norsken er en gammel Plante, . . . saa er Ny-Norsken en ung, naturfrisk Livsvæxt.' Garborg, *Den ny-norske Sprog- og Nationalitetsbevægelser*, ibid., 31.
[34] 'Enhver folkelig Individualitetsdannelse, enhver Folke-Enhed, det træder distinkt og klart ud af Barbarismens Formløshed og Massetilværelse, er en historisk Seier. Det er en Seier for selve

It was therefore possible, according to Garborg, to speak *landsmål* and yet be a member of a modern European nation state (an argument still promoted strongly by nationalist political parties on the left of European politics). The paradox between the notion of an original individuality (the defining character of Garborg's regional identity) and the political goal of national unity was resolved, according to Garborg, by the idea of *landsmål* as a form of genealogy:

> Speech is precisely the natural expression of inner kinship. If we are truly to be brothers, we should at any rate speak together in the same tongue. There can and must be differences in dialect, just as in actual families each individual has their own way of talking; but there must be a common idiom; everyone must feel one and the same language as theirs, even if, for example, the Intelligentsia have it in its Sunday clothes, its nobler and more idealised form, while the people have it more in its 'natural condition'.[35]

For Garborg, therefore, *landsmål* was both the symbol and expression of a higher state of community, whose spirit, he believed, would naturally lead to Norwegian independence. To oppose *landsmål* was not only to deny Norway's true political status but would effectively constitute an assault on the natural order of things. Garborg ultimately believed that 'the people are recognised and judged according to their language, their spiritual independence, their originality, their moral power, in one word: their right to exist'.[36]

Grieg's choice of Garborg's poetry suggests that he was at least sympathetic to some of the political ideals that lay behind the language debate, and their correspondence indicates that they shared a common understanding of the qualities of *landsmål* itself. Following an early performance of the *Haugtussa* songs in Christiania on 7 November 1899, for instance, Garborg wrote warmly to Grieg:

> It is precisely that deep, gentle, subdued, underworld music, which in my own way I tried to sing into words and verse, but which you have captured. And then suddenly again the sparkling shining sun and summer rapture as in the splendid 'Killingdansen' ('Kidlings' Dance') [op. 67/6]. But one of the most trollishly

Kosmopolitanismen; thi den sande Kosmopolitanisme er netop baseret paa Nationalitetsprincipet, d.e. paa Folkeindividualiteternes Originalitet, paa Arbeidets Deling.' Garborg, *Den ny-norske Sprog- og Nationalitetsbevægelser*, quoted in Time, 'Språk og nasjonalitet', 163.

[35] 'For det indre Slægtskab er jo netop Sproget det naturlige Udtryk. Skal vi virkelig være Brødre, saa maa vi idetmindste kunne tale sammen i samme Tungemaal. Der kan og maa være Dialektforskjelligheder, ligesom i den virkelige Familie hvert enkelt Individ har sin særegne Maade at tale paa; men Idiomet maa være fælles; Alle maa føle et og samme Maal væsentlig som sit, omend f. Ex. Intelligentsen har det i dets Søndagsdragt, dets ædlere og idealiserede Form, medens Folket har det mere i «Naturtilstand».' Garborg, *Den ny-norske Sprog- og Nationalitetsbevægelser*, quoted in ibid., 169–70.

[36] Sørensen, 'Development', 32.

enchanting is 'Bekken' ('The Brook') [op. 67/8]. Yes, I am now glad and proud, unashamedly proud, because you could use these verses. Thanks![37]

Grieg replied to Garborg in more detail, setting his thoughts in the broader context of the language debate and answering the criticisms of one of *landsmål*'s most outspoken opponents, Bjørnstjerne Bjørnson ('B. B.'):

> I am delighted that you like my *Haugtussa* songs. And doubly glad because Fru [Eva] Nansen did them splendidly. And I am certain that Fru [Agathe Backer] Grøndahl was the best in the country at the piano.
>
> It is not many weeks since I argued with B. B. about the language issue. Unfortuately we are in complete disagreement. It is a great nuisance that we do not have B. B. with his overpowering talents on our side. And yet I think that his opposition is good in so far as it gives the fanatics something to think about. What should we beggars do, who were born of a Danish-speaking mother and father who only have the gift to love the language, but without being able to write and talk it? Should we therefore be regarded as enemies by the language fanatics? That is unfair and unwise. I regard neither city dweller nor farmer as the patent holder of the soul's and heart's delicacy, and I do not believe that language makes any difference to those who possess that for which language is simply an expression, whether it is *Rigsmål* (damned word) or *Bondemål*. But B. B. and his colleagues have overlooked two things, which I believe are of the greatest importance:
>
> 1. Our Danish language is forced upon us through school and church. Justice suggests that which is now only peasant language should have the same right. This might take place in a few generations (or perhaps in only one). I am not afraid for the peasant culture. It gives us richness and will eventually form a higher unity with the town culture. I am certain that the language of the future will come from that.
>
> 2. B. B. does not mention that it is four-fifths of the nation that speak *Bondemål*. That is decisive for me.[38]

[37] 'Det er netop dette dybe, bløde, dæmpede, den underjordiske Musik, som jeg paa min Vis søgte at synge ind i Ord og Vers, men som De har fanget. Og saa pludselig igjen tindrende straalende Sol og Sommerfryd, som i den velsignede Killingdansen. Men noget af det mest troldsk betagende er Bekken. Ja jeg er nu glad og kry, rent utilladelig kry, fordi De kunde bruge disse Versene. Tak!' Letter dated 7 November 1899, *Brev*, I, 176.

[38] 'Jeg er lykkelig over, at De liker mine Haugtussa-Sange. Og dobbelt glad er jeg fordi da må Fru [Eva] Nansen ha gjort dem bra [on 2 November]. Og at Fru [Agathe Backer] Grøndahl har været den Bedste i Norges Land ved Pianoet, er jeg sikker på.

Det er ikke mange Uger siden jeg disputerede med B. B. om Målsagen. Desværre er vi helt uenig. Det er helt forbandet at vi ikke skal have B. B med sin henførende Evne på vår Side. Og dog tror jeg, hans Modstand er forsåvidt god, som den gir *Fanatikerne* Noget at tånke over. Hvad skal vi Stakkarer

In a letter written later the same month (November 1899) to Frants Beyer, Grieg complained, 'and what is it fundamentally that they have against the *landsmål?* That it is more difficult! Who cares about that?' In response, he argued, 'it is *ours*, that is the issue', and aligned characteristics of the western Norwegian topography with those of the dialect language: 'It is also more difficult to get up our fells than to go along the road, but they are ours, and they give greater pleasure in spite of the difficulties precisely because they are ours.' Hence, for Grieg, landscape and language appeared to be intimately (and naturally) linked. Bjørnson's opposition, he concluded, 'was formed in his private laboratory and not in the world of reality'.[39] Grieg wrote to Bjørnson himself in similar terms, but sought to take a more conciliatory approach, stressing his own sense of regionalism as justification for his position on the debate:

> How sad for me, and many with me, that *you* with your overpowering talents should stand on that side [of the language debate]! I believe now that out west we feel more positively about the language, because it is so much lovelier and often gives expression to the noble aspects of the folk character. If, like me, you had spent 1½ years in Hardanger at an important point in your development, you would understand me more easily. But of this I am in no doubt for an instant: your appearance has done some good regarding the 'language fanatics', those narrow-minded people who go so far as to look down upon those of us who *only* love the language, but cannot speak it![40]

gjøre, som er født av en dansktalende Mor og Far som bare har fåt den Gave at *elske* Målet, men uden at kunne skrive og tale det? Skal vi derfor af Målsagens Fanatikere betragtes som Fjender? Det er uretfærdigt og uklogt. Jeg betragter hverken Bymand eller Bonde som Patentindehaver af Åndens og Hjertens Finhed og jeg tror ikke at Sproget gjør Noget til Sagen for den som ejer det, som Sproget bare er udtryk for, enten det nu er «Rigsmål» (forbandet Ord) eller Bondemål. Men to Ting har B. B. og hans Meningsfælder ikke nævnt, som jeg synes er af største Betydning:

1) Vort danske Sprog er os *påvvunget* gjennem Skole og Kirke. Retfærdighed fordrer da, at det som nu bare er Bondemål, får samme Ret. Det må i nogle Generationer (eller bare i én) påtvinges. Bondekulturen er jeg ikke bange for. Den giver os Stofrigdom og vil gå op i en højere Enhed med Bykulturen. Deraf vil da fremgå det Fremtidssprog, jeg tror på.

2) B. B. nævner ikke at det er *fire Femtedele* af Nationen, der tale Bondemål. Det er for mig afgørende.' Letter dated 9 November 1899, ibid., 176–7.

[39] 'Og hvad er det i det Hele for Grunde mod Landsmålet, man bringer tiltorvs? At det er vanskeligere! Hvem spør om det? Det er *vort*, det er Sagen. Vore Fjelde er også vanskeligere at komme op på, end at gå Landevejen, men de er *vore*, og de gir større Glæde trods Vanskeligheden, netop derfor, at de er vore. . . . B. B. henter sine Grunde fra sit private Laboratorium og ikke fra Realitetenes Verden.' Letter dated 25 November 1899, Grieg, *Brev til Frants Beyer*, 241.

[40] 'Hvor trist for mig og mange med mig at *Du* med Din henførende Evne skal stå der! Jeg tror nu, at vi der vesterpå føler varmere for Målet, fordi det der er så meget vakkere og ofte gir Udtryk for det noble i Folkekarakteren. Havde Du som jeg, på et vigtigt Punkt i Din Udvikling levet 1½ år i Hardanger, så vilde Du lettere forstå mig. Men, derom er jeg intet Øieblik i Tvivl: Din Optræden har gjort godt ligeoverfor «Målfanatikerne», dette snæversynte Folk, der går så vidt, at de ser ned på os, der *bare* elsker Målet, men ikke kan tale det!' Letter dated 16 January 1900, *Brev*, I, 82. Benestad notes that Bjørnson had given a lecture in Christiania on 23 October 1899 entitled 'Målsagens Stilling

Grieg's personal friendship with Bjørnson, and his association with the so-called 'Lysaker circle' of artists, intellectuals and politicians centred around the figure of Fridtjof Nansen,[41] meant that he ultimately adopted a more diplomatic approach to the language issue than that taken by Garborg. Indeed, following the achievement of Norwegian independence in 1905, Grieg evidently began to feel that Garborg's position had become too isolationist. 'Garborg seems no longer to be a European', he complained to Frants Beyer, 'barely even national in its wider sense. He has become more and more encircled in trifles and narrow-mindedness.'[42] Similarly he wrote to Bjørnson in the very final year of his life, that 'since the language debate has become a matter of political power, I have distanced myself from it'.[43] But Grieg remained committed to *landsmål*, and to Garborg's poetry, precisely for its regional qualities. Hence, he wrote to Beyer, 'what remains in compensation is fortunately the wonderful descriptions of nature. They are truly felt and they appear lived through', even if he still criticised Garborg for being 'all too swiftly lost in language fixation and obstinacy'.[44]

Grieg was drawn to Garborg's verse novella *Haugtussa* for a number of reasons. Writing to the German pianist and composer Oscar Meyer, for instance, he described *Haugtussa* as 'a masterpiece, full of originality, simplicity and depth, and with an utterly indescribable strength of colour',[45] qualities which he also ascribed more generally to *landsmål*. Writing to Anders Hovden from Denmark, shortly before reading *Haugtussa* for the first time in 1895, Grieg added wistfully: 'write more in that splendid language! It sounds to me like the most beautiful music.'[46] But in a letter to August Winding, having discovered the book, Grieg stressed that it was Garborg's descriptions of nature that had attracted him: 'that brilliant author in *landsmål*, Arne Garborg, has just published a novel, consisting simply of poetry, called *Haugtussa*, and it is so full of nature mysticism that I could not

---

i vort Kulturliv' ('The Language Debate's Position in Our Cultural Life'), in which he was highly critical of *landsmål*.

[41] See Steensen, 'Borgelig nasjonalisme og bygdenasjonalisme', especially 163, for a discussion of the 'Lysaker circle' in the context of the language issue. Nansen attempted to steer a paternalistic middle way between the opposing sides in the debate, and sought to promote a *samnorsk* which combined elements of both western and eastern Norwegian dialects (160).

[42] 'Garborg synes ikke mere at være Europæer, ja neppe nok national i større Betydning. Han er bleven mere og mere incirklet i Smätterier og Trangsyn.' Letter dated 17 November 1904, Grieg, *Brev til Frants Beyer*, 313.

[43] 'siden Målsagen er bleven en politisk Magtsag, har jeg tat Afstand fra den.' Letter dated 16 May 1907, *Brev*, I, 97.

[44] 'Hvad der holder én skadeløs, er heldigvis de vidunderlige Naturskildringer. De er isandhed følt og de sete gjennemoplevet. Men altfor snart afløses de af Målbundethed og Kjævlelyst.' Grieg, *Brev til Frants Beyer*, 313.

[45] 'Det er et mesterverk, fullt av originalitet, enkelhet og dybde og med en ganske ubeskrivelig fargekraft.' Letter dated 7 June 1898, reprinted in *Brev*, II, 523–4 (originally in German).

[46] 'Skriv mere på det herlige Mål! Det klinger for mig som den skjønneste Musik.' Letter dated 12 February 1895, reprinted in *Brev*, I, 462.

resist it.'[47] Hence, it appears to have been *Haugtussa's* qualities as *Heimatkunst* that ultimately attracted Grieg to the work, rather than its language alone. The combination of landscape, nature, myth and folklorism appealed to Grieg's strong sense of regional identity. But it must also have suggested certain kinds of structural shapes and musical gestures associated with folk music and the natural world that Grieg had already begin to explore in the *19 norske Folkeviser*. In that sense, Garborg's novel served as both a continuation and intensification of compositional issues which had preoccupied Grieg in his previous work. Closer examination of Grieg's setting of Garborg's poetry therefore adds new perspectives to our understanding of his creative response to contemporary debates about Norwegian national identity, while simultaneously deeping our appreciation of the way in which landscape becomes sound and gesture in Grieg's music.

Veslemøy's death: landscape and nature in Grieg's Haugtussa

Arne Garborg's verse novel *Haugtussa*, published in spring 1895, is set in the remote mountains of central south-western Norway, supposedly close to where Garborg himself had grown up. The novel's principal character is a young shepherd girl known as Veslemøy (literally meaning 'little maiden'), who possesses a hallucinatory sixth sense that allows her to experience supernatural images, sounds and visions. For the most part, these visions are taken from Norwegian mythology: trolls, demons and *huldres* appear in various forms, most significantly the figure of a 'fine blue mountain troll' ('ein haugkall fager og blå') that first appears amid the midwinter festivities of the chapter 'Jol' ('Yuletide') to seek Veslemøy as his earthly bride. But occasionally Veslemøy also experiences images that foreshadow the real world, premonitions of future events, or characters drawn from her own family such as the figure of her sister 'fair, light and cheerful in a serious way' ('fager og ljos og ålvorsblid'), who appears in the very final poem of the novel to lead Veslemøy into a hazy and distant future. Veslemøy herself first appears at her spinning wheel, an archetypal image that suggests the unscrolling of a mythic narrative ('spinning a yarn') or the unravelling of fate. The rocking motion of the wheel triggers her first hallucinatory visions, the stormy autumn weather outside serving as a metaphor for her turbulent emotional state. The following poem, 'Kvelding' (evening), is both an actual and a psychological twilight partly induced by Veslemøy's sixth sense. The story of the *huldre* (fairy enchantress) that Veslemøy narrates in 'I Omnskråi' foreshadows her own doomed romance with the local village lad, Jon of

[47] 'Den geniale Forfatter på Landsmålet, Arne Garborg, har nemlig udgivet en Fortælling, bestående af bare Digter, der hedder "Haugtussa", og som er så fuld af Naturmystik, at jeg ikke kunde modstå den.' Letter dated 19 June 1895, ibid., 275.

Skare-brot, which occupies the heart of the novel and takes place entirely within the short summer months (the central chapter 'Sùmar i Fjellet'). Veslemøy initially seeks solace in the waters of the brook ('Ved Gjætle-bekken'), but the latter part of the novel is a remarkable extended vision of the troll kingdom in which Veslemøy loses herself ('På Skare-kula'). It is only through an immense effort of will ('Den store Strid') in the final section of the novel that Veslemøy eventually brings herself back into the cold wintry world of reality.

The mood of Garborg's novel is remote from the kitsch romanticism of Norwegian fairytale. Rather, its supernatural figures can be understood as a form of ecology. They are animating spirits which inhabit Veslemøy's environment such as wind trolls, forest ghosts and mountain gods, natural forces that lie outside immediate human control or understanding. Much of the novel's earthiness or *Heimatkunst* flavour comes from its detailed descriptions of this rural environment. The opening prologue, 'Til deg, du heid og bleike myr . . . eg gjev mitt kvad' ('To you, you heath and pale swamp . . . I give my song') for example, is a performative utterance that serves as both a framing device and an invocation to the spirits of the natural world. Veslemøy's hallucinations not only access an elemental form of nature, they also provide momentary glimpses into her unconscious feelings and desires. In this sense, Garborg's work is closer to the *Nervenkunst* of Strindberg or Knut Hamsun with which it is immediately contemporary than the radical social realism of Ibsen's plays from the 1880s. The novel can also be understood as a pre-Freudian discourse on the nature and function of dream, a reading supported by the recurrence of the verb *drøyme* throughout. Veslemøy's psychological instability is not simply the result of external natural forces acting upon her daily life, but caused by her ability to perceive areas of human consciousness which normally remain hidden. The bestial character of the troll scenes in 'Jol' and 'På Skare-Kula' therefore becomes a reflection of the more animalistic side of human nature.

Haugtussa is also concerned with issues of temporality. It explores different kinds of narrative time, the fragmentation of a single narrative progression (centred around Veslemøy's failed romance) through various diversions, reported speech, inner monologues, visions and symbolic foreshadowings. The novel's action takes place within various different temporal cycles. Seasonal time is structurally significant, namely the transition from autumn through winter to summer and back into winter once again, since it colours the quality of the action that takes place as the novel progresses. Mythical time is also important, not least since the trolls and ghosts that appear during Veslemøy's supernatural visions seem to occupy a different temporal dimension from that of events in the real world around her. In the poem 'Laget' ('The Party') in 'Jol', for instance, time appears to stand still even as the demonic dance whirls past, accentuating the feeling of disembodiment in such passages. The novel is also marked by religious time, such as the sound of church bells and the recitation of the hellish 'svarte-katekisma' ('black catechism') in 'På Skare-Kula'. Meanwhile, Veslemøy's daily routine is organised according to the rhythms of her rural domestic life (harvesting, minding the animals, baby-sitting and spinning). In addition to these cyclic structures, *Haugtussa* is also concerned with polarisation and inversion. Events revolve around two key festival dates in the folk calendar: midsummer night and midwinter. Similarly, the novel focuses on the tension between waking and sleeping, and the associated functions of remembrance and forgetfulness. The prominence of the verb *drøyme* noted above is paralleled by the frequent appearance of *gløyme* ('to forget'), a coupling which seems to have attracted Grieg in particular. Finally, the novel engages with metrical time. Garborg employs a wide range of different verse forms and metres, some borrowed from old Norwegian poetry, and including several dance forms (*hallings* and *springars*) which find a correlate in Grieg's setting.

Grieg appears to have responded to much of this formal complexity when he came to compose his song cycle. The compositional genesis of the work has been described in detail both in the critical edition[48] and in a journal article by James Massengale.[49] As Massengale notes, Grieg appears to have undergone a compositional crisis while working on *Haugtussa*: though the music was written in an initial flurry of enthusiasm shortly after Grieg first read the book immediately following its publication in 1895, he did not publish his song cycle until three years later. Massengale suggests a number of reasons for this delay, including Grieg's doubts about his perceived inability to work with large-scale musical structures and a more general sense of disillusionment with his composition. Hence, for Massengale, '*Haugtussa* as a cycle lies under a peculiar cloud of failure, or at least of serious and long-lasting frustration'.[50] Grieg certainly seems to have experienced doubts about the work's ultimate shape. In September 1895, for example, he mentioned to the younger Norwegian composer Iver Holter: 'I am writing music to *Haugtussa* by Garborg. It will be something for voice and orchestra; the form I haven't quite finalised yet. It is a brilliant book that has gripped me.'[51] Musical evidence for this more ambitious project survives in the source material preserved at the Grieg Archive in Bergen (summarised in the critical edition). In the 'Kladdebok fra 1890-

[48] Grieg: Songs with piano accompaniment, op. 58–70 and EG 121–57, *Samlede verker*, XV, ed. Dan Fog and Nils Grinde (Frankfurt: Peters, 1991).
[49] Massengale, '*Haugtussa*'.
[50] Ibid., 131.
[51] 'Jeg skriver Musik til "Haugtussa" af Garborg. Det blir Noget for Sang og Orkester, Formen har jeg endnu ikke ganske på det Rene. Det er en genial Bog, som har grebet mig.' Letter dated 10 September, reprinted in *Brev*, I, 434.

årene' which contains the compositional sketches and drafts for *Haugtussa*, various instrumental indications can be identified in projected settings of 'Sporven' ('The Sparrow'), 'Dømd' ('Doomed') and 'Ku-lok' ('Cow Lure'), none of which were included in the final cycle.[52] Of the thirteen songs which Grieg eventually completed, five remained unpublished. Massengale argues that the most pressing reason why Grieg hesitated before publishing *Haugtussa* was 'that he had not succeeded in doing what he had set out to do, and that his final set of songs was neither a logical and a completely coherent cycle nor simply a sampling of Garborg's poetry'. Hence, Massengale claims, 'not only was his work a sorry remnant of the dream of a cantata with orchestra and multiple voices; it even made little sense compared to the psychological depth and the monumental structure of the verse novel.'[53] Other commentators, however, have been more positive and have drawn attention to the symmetry of Grieg's final design. Torstein Volden, for example, has argued that the eight songs constitute a carefully constructed arch, in which the vivid nature mysticism of the two outer numbers ('Det Syng' and 'Ved Gjætle-bekken') supports two more intimate psychological portraits ('Veslemøy' and 'Vond Dag' ('Hurtful Day')), which in turn support the playful nature moods of 'Blåbær-Li' ('Blueberry Slope') and 'Killingdans' ('Kidlings' Dance'). The apex of this design are the two central love songs, 'Møte' ('The Tryst') and 'Elsk' ('Love'), which form a structural and expressive highpoint.[54]

It is surely possible to mediate between the sense of structural failure identified by Massengale and the idea of a balanced symmetrical design proposed by Volden and others. Massengale dwells particularly on the unsatisfactory narrative closure in the final song.[55] The apparent absence of conclusive resolution, however, is not simply an archetypal generic function of the nineteenth-century song cycle (the reference to Schubert's *Die schöne Müllerin* is surely so obvious that it hardly needs to imply conscious modelling on Grieg's part). Rather, it can be understood as a function of tensions within the song cycle itself, between representations of nature and Veslemøy's individual subjectivity, and between the material's *volkische Heimatkunst* qualities and the more modernist impulses that underpin the cycle's psychological drama. These tensions are apparent in the very first song 'Det Syng' ('The Enticement').

---

[52] The draft of the cycle in Bergen Offentlige Bibliotek also includes an attempt to orchestrate the piano accompaniment of the final song, 'Ved Gjætle-bekken' for flutes and upper strings (pp. 39–40), which Grieg evidently abandoned after a single bar.

[53] Massengale, '*Haugtussa*', 150.

[54] Torstein Volden, 'Studier i Edvard Grieg's Haugtussasanger, med særlig henblikk på sangenes opprinnelse og på forholdet mellom poesi og musikk', hovedoppdrag (master's thesis), University of Oslo, 1967, 49–50. I give translations of songs 1, 2 and 8 in an appendix.

[55] Massengale, '*Haugtussa*', 150.

The opening number, a setting of three stanzas from the fifth poem in the first chapter of Garborg's book, is partly a dream vision and partly an invocation, 'Å veit du den Draum, å veit du den Song' ('Oh, if you know the dream, if you know the song'). The song serves as a substitute for the narrative framework created by Garborg's own prelude (for which Grieg in fact sketched a setting that he never completed). In the novel, the poem is the voice of the blue mountain troll inside Veslemøy's imagination, whose identity is only revealed at a later stage. But in Grieg's cycle, the song becomes a more universalised expression of bewitchment, like the opening 'Kulokk' of op. 66: it serves simultaneously as a threshold into an enchanted mountain nature realm and the gateway to an inner psychological state of heightened sensory awareness. Musically the process of enticement, as in *Den Bergtekne*, is once again associated with a pattern of harmonic evasion (Ex. 3.1). The piano's initial sonority is a *Naturklang* of the type identified by Dahlhaus discussed in Chapter 2 with reference to the opening of op. 66. It consists of a dissonant complex of 'superimposed fifths and octaves' (here a pair of fifths, b♭–f, g–d, plus octave transfer), which unfolds registral space while avoiding a strong sense of metrical articulation, thereby 'suggesting that processual cognition has been suspended'.[56] The slow rising arpeggiation provides a further folkloristic allusion, namely to the ballad singer's harp, a familiar rhetorical device in nineteenth-century music (compare for example the opening gestures of Chopin's *Polonaise-Fantasie* and the First Ballade in G minor, op. 23). Here, the harmony suggests a supertonic seventh chord in third inversion,[57] but immediate diatonic resolution is denied firstly by the silence at the end of the third bar (as the chord reaches the outer upward limit of its registral range) and secondly by the articulation of a tonic *minor* chord in bar 4. This modal interruption highlights the song's schizophrenic character, initially stern and epic and then distant and other-worldly. The sense of suspense created by the opening three bars is intensified by a pair of antecedent four-bar phrases, Grieg exploiting the enharmonic relationships c♭–b♮, f♭–e♮ and approaching the dominant via two German sixths (bars 5 and 10). The tension between such sophisticated harmonic elisions and the apparent *Heimatkunst*-like simplicity of the musical surface could arguably be heard as a reflection of Veslemøy's character, with her hidden wisdom or supernatural forsight. The lack of harmonic resolution is perpetuated even by the transition to the second half of the stanza. Marked *Poco più lento*, like the *tryllt* ('bewitched') section of *Den Bergtekne* (bars 81 ff.), this contrasting

---

[56] Dahlhaus, *Nineteenth-Century Music*, 307. This opening sonority can also be heard as a chain of thirds rising from g, an alternative reading which reinforces the nature associations analysed by Dahlhaus.
[57] The exact analytical status of such chords is debatable: ii⁴₃ is arguably correct in terms of regular diatonic syntax, but the chord functions more like a subdominant with added sixth, a dissonant appoggiatura that remains unresolved.

Example 3.1. Grieg: *Haugtussa*, 'Det Syng', first strophe

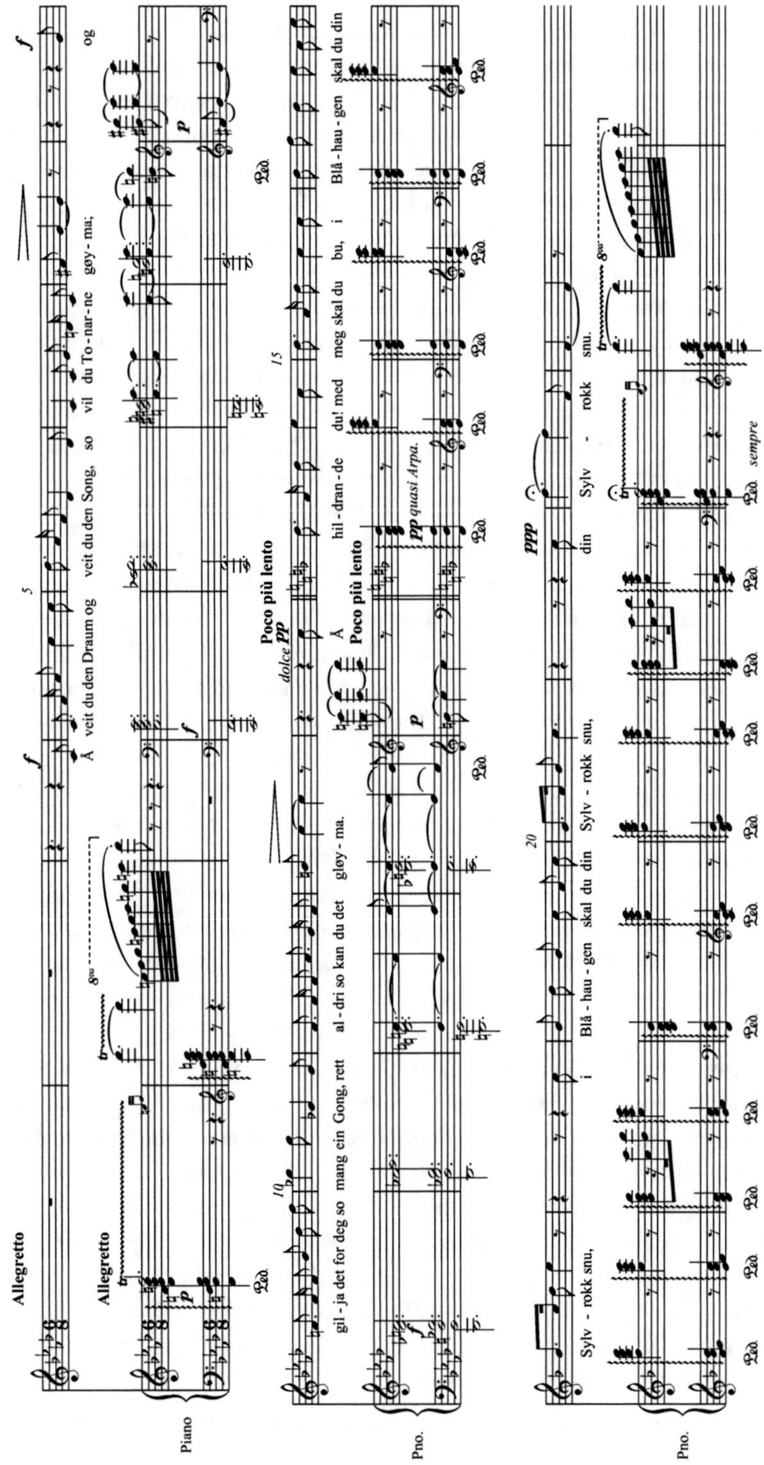

passage foreshadows Veslemøy's own later infatuation with Jon, simultaneously emphasising a return towards the dissonant nature music of the opening.
The vocal line dwells on $\hat{5}$, $\hat{6}$ and $\hat{7}$, straining upwards but touching the upper
tonic ($\hat{8}$) only once briefly,[58] while the harmony oscillates gently between 'off-
tonic' chords based on the submediant and mediant. The voice reaches its
goal pitch conclusively at the end of the refrain, but even here Grieg avoids
harmonic closure, instead returning to the chord of the opening. The song
remains harmonically open, in spite of a three-bar codetta which symmetrically balances the initial prelude. The piano's drooping *dolce* melodic figure,
recalling the languid octave descents of the voice previously at the end of
each stanza, is followed by a simple tonic perfect cadence, but the accented e^2
is left hanging unresolved, anticipating the key centre of the following song,
a portrait of Veslemøy herself. The tension between the two pitch classes, f
and e, becomes one of the principal structural ideas in the cycle.

A different kind of nature music is presented by one of the songs that Grieg
eventually chose to omit from his cycle, 'Ku-lok'. The text is taken from the
same chapter, 'Sùmar i Fjellet', that forms the basis for the doomed romance
that dominates Grieg's cycle. The poem is sung by Veslemøy as she tends her
herd on the high summer pastures, listening to the sound of the cowbells.
The principal themes are distance, yearning and, ultimately, isolation. Grieg
may have chosen to withdraw the song from his final set because it was
incompatible with the symmetrical arch-like design subsequently identified
by commentators such as Volden, or simply because he was uncertain about
its quality (as appears to have been the case with the other songs that did
not appear when the cycle was published). Indeed, the final draft of the song
is in a key (F sharp minor) that plays little part in the tonal design of the
finished cycle with the notable exception of the final song, suggesting that its
inclusion might have seemed structurally anomalous without transposition.
But the eventual omission of 'Ku-lok' may also have been decided because
in many senses the song is more radically austere than the other numbers
in the collection. With the exception of the final ten bars and the short
piano postlude, the song consists exclusively of a simple antiphonal dialogue
between the solo voice and a single line 'echo' in the right hand, a theatrical
device that mirrors both Veslemøy's environment and her supposed state
of mind. Grieg's sketches even include instrumental indications for oboe
and cor anglais, strengthening the reference to other nineteenth-century
musical evocations of longing and natural isolation such as the 'Scène aux
champs' from Berlioz's *Symphonie fantastique*, or the opening of Act 3 from
Wagner's *Tristan und Isolde* where the boundary between dream world and
reality seems especially permeable.

[58] Of course, the voice has already 'overshot' its target earlier, reaching g♭ in bar 10, a gesture that
perhaps adds to the sense of yearning in the refrain.

Example 3.2. Grieg: *Haugtussa*, 'Ku-lok' (conclusion)

Å Ky - ri, å Ky-ri mi ve-ne, å Ky-ri mi!

The textural shape of the song (an extended solo lure, here in dialogue with its echo, followed by delayed cadential contextualisation) parallels that of 'Aften på Höyfjellet' from the *Lyric Pieces*, op. 68, discussed in the preceding chapter, suggesting that Grieg's thoughts might have been preoccupied with images of loneliness and alienation in 1895–6 over and beyond the *Haugtussa* project itself. Furthermore, 'Ku-lok' reaches out from the immediate surroundings of the Garborg sketches and draws on an actual folk source, apparently the only time in the *Haugtussa* project in which Grieg chose to use such material. The piano postlude is based on the three-note figure of a *bukkehorn* call: a transposition of precisely the same call, in fact, which Grieg had heard at Skagastøl in 1887 and notated in his letter to Niels Ravnkilde of 17 October. It is tempting to read 'Ku-lok' therefore as containing an element of enacted autobiography (another reason, perhaps, why Grieg may ultimately have wished to omit the song from the final cycle).[59] The song could concern not just Veslemøy's sense of isolation and her longing for Jon, as in Garborg's novel, but Grieg's own sense of creative loneliness and the perceived peripheralisation that recurs in much of his own correspondence around this time. But since such autobiographical readings ultimately seem one-dimensional, the song is perhaps best heard as a more universalised expression of the human relationship with nature. In that sense, 'Ku-lok' is best compared with the opening number of the op. 66 set. Like the earlier folk-song setting, the song becomes a gradual withdrawing towards a distant harmonic vanishing point. The pivotal moment in this process is bar 35 (Ex. 3.2), since this is where the piano finally breaks the pattern of call–response (voice–piano) that has prevailed up until this point. The harmony is a subdominant seventh chord, a sonority that sounds stable, or at least static (since it lacks a strong dominant pull towards the tonic), but is also dissonant and demands resolution. However, immediate resolution of the chord is delayed first by the singer's repeated calls, and then by an even more dissonant echo, the entirely non-functional appoggiatura in bars 38–40.[60] Harmonic closure is only achieved once the bass has slipped down to the tonic via G♮ (bars 41–2), and the inner parts have dwelt on the chromatic inflection b♭ (an enharmonic anticipation of the raised third, a♯, in the final tonic major cadence). As in op. 66/1, therefore, pictorial and structural (voice leading) representations of landscape are combined in the creation of a directed sense of expectation or perspective, leading to an eventual harmonic goal or vanishing point.

The role of nature in *Haugtussa*, and in 'Ku-lok' particularly, can be seen as both a negation and affirmation. It serves as a sign of human presence in the landscape, represented through Veslemøy's relationship with her natural environment. Ultimately, however, it denies any sense of individual subjectivity: the comfort and solace offered by Nature in the final song results in

---

[59] Grieg's music rarely presents itself as an autobiographical text in the way, for example, that the work of Mahler or Alban Berg does, although the String Quartet in G minor is perhaps an exception. See, for example, Benestad and Schjelderup-Ebbe, *Edvard Grieg*, 216–19, for a discussion of the 'first Hardanger period'.

[60] I have found no satisfactory way of analysing this sonority in diatonic terms other than as a passing chord as part of a broader voice-leading progression from IV⁷ via the French sixth in bar 41 towards the tonic.

dissolution. In this sense, Grieg's use of landscape is similar to that in the music of Mahler. For both Mahler and Grieg, landscape is a special category, rather than a general property of their musical works, and is concerned primarily with the evocation of distance. As Julian Johnson has written, 'what is heard as spatially distant in Mahler's orchestra not only signals the idea of temporary distance (reminiscence and anticipation), but furthermore signals the idea of difference itself'.[61] The same quality, namely the sense of alienation which lanscape suggests, is true equally of Grieg's music. But for many critics, notably Theodor W. Adorno, Mahler's landscapes arguably fracture the musical surface of the work so that they become aspects of an ironic gaze. Landscape in Mahler's music deconstructs itself, through the unexpected intrusion of 'real' natural effects such as cow bells or animal calls within the domain of a bourgeois high art aesthetic, only to reaffirm its aesthetic presence (as a window on an alternative world view or natural order).[62] There is little comparable sense of irony in Grieg's music, however. Landscape for Grieg seems to point inwards, rather than outwards as in Mahler's work, leading towards a contemplative inner realm that is fully enclosed instead of revealing, in Johnson's words, 'the formal articulation of the work's failure as discourse' by pointing to a resolution beyond its own boundaries.

This sense of interiorised closure is especially strong in the final number of Grieg's cycle, 'Ved Gjætle-bekken' (Ex. 3.3). The song follows a varied strophic model, and is structurally the most complex in the set. The first two verses are sung to the first strophe, which is repeated. The third and fourth verses of the poem occupy an expanded central strophe (bars 21–65), reflecting the critical shift of poetic emphasis from 'her vil eg minnast' ('here I will remember') at the end of the third verse, to 'her vil eg gløyma' ('here I will forget') at the end of the fourth. This central strophe is prolonged by two descending chromatic bass movements (c♮–F♯, bars 24–40, and A–D, bars 55–64), followed by an extended final strophe that recalls the bass movements of the preceding strophe at the close (bars 90–3). The tension between this essentially static strophic design and the developmental tendencies of the central strophe parallels the structure of Garborg's poem, in which the frequency of the internal rhymes within each stanza ('Du surlande Bekk/du kurlande Bekk', and so forth) creates a sense of circularity, while the progression in the final lines (from 'her vil eg kvila' ('here I will rest') in the first verse to 'her vil eg blunde' ('here I will sleep') in the last) simultaneously creates a feeling of onward motion and renewal.

---

[61] Julian Johnson, 'Mahler and the Idea of Nature', in *Perspectives on Gustav Mahler*, ed. Jeremy Barham (Aldershot: Ashgate, 2005).

[62] See, for example, the discussion of Adorno's analysis of Mahler's landscapes in Peter Franklin, '". . . His fractures are the script of truth" – Adorno's Mahler', in *Mahler Studies*, ed. Stephen E. Hefling (Cambridge: Cambridge University Press, 1997), 271–94, here 281–2.

Example 3.3. Grieg: *Haugtussa*, 'Ved Gjætle-bekken'

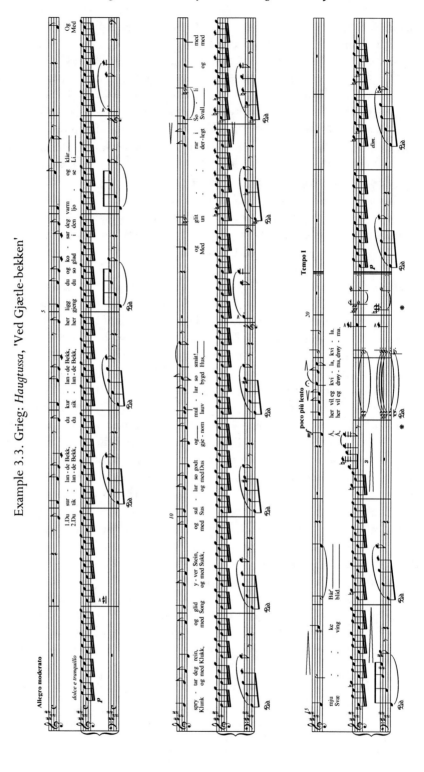

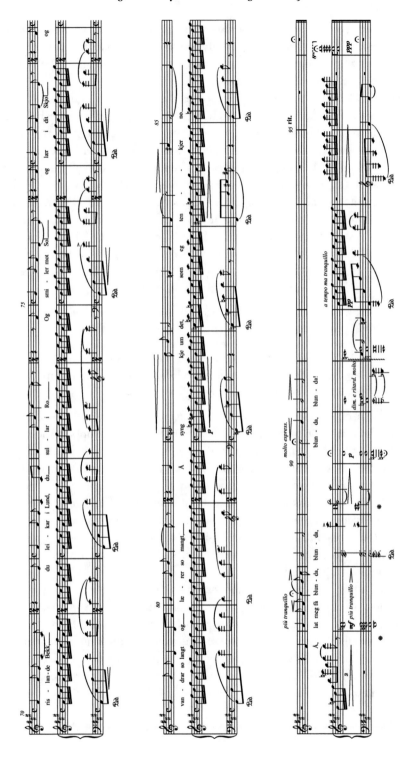

Grieg captures this sense of looking both forwards and backwards in the final bars of the song, returning briefly to the opening bars but withholding the voice, whose silence as in the final number of Schumann's *Dichterliebe* signals both absence and closure.

The tonal centre of the song reinforces the sense of openness that characterises the final bars. A major has been heard only once previously in the cycle, in the fourth song 'Møte' ('The Tryst'), where a sudden magically *pianissimo* modulation to A major in bar 12 is associated with the text 'Då gjeng det som ei Hildring yver Nuten' ('Then it appeared like an apparition over the fell top'). In other words, A major is marked both as a special sonority within the overall tonal design of the cycle, and is associated with the idea of enchantment or bewitchment that characterises the final number in particular as Veslemøy seeks release from her worldly suffering. This is a familiar rhetorical device in the Romantic song cycle as a genre. Richard Kramer, for example, has argued that in Schubert's Heine cycle from *Schwanengesang*, 'the inexorable pull toward a final tonic is rejected'. Instead,

> the final tonic . . . contradicts what we must take to be the central and generating tonic. The true tonic becomes a poetic image, a figure of ambiguity that hovers somewhere in the midst of the cycle. And that accords well with the sense of most Romantic song cycles, for it is not structural closure that they are about but rather reminiscence and longing and dissolution.[63]

A similar process takes place in Grieg's *Haugtussa*: F major functions as the cycle's default tonic by virtue of its relative frequency of appearance (it is the key of the first, third and fourth songs; the fifth song is in the closely related key of C, while the seventh is in F minor). A major in contrast constitutes an idealised figure rather than a genuine tonal goal, a 'poetic image' that represents an elevated state of being. The final song articulates closure through a sense of transcendence rather than through balanced symmetrical resolution. 'Ved Gjætle-bekken' offers a glimpse of a remote harmonic domain whose presence, in relation to the other songs in the cycle, is deliberately distanced.

This feeling of remoteness and finality is immediately created by the opening bars of the song, and by the musical signs of closure which pervade its surface. Harmonically, the song opens with a broken triad that, for the first bar until the entry of the left hand (as a cue for the singer's first note), suggests either the tonic plus added sixth, or a submediant seventh chord in first inversion. Indeed, this dual function is retrospectively reinforced by the harmonic pattern of the opening phrase (bars 3–7), which begins by moving

---

[63] Richard Kramer, *Distant Cycles: Schubert and the Conceiving of Song* (Chicago: Chicago University Press, 1994), 87.

from I to vi, and by the pivotal cadence on F sharp minor that divides the third and fourth verses (bars 40–1). The oscillating accompanimental figuration, however, immediately suggests the rippling waters of the brook in which Veslemøy seeks solace. But the repeated echoing triadic pitch content could also be heard as the stylised representation of a bell sound, the more complex components of the bell spectrum diffused as though through a prism. The reference to bells is surely significant: as analysis of 'I Ola-Dalom, i Ola-Kjønn' (also in an enchanted A major), in the previous chapter suggested, bells are conventionally associated with closure, loss and remembrance, a mood that is equally applicable to 'Ved Gjætle-bekken'. Furthermore, bells are concerned with the suspension of regular (linear) time: their effect is temporally disruptive, since their sound suggests a ritualistic circularity or cyclism. In 'Ved Gjætle-bekken', this sense of cyclism is created by the perception of multiple levels of musical motion. The semiquaver figuration of the accompaniment in the right hand represents the first level, the repeated rising arpeggios in the left hand (which, in the final verse, begin to echo the voice in a poignant dialogue) the second, and finally the voice itself, which can be heard as an augmentation of the right-hand figuration, is the third. The cadential passages at the end of each verse therefore assume an even greater structural weight. They not only provide a sense of temporary harmonic arrival, but also function as temporal landmarks, allowing a momentary pause for contemplation from which the preceding music can be contexualised.

Poignant echoes of the temporal brook/bell music that underpins 'Ved Gjætle-bekken' can be found in other solo piano works, reinforcing the impression that the compositional ideas which preoccupied Grieg during the *Haugtussa* project were not limited to the song cycle. Two numbers from the op. 62 collection of *Lyric Pieces*, 'Bekken' ('The Brook') and 'Drömmesyn' ('The Phantom' or, more literally, 'Dream Vision'), composed alongside the *Haugtussa* songs in 1895, offer contrasting perspectives on the brook material. The first of these two numbers, 'Bekken', invites a comparison on the basis of its title alone. Like 'Ved Gjætle-bekken', the texture of 'Bekken' is dominated by ostinato figuration that could be heard as an environmental acoustic, a musical representation of the sound of running water. Tonally, however, 'Bekken' is set in a minor key, an altogether icier environment than the hazy midsummer major tonality of the song. Furthermore, it is structurally concerned almost exclusively with a process of chromatic saturation. After an initial eight-bar phrase (a harmonically static four-bar opening gesture followed by a cadential unit with descending bass line, which is repeated), a contrasting eight-bar episode articulates a gradual sequential intensification. The chromatic tension of bars 17–30 is released only once the texture has been liquidated by a descending chromatic scale (Ex. 3.4).

Example 3.4. Grieg: 'Bekken', op. 62/4 (opening strophe)

Example 3.5. Grieg: 'Drömmesyn', op. 62/5 (opening strophe and conclusion)

The whole cycle (statement, intensification and release) is then repeated before closure is achieved, principally through registral means, in the coda. As in 'Klokkeklang', the apparently single-minded pursuit of a purely structuralist agenda in 'Bekken', namely the generation and resolution of chromatic tension, coupled with the prevailing four-square phrase rhythm, threatens to challenge and undermine the music's pictorial associations. No other number among the *Lyric Pieces* comes closer to the texture of an *étude*. The piece therefore offers a strangely objective, distanced representation of the natural world, which offers a less comforting evocation of nature than that suggested by the title and the generic territory of the set.

'Drömmesyn' offers a very different kind of representation of the natural world, and one that ultimately seems closer to that unfolded at the end of *Haugtussa*. Tonally, 'Ved Gjætle-bekken' and op. 62/5 occupy almost identical tonal domains: A major with a strong inflection towards the relative minor. Harmonically the opening bars are identical, and the texture is likewise dominated by ostinato arpeggio figuration (Ex. 3.5). The overall harmonic shape of 'Drömmesyn' is very different from that of 'Bekken'. Whereas the emphasis in the earlier number is almost exclusively on forward momentum and goal direction, the effect in the later piece is more static and contemplative. Indeed, the title suggests a meditative or hallucinatory state of mind (enchantment) that is successfully evoked by the work's repetitive figuration and melodic material. Like 'Ved Gjætle-bekken', voice-leading parameters also play an important role in this process. The whole piece is essentially built from two strophes, each underpinned by a slow chromatic bass descent from the tonic to the dominant (bars 1–20; 26–44). The chromatic steps in these descents support a chain of enharmonic echoes (bars 6–9; 14–17), whose other-wordly quality is reinforced by their subdued dynamic level (*pp* against a general *piano cantabile*). The echoes also articulate a process of melodic expansion, stretching the compass of the preceding four bars outwards (if only by a semitone) so that their effect is to intensify the sense of yearning within each phrase. Though 'Drömmesyn''s likely cultural and generic associations – an enchanted mountain nature realm, the midsummer night, bewitchment – suggests that it can be heard as the musical representation of some kind of erotic encounter, the expected moment of consummation at the end of the second strophe is missing. Rather, the coda effectively functions as a third varied strophe: the bass descents from the preceding two are stretched so that they now become a single octave transfer from e to E (bars 44–52). The melodic material in the right hand, which was minimal in any case, is replaced by an inverted pedal so that the piece audibly appears to be receding into the distance. The 'Drömmesyn', or dream vision, of the work's title therefore seems to be built into its design: the creation of a sense of imminent arrival (based on cumulative repetition) that is suspended and then ultimately withdrawn without resolution. Indeed, some sense of symmetrical balance is only offered by the following piece, 'Hjemad', where chromatic elements from 'Drömmesyn', notably the ♮III–I progression in the coda (bars 55–6), are finally gathered up and resolved in a celebratory cadential context.

A final echo of 'Ved Gjætle-bekken' can be found in 'Fra Ungdomsdagene' ('From Early Years'), the first of the op. 65 *Lyric Pieces* composed shortly after Grieg had abandoned plans for a large-scale setting of Garborg's work. In this later solo piano piece, a lively *springar* (energised by leaping dotted rhythms and strong Lydian modal inflections) is nested within statements of more anguished and expansive ballad-like material, suggesting the recollection of a distant happy past from a more troubled present: a narrative archetype that could also be read in 'Ved Gjætle-bekken'. Grieg explicitly recalls the keyboard texture of the song, a rippling ostinato in the right hand and rising arpeggios in the left, in the codetta of the ternary outer ballad sections (bars 50–8 and 156–69) (Ex. 3.6). The function of this material, initiated by a simple cadential figure (the semiquaver tag first heard in bar 44), is principally transformational. It provides a link, both texturally and in temporal terms, between the immediate declamatory style of the ballad and the folk-inspired dance music of the retrospective central episode and back again. The first time this material is heard, it liquidates the troubled chromatic discourse of the opening ballad, providing a greater sense of textural continuity and linear harmonic direction towards a German sixth (bars 57–8), resolved by the entry of the *springar*'s pedal fifths. On its second appearance, the function of the codetta is more clearly closural, modulating away from the tonic minor of the ballad reprise back towards the major mode of the *springar*. Any possibility of optimistic major-key resolution is denied, however, by an epigrammatic coda, similar in design to those that conclude many of the earlier songs in *Haugtussa*, which closes the work decisively in the minor mode. (Conclusive tonic major resolution arguably is provided only by the final number in the set, the famous 'Bryllupsdag på Troldhaugen'.) The significance of the transition passage, like the coda in 'Drömmesyn', is therefore dependent on its sense of suspension, the way in which it inhabits an alternative musical domain. As in *Haugtussa*, the texture appears to be associated with both remembrance (leading to the stylised recollection of a folk dance from childhood) and forgetfulness. It therefore performs a dual function, creating a sense of circularity or openness similar to that which underpins the whole of the *Haugtussa* cycle.

Remembrance and forgetfulness collide in the climax of 'Ved Gjætle-bekken' at the end of the fourth verse (bars 53–65). The vocal line reaches its registral peak in the song, f♮ (anticipated only once enharmonically by the e♯ in bar 40), and replays the critical moment of realisation in *Den Bergtekne*:

Example 3.6. Grieg: 'Fra Ungdomsdagene', op. 65/1 (transition to middle section)

'Tru nokon du såg so eismal som eg?' ('Have you ever seen anyone as lonely as I?'). In both songs at this point, the process of enchantment is revealed as empty and illusory. Veslemøy's subsequent repeated lament, 'her vil eg gløyma' ('here I will forget'), over the piano's chromatic cadential descent, anticipates the final bars. To all intents and purposes, the song is structurally and narratively closed at this point and necessitates no further continuation. The fifth verse consequently assumes a retrospective quality, and the coda, as Veslemøy sings 'Å lat meg få blunda, blunda' ('here will I slumber'), is a poignant leave-taking. Here the music draws particularly on structural elements from both 'Drömmesyn' and 'Fra Ungdomsdagene': the sense of cyclic closure or remembrance, and the gradual withdrawal to a seemingly infinitely distant vanishing point. Though the vocal line dwells on $\hat{2}$ and $\hat{1}$, emphasising closure, the accompanying harmonic support gently refuses to coordinate the root-position tonic chord with the final melodic moment of arrival.[64] The last five bars offer a fragment of the opening figuration and an ethereal closing chord, which returns to the registral range associated with the enchanted nature realm at the start of 'Det Syng'. In Grieg's cycle, to a much greater extent than Garborg's novel, Veslemøy falls asleep, or dies, through a process of diffusion, by becoming part of her natural environment. Landscape thus functions as a framework, both for Grieg's paraphrase of Garborg's narrative and for the structural, registral and harmonic parameters that musically define the song cycle, and also as a locus of identity, as the embodiment of Veslemøy's ultimate sense of being and place.

Haugtussa offers a uniquely concentrated example of the ways in which landscape operates in Grieg's music. Garborg's novel had presented a series of images of western Norwegian nature whose meaning and significance was defined by their historical context, as part of a broader *Heimatkunst* movement that sought to promote Norwegian cultural and political independence. Grieg's song cycle can be heard on this level, and his enthusiasm for *landsmål* illustrates his commitment to the political aspects of Garborg's project. But *Haugtussa* also concerns landscape in an abstract, structural sense, and it is arguably this idea of landscape as representation that attracted Grieg more deeply. Like the folk-song arrangements, Grieg's song cycle intensively explores the structural implications of certain kinds of musical gestures conventionally associated with landscape: diatonically dissonant sonorities, linear chromatic voice-leading progressions and various categories of nature sounds. The evocation of space and distance are of fundamental importance in every aspect of Grieg's work on the *Haugtussa* material, not simply the eight songs that he eventually chose to publish as a finished cycle. *Haugtussa*

---

[64] For a remarkably similar closing effect, all the more striking given the fundamental aesthetic differences between the two composers discussed above, compare the conclusion of 'Der Abschied' from Mahler's *Das Lied von der Erde* (1909–11).

is also concerned with various kinds of temporal structures: linear narratives, seasonal cycles, remembrance and forgetfulness. The image of nature that *Haugtussa* ultimately seeks to present is largely a nostalgic one. In this sense, it can be heard as a form of *Heimatkunst*, which looks back to a supposed golden age of folk wholeness and purity while simultaneously looking forward towards a more modernist objectivity. But the sense of retrospection at the end of Grieg's cycle seems unusually hollow and enclosed, and unlike anything in Garborg's text. Landscape, for Grieg, seems inextricably linked with a sense of loss. Perhaps this is why the emptiness of the closing bars, as Veslemøy sleeps silently, seems so final.

CHAPTER FOUR

Modernism and Norwegian Musical Style:
The Politics of Identity in the *Slåtter*, op. 72

In *Haugtussa* and the *19 norske Folkeviser*, landscape emerges in Grieg's music as an essentially nostalgic presence. It is concerned, above all, with the evocation of space and distance, and with the suspension of regular musical time, so that it dwells ultimately on a sense of hollowness, isolation and loss. This can be read as a metaphor for Grieg's own creative conditition, particularly his sense of alienation from perceived mainstream centres of musical progress. But it is more deeply concerned with a powerful sense of regionality, embodied both in the dialect language forms that were synthesised by *landsmål* and in the locations associated with particular tunes or poems. As argued in the preceding chapter, Grieg's work becomes a form of *Heimatkunst*, dedicated to the creation and promotion of a particular regional identity in music, a process that was part of a broader cultural-political project in Norway at the end of the nineteenth century. But landscape in Grieg's music can also be heard as a form of structural discourse, as a means of organising specific musical gestures and events such as nature sounds, folk songs and lures. The more abstract aspect of Grieg's work, involving the systematic use of register, motivic cells and voice-leading progressions, cuts against the associative aspects of landscape. Landscape therefore highlights a creative tension in Grieg's music, between its representational function (particularly the evocation of visual modes of perception) and its structural character.

This tension is intensified in the *Slåtter*. In both scale and tone, the *Slåtter* are Grieg's most ambitious and radical response to Norwegian folk music. Unlike the *19 norske Folkeviser*, which are primarily vocal in origin, the *Slåtter* are based on Hardanger-fiddle tunes, using transcriptions prepared by Johan Halvorsen from the playing of Knut Dahle (1834–1921), a *spelemann* from Telemark in southern Norway. They are therefore linked to a particular sense of place to a greater degree, perhaps, than any of Grieg's other works. At the same time, however, the *Slåtter* are also more clearly international in outlook than the earlier folk-music arrangements. Their critical reception underlines their cosmopolitan character: the set was initially more positively received abroad by composer-pianists such as Ravel, Bartók or Percy Grainger than at home in Norway. This chapter will summarise the compositional history of the *Slåtter*, consider Grieg's attempts to notate Hardangerfiddle music, and examine the intricate rhythmic characteristics of selected dances from the set. Commentators have often drawn attention to the *Slåtter*'s rigorously modal harmonic language, but close reading of dances such as 'Knut Luråsens Halling II' suggests a more complex relationship with diatonic and modal systems. Consideration will also be given to the critical status of the set, including recent attempts to 'reclaim' the so-called *Grieg Slåtter* by contemporary folk musicians and scholars such as Sven Nyhus. The *Slåtter* continue to provoke heated questions about ownership and identity, so that in western Norway, at least, Grieg's most sustained engagement with a specific folk repertoire remains a problematic and controversial work. Landscape in the *Slåtter* can be understood as an aspect of these debates. It is part of the music's sense of authenticity, its claim to groundedness in a closely defined folk tradition, as well as its sense of rhetorical directness or 'plain speaking', a quality which Grieg appears to have associated more generally with the dialect language and folk music of western Norway. But it also becomes an integral part of the music's discursive character, an element in the abstract structural play with particular musical parameters within a tightly controlled formal framework that characterises the work. This compositional 'writerliness' is perhaps why the *Slåtter* appealed so powerfully to later modernist figures as Bartók. As in *Haugtussa*, therefore, a tension exists between two different forms and functions of landscape: representational or associative on the one hand, and compositional or constructive on the other. This structural conflict points not only to an inherent contradiction in the musical definition of landscape, but also to a fundamental structural dissonance in Grieg's work. Grieg's music thus encourages us to reflect back on the representation and perception of landscape in music, and to reconsider its historical and theoretical contexts from a new critical perspective.

Imagined Traditions: Grieg, the Hardanger fiddle and Norwegian folk music

The Hardanger fiddle has often been at the centre of debates about the nature and status of a distinctively Norwegian folk tradition. In a letter to the Norwegian folk-music magazine *Spelemannsbladet* in 1951, for example, Hardanger fiddler Johannes Skarprud wrote:

> Folk music is a true sapling of the Norwegian folk character. It is Norwegian nature in its changing moods, with its mountainous country and sheltered valleys, wild waterfalls and still, dreamy

fjords. It is the whisper of wind through leaves and cowbells ringing in mountain meadows and in home pastures that give melody to folk music.

Such a music can't flourish in the city or on the plains. Echoes can't ring there, or waterfalls exult. And the spirits that fiddle beneath the waterfalls can't teach young lads there.[1]

The 1950s were a decade of significant consolidation in the Norwegian folk movement. In the years following the Second World War, the need to reassert a specifically regional Norwegian folk identity appears to have been especially compelling. This period not only saw a substantial increase in academic interest in folk music, including the inauguration in 1954 of the monumental Norsk Folkemusikk series, a national collection organised according to scholarly ethnographic principles and initially led by Ole Mørk Sandvik, but also witnessed a more general public revival of folk customs.[2] Skarprud's letter summarises many of the images associated with the idea of a Norwegian folk tradition since the nineteenth century, including biological metaphors of organic growth and cultivation (a 'true sapling of the Norwegian folk character'), and the link between Norwegian topography (fjords, narrow valleys, mountain pastures), folk music and mythology. For Hardanger-fiddle players, the legendary figure of the *fossegrim* or *nøkken*, the water sprite that inhabited waterfalls in the mountains and enchanted unwary passers-by with the sound of his music within the water, was a particularly powerful image. Stephan Sinding's commemorative statue on Ole Bull Plads in the heart of Bergen (unveiled on consitution day, 17 May 1901) clearly draws on this mythic topic. The famous violinist is set heroically on top of a crag with the figure of *nøkken* reaching upwards from the water below. Skarprud's letter reinforces such mythical accounts of music and its origins in the natural world. But it also serves a more exclusive purpose in the formation of a Norwegian cultural identity. It defines Norwegian folk music as specifically rural and regional in character. Hence, Norwegian folk music properly belongs in the Norwegian mountains: 'such a music can't flourish in the city or the plains'. This isolationist tendency runs even deeper as Skarprud's letter proceeds. He observes that 'you can dance to an accordion or German fiddle; they have rhythm in them, but lack Norwegian feelings and beauty. They lack tradition; they're not ours.' For Skarprud, the Hardanger fiddle is the proper instrument on which Norwegian folk music should be played. In contrast, the ordinary (German) fiddle or *flatfele*, is inadequate, since it lacks the extra set of sympathetic strings strung underneath the fingerboard that gives the Hardanger fiddle its characteristic sound. 'It's only the Myllargut-fiddle that can do the job', Skarprud maintains, since 'it

---

[1] *Spelemannsbladet* 1951 (6), 8–9. Translated and analysed in Goertzen *Fiddling for Norway*, 34–5.
[2] See especially Goertzen, *Fiddling for Norway*, 35–46.

has the Norwegian resonance.' According to Chris Goertzen, this attitude has prevailed in the Norwegian folk community until relatively recently. The *flatfele* has been seen as a poor relative (or worse, a foreign import), whereas the Hardanger fiddle has been celebrated as the authentic national instrument. The instrument has therefore become emblematic of the way in which, at the end of the nineteenth century, a particular regional identity or cultural practice was elevated to the status of a national symbol.

For Skarprud, evidence of the Hardanger fiddle's pre-eminence as a national instrument can be found not just in its characteristic timbre, but also the historical playing tradition with which it was associated. This sense of tradition was defined both in terms of a particular repertoire of melodies and through a series of influential performers:

> The Hardanger fiddle has more and subtler tones than any other instrument if one has the gift to play it correctly. A Myllarguten, Giböen, Flatland, Helgeland, Löndal, Haugerud, Örpen, Fykerud, Borgen, and several contemporary players such as Roheim, Haugen, Manheim and others can interpret our rich and large body of tunes, a repertoire so rich that our greatest composers, such as Grieg and Halvorsen and others, drew on these Norwegian sources and thereby made names for themselves well outside Norway.[3]

Skarprud's argument attempts to create a synthesis of regional and universal impulses. A highly localised culture of performance, defined by individual players as well as a common set of musical materials, forms the basis for the cosmopolitan art of Norway's 'greatest composers', Grieg and Halvorsen. Skarprud thereby implicitly invokes a hierarchical model of musical development, in which an art music of international importance and orientation is built upon (or grows naturally out of) a folk tradition of explicitly local character. But the tensions and contradictions upon which this model rests, both with reference to Grieg's folk-music arrangements and to the very notion of a fixed Norwegian folk tradition itself, are inevitably deeper and more complex than Skarprud's argument suggests.

The compositional genesis of Grieg's *Slåtter* can be followed in the editorial commentary acompanying the relevant volume of the Complete Edition, and is summarised in the biography by Finn Benestad and Dag Schjelderup-Ebbe.[4] Grieg's first contact with Knut Dahle, the *spelemann* who eventually provided the tunes for his collection, was a letter from Dahle dated 8 April 1888. Their subsequent correspondence has been published in an article edited by Øyvind Anker.[5] Dahle's letter began by introducing himself as

---

[3] Ibid., 34.
[4] Benestad and Schjelderup-Ebbe, *Edvard Grieg*, 363–70.
[5] 'Knut Dahle – Edv. Grieg – Johan Halvorsen', ed. Øyvind Anker, originally published in *Norsk*

'an elder national Hardanger violinist', and he claimed to have learnt from two of the nineteenth-century's leading Hardanger players, Håvar Gibøen (1809–73) and the famous 'Myllarguten', Torgeir Augundsson (1801–72). Whether factually accurate or not, Dahle's claim is perhaps less important than the impression of an inherited tradition that his letter creates. The construction of a personal genealogy serves to represent the transmission not just of the individual tunes themselves but of a complete performance practice, including the use of ornamentation, the style of bowing and the type of rhythmic articulation. Such genealogies were especially important in a rural Norwegian context, since they served to strengthen communal ties in a remotely populated area. But they also constituted a claim to ownership and authorial control, concepts that were later to prove problematic in the critical reception of Grieg's work. The titles of pieces, which often referred to players such as Gibøen or Myllarguten as well as to a particular generic dance form, therefore became an additional sign of their authenticity, their place within an imagined tradition, as much as a mark of their (notional) points of origin.

Grieg had previous direct experience of this Hardanger tradition before he received Dahle's first letter in 1888.[6] His encounters with folk music in its local environment have been described in detail by a later Norwegian folk-music collector, Arne Bjørndal (1882–1965), who was himself a proficient fiddler.[7] According to Bjørndal, Grieg first immersed himself in Norwegian peasant culture in the summer of 1877 at Øvre Børve in Hardanger, the period during which he worked on *Den Bergtekne* (discussed in Chapter 2), as well as the Vinje songs, op. 33. Bjørndal remarks that when Grieg met the Hardanger fiddler Ola Mosafinn (1828–1912) at Ullensvang in 1879, 'it wasn't the first time that he had heard folk music upon the Hardanger fiddle'.[8] Mosafinn is supposed to have a performed a series of dances for Grieg's birthday on 15 June 1879 at the invitation of Ole Bull, and Bjørndal comments that 'I do not know how many dances Mosafinn

musikkgransknings årbok, 1943–6, reprinted in *Grieg og Folkemusikken: en artikkel-samling* (Oslo: Landslaget Musikk i Skolen, 1992), 44–58.
[6] Carl O. Gram Gjesdal states: 'Grieg was well versed in the Hardanger fiddle. As early as the 1860s he had become familiar with it at Valestrand in the inspiring company of Ole Bull. He subsequently heard skilled fiddlers play in Bergen, at Voss, at Lofthus in Hardanger and elsewhere.' Notes for Simax CD PSC 1102, 'Grieg: Norwegian Folk Songs and Dances from op. 66 & op. 72' (Oslo: Pro Musica, 1993), 14.
[7] Bjørndal, 'Edvard Grieg og folkemusikken'. More material can be found in the archives of the Arne Bjørndal samling in Bergen, which is one of the most important sources for research on the history of Norwegian folk music. Much of Bjørndal's information is anecdotal, and is based on his own personal relationships with other folk musicians. Though he does not always provide substantial documentary evidence of Grieg's meetings with *spelemenn* such as Mosafinn or Sjur Helgeland, there seems no reason to cast doubt on the accuracy of Bjørndal's account.
[8] 'Då Edvard Grieg i 1879 møtte Ola Mosafinn i Ullensvang (1828–1912) var det ikkje fyrste gangen han høyrde slåttemusikken på hardingfela.' Ibid., 10.

played on that occasion. But both Grieg and Ole Bull set great prize upon his playing, even if he himself was not compelled.'[9] Another prominent *spelemann* with whom Grieg became aquainted, according to Bjørndal, was Sjur Helgeland (1853–1924). Helgeland won first prize in the inaugural Hardanger-fiddle competition held by the Vestmannalaget, the western Norwegian folk association, in Bergen in 1896.[10] On this occasion Frants Beyer, Grieg's closest friend and walking companion (who had transcribed most of the mountain melodies Grieg used in op. 66), was a member of the jury, while Grieg himself listened in the front row of the audience. 'Sjur Helgeland affected and inspired Edvard Grieg', Bjørndal records, so that when the two musicians met at Stalheims hotel, perched high on a dramatic cliff overlooking the Nærøyfjord between Bergen and Voss, during the summer, 'Grieg sat with a notebook and pencil and wrote'.[11] In other words, Grieg had already attempted to transcribe Hardanger-fiddle music before he turned to the composition of the *Slåtter* in 1901–2, an activity that is supported by the survival of several pages of undated sketches in the Grieg collection in Bergen public library (Figs. 4.1 and 4.2). Grieg also appears to have shared a sense of the Hardanger fiddle's 'authentic' regional character as a rural instrument. Bjørndal recalls that Grieg apparently preferred Helgeland's original free composition (*lydarslått* or 'listening piece'), 'Budeione på Vikafjell' ('The Dairy Maidens at Vikafjell'), to Ole Bull's famous 'Sæterbesøget' ('The Visit to the Mountain Pasture'). 'Bull was a town boy, you are a country boy; he yearned for the mountains, you live in the mountains.'[12] Landscape and topography are once again invoked as a sign of aesthetic integrity. For Grieg, as for Bjørndal and other later folk-musicians, Norwegian music is properly rural in character: music from an urban context (even when composed by Ole Bull) cannot be admitted into the privileged category of 'folk'.

It is this concern with authenticity, of the perceived groundedness of Norwegian music in its natural environment, which often appears to have motivated Grieg's relationship with the Hardanger repertoire. In conversation with a third prominent *spelemann*, Olav Moe (born *c.* 1872) from Valdres (whom Grieg first met at the 1898 competition held by the Vestmannalaget), Bjørndal records Grieg as saying:

[9] 'Kor mange slåttar Mosafinn spela ved dette høvet, veit me ikkje. Men både Grieg og Ole Bull sette stor pris på spelet, endå om han sjølv ikkje var nøgd.' Ibid.

[10] Goertzen notes (*Fiddling in Norway*, 25) that the first formal folk-music contest in Norway was organised in 1881 by the Norwegian Tourist board and Norwegian Youth Organisation (Noregs Ungdomslag), and was a competition for the *lur*. It was followed by a local contest for the Hardanger fiddle in Telemark, 8 July 1888, and the first Vestmannalaget competition (*kappleik*) in Bergen, 16 May 1896.

[11] 'Sjur Helgeland påverka og inspirerte Edvard Grieg. . . . Grieg sad med noteblokk og blyant og skreiv.' Bjørndal, 'Edvard Grieg og folkemusikken', 11 and 12.

[12] 'Jeg liker dette bedre enn *Sæterbesøkt*. Bull var bygutt, du landsgutt; han lengtet til fjellet, du bor i fjellet.' Ibid., 12.

Folk music must be kept up, because it will form the foundation for all future composition in Norway. The Norwegian peasant musician should treat the old peasant dances with care. And if one creates something new, it must not be blended together and confuse the original motives, but should stand entirely on its own account. . . . Keep away from the accordion, because it will completely ruin Norwegian folk music. This is a mission you should set yourself, namely to travel round the country to play and collect the Norwegian peasant dances.[13]

Grieg's comments rest on assumptions that are historically contestable, such as the presumed antiquity of the peasant dances, and the 'foreign' status of the accordion as opposed to the Hardanger fiddle (a polemic that recalls the prejudice against the *flatfele* discussed by Goertzen). But his attitude to Norwegian folk music (as reported by Bjørndal) can be compared with other broader nationalist discourses, as discussed in Chapter 1. It presents a double temporal vision of the kind identified by Benedict Anderson and others. Retrospectively, Grieg evokes the idea of a historically defined folk tradition (which, in common with many folklorists at the end of the century, Grieg believed was somehow threatened or in decline). Prospectively, however, Grieg holds out the promise of the future renewal of an authentically Norwegian music through the study and revival of traditional folk customs. This sense of revival and renewal is one of the recurrent themes in his correspondence with Johan Halvorsen about the transcription of Knut Dahle's *Slåtter*. Though Grieg had responded swiftly to Dahle's initial inquiry in 1888, nothing had taken place, and Grieg evidently failed to follow up a second approach from the folk musician in late 1890.[14] Dahle travelled to America in the meantime, and it was not until a decade

---

[13] 'Folkemusikken må holdes oppe, ren og egte, for den skal danne grunnlaget for all fremtidig tonedikting i Norge. Den norske bondespillenmanden bør fare varsomt med de gamle slåttane. Og laver man noget nytt, må det ikke blandes sammen og forvakle de ophavelige motiver, men ma stå helt for egen regning . . . Få vekk trekkspillet, for det vil ødelegge hele den norske folkemusikk. Det er en misjon du bør sette dig, nemlig å reise rundt i landet å spille og samle inn de norske slåttene.' Ibid., 13. Though the anecdote is undated, Grieg's comments were perhaps motivated by an encounter with Moe's playing in 1902 that he appears to have found disappointing. In a letter to Frants Beyer dated 24 July, he complained: 'yesterday the fiddler Ole Moen [*sic*] was here and played his best down in the bar while I was up here in my room. Partly because I did not feel well enough to socialise, but partly because he played so out of tune, in my opinion, that I was glad when he finished. He has much technique and a good tone. But his Slåtter contain so little spirit and devilry of the good old kind. I will detest this hybrid style until my death. And yet it is the consequence and the natural punishment because Norway did not understand how to look after the treasure it owned.' ('Igårkveld var Spillemanden Ole Moen her og gav endel til beste nede i Salonen, mens jeg var heroppe på mit Værelse. Dels følte jeg mig ikke vel nok til at blande mig med Folket, og dels spillede han til min Forundring så urent, at jeg bare var glad, da han holdt op. Han har megen Teknik og en god Tone. Mens hans Slåtter indeholder så altfor lidt av Sprit [*sic*] og Dæmonik af det gode gamle Slags. Denne Overgangsstil kan jeg ikke for min Død fordrage. Men den må jo bli Enden og er den naturlige Straf, fordi Norge ikke forstod at tage Vare på den Skat, det ejed.') Grieg, *Brev til Frants Beyer*, 273.

[14] 'Knut Dahle – Edv. Grieg – Johan Halvorsen', 44–8.

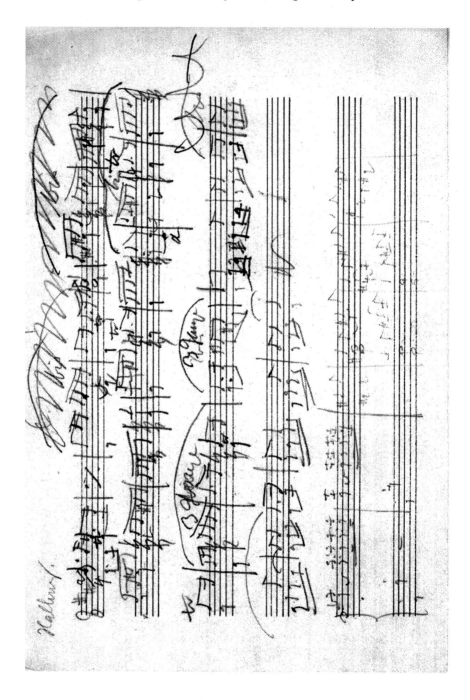

Fig. 4.1. Grieg: Hardanger fiddle notation (for a Halling).
Courtesy Bergen Offentlige Bibliotek

Fig. 4.2. Grieg: Hardanger fiddle notations (for a Nøringslått,
'Thomasklokken', Ganger, Springdans).
Courtesy Bergen Offentlige Bibliotek

later that he contacted Grieg again. On this occasion, Grieg's reply (dated 18 October 1901) betrayed both a greater sense of urgency and also an awareness of the national context in which he now valued the Hardanger repertoire:

> Mr Knut Dahle,
>
> I have just received your letter. My interest in the peasant dances is naturally the same as before, but at present there is nothing I can do personally, since I am unwell and otherwise unable to meet with you. But one thing is very important: the peasant dances must be written down by a violinist (I am a pianist) because of the bowing, tuning, fingering, and for the sake of the tone colour. The parliament has previously paid people to collect folk tunes but they do not understand that to collect folk dances requires a specialist. Thank you for writing. I feel stronger than ever before that something must, can and should be done. I will write to Kristiania today about the matter. If a violinist can be found there who understands how to notate and has a sense of this kind of work, he must either travel to you or, if that cannot happen, you must travel to him in Kristiania if you are able to undertake such a trip. The expenses involved will be covered in one way or another. I shall request an immediate response from Kristiania and as soon as I have it, you shall hear again from me.
>
> When you have the opportunity tell me how old you are, when you were in America and how long you were there and where you performed publically.
>
> Yours sincerely,
> Edvard Grieg.[15]

Though strongly supportive, Grieg's letter nevertheless points to a tension between urban and rural contexts that continues to underpin

[15] 'Hr Knut Dahle.

Jeg har netop modtaget Deres Brev, Min interesse for Slåtterne og Deres Opbevaring er selvfølgelig den samme som før, men for Øjeblikket kan jeg personlig Intet gjøre, da jeg er sygelig og også ellers forhindret fra at opsøge Dem. Men der er en meget vigtig Ting: Slåtterne må opskrives af en Violinspiller (jeg er Klaverspiller) både for Buestrøgenes, Stemningens, Fingersætningens og Klangfarvenes Skyld. Strotinget har betalt Folk forat samle Folkeviser men har ikke havt Forstand på, at tilat samle Folkedansene hører der en Spesialist. Tak fordi De skrev. Thi jeg føler stækere end nogensinde, at Noget må, bør og skal gjøres. Jeg skriver idea til Kristiania om Sagen. Hvis en Violinspiller derfra, som forstår sig på at nedskrive og har Sansen for dette Arbejde, kan fåes, så må enten han rejse til Dem og hvis det ikke kan ske, så må De rejse til ham i Kristiania, om De endnu arker en slig Rejse. Udgifterne må besørges dækket på en aller anden Måde. Jeg skal forlange øjeblikkeligt Svar fra Kristiania og straks jeg har det, skal De atter høre fra mig.

Fortæl mig ved Lejlighed hvor gammel De er, hvad Tid De var i Amerika, hvorlænge De var der og hvor De optrådte offentlig.

Med venlig Hilsen

Edvard Grieg'

Ibid·48.

his correspondence with both Dahle and Halvorsen, and which points towards one of the underlying structural conflicts in op. 72. Collection of the peasant dances must be undertaken by a Kristiania-based violinist with prior experience of the repertoire, Grieg maintains, rather than being left to his own more amateur abilities. Although, as in the earlier folk-song arrangements op. 17 and op. 66, Grieg was content to rely upon someone else's transcriptions of the original melodies and was not directly engaged with their collection himself, he seems to have conceived of the project in more professionalised terms. This suggests a consciously ethnographic approach on Grieg's part, as well as reinforcing the more modernist character of op. 72.

On the same day that Grieg replied to Dahle, he also wrote to Johan Halvorsen about the work involved with the transcription, enclosing Dahle's letter. Expressing similar concerns about the need for specialist expertise and stressing the urgency of the situation within a larger political context, Grieg asked:

> What should now be done? To get Møllarguten's dances secured in their original form, that is the task, which cannot be postponed for another single day since Knut Dahle is an old man. I would rather that you undertook the task. But you are surely too busy, even if I could persuade Dahle to travel down to Kristiania and come to you one morning in a few weeks. If no wealthy man will cover his travel and board, I shall do it myself from here. So we will not give the finanical side much thought. Rather, just think if you did this and then I set them for piano afterwards and so we made them famous through Peters right in front of the nose of this barely national yet unnational parliament! If you simply do not have the time, there is obviously Gustav Lange, who no doubt has as little time to spare. But I think that the possible loss of teaching and other time could be made up for in other ways, for example through publication.
>
> So the question, if you would be so good as to answer the following, is therefore this: can you either receive Dahle, or can you pass me on to another, suitably qualified man in Kristiania, or, let me say, in Norway?[16]

---

[16] 'Hvad skal der nu gjøres? At få Møllargutens Slåtter fæstet i sin originale Skikkelse, det er Opgaven, som ikke kan udsættes en eneste Dag, da Knut Dahle er en gammel Mand. Jeg vilde helst at *Du* skulde overtage Opgaven. Men Du er vel for optaget, selv om jeg kunde formå Dahle tilat rejse ned til Kristiania og komme til Dig en Morgentime i nogle Uger. Hvis ingen Rigmand vil betale hans Rejse og Ophald, skal jeg nok påtage mig det herfra. Så den financielle Side vil vi ikke offre en Tanke. Nej tænk, om Du gjorde dette og om jeg bagefter sat Slåtterne for Klaver og så gjorde vi dem verdensberømt gjennem Peters midt for Næsen af det af bare Nationalitet unationale Storting! Skulde Du nu rent umulig kunne offre Tiden, så har vi naturligvis Gustav Lange, som dog vistnok har ligeså lidet Tid at bortgive. Dog jeg tror nok at det eventuelle Timetab og andet Tidstab vilde kunne godtgjøres på anden Måde, f. Ex. gjennem Offentliggjørelsen.

Grieg wrote again on 23 November in even stronger terms, regretting Dahle's poor physical condition, but adding that 'the stamp of authenticity is the main thing'. He also instructed Halvorsen that 'obviously you should transcribe with the original tuning. I hope my brain can still work it out',[17] a potentially significant detail given Grieg's later reading of at least one of Halvorsen's transcriptions discussed below. Halvorsen had already written to Grieg during the transcription process with Dahle, describing the 'small leaps and trills' in Dahle's melodies, 'which are like a little trout on a string. As soon as you try and catch them they are gone', and on 28 November he compared the ornamentation with *rosemaling* ('rose painting'), the floral patterning or carving traditionally associated with western Norwegian folk art.[18]

Grieg received Halvorsen's transcriptions the following month, and was evidently pleased with the result even though he was immediately struck (and puzzled) by the modal character of the dances. His reaction also betrayed a sense of inferiority or uncertainty. In a letter to Halvorsen dated 6 December, he wrote:

> I have just received your *Slåtter* and read them through, while chuckling to myself with delight. But at the same time I have also cursed and raged for not being a fiddler. How I detest this Conservatory in Leipzig!
>
> But to the issue: as you say, this 'oddity' with G♯ in D major was what drove me wild and mad in 1871. Of course I stole it straight away in my 'Scenes from Folk Life' [op. 19] This sound is something for scholars. This augmented fourth can also be heard in folk song. It is a ghost from one or other ancient scale. But which? It's incomprehensible that no-one here has devoted himself to the study of national music, when we possess so many rich sources in our folk music for those that have ears to hear with, hearts to feel with, and the understanding to write them down.
>
> At present I feel it would be like a sin to arrange the peasant dances for piano. But I will commit this sin sooner or later. It is too tempting. I heartily thank you for your work, through which you have given me so much pleasure, and in the future it will appear that you have done much more than that.[19]

Spørgsmålet som Du godhedsfuldt må besvare omgående, er altså dette: Kan Du enten selv modtage Dahle eller kan Du opgive mig nogen Anden, *dertil skikket* Mand i Kristiania – eller lad mig sige, i Norge?'
Ibid. 49, also in *Brev*, I, 369–70.
[17] 'Hovedsagen er *Ægthedens Præg* . . . Selvfølgelig optegner Du i Originalstemningen. Jeg håber min Hjerne endnu duer tilat regne den ud.' (original emphasis). *Brev*, I, 371.
[18] 'Små spræt og triller, der er som en liden ørret i et stryg. Når man skal lage dem, er de borte.' Letter dated 17 November 1901, ibid., 372.
[19] 'Jeg har netop fåt Dine Slåtter og har just fåt læst Dem igjennem, mens det formelig har klukket

This letter suggests that Grieg seems to have been anxious at an early stage to draw attention to his status as an outsider, both in terms of specific instrumental training (as a pianist working with fiddle music) and broader musical education (his period at the Leipzig Conservatory), while simultaneously underlining the potentially national context for such folk-music research. Grieg's comments also reveal a tension between his conception of the peasant dances as a naïve, innocent source of antique purity in need of preservation, and his desire to present them in a modern setting arranged for piano: a perceived conflict of interests that is recurrent throughout his work on op. 72. Similar concerns are evident in his later correspondence. To Iver Holter, for example, he described the peasant dances as 'so genuine and so wild and bursting with energy and yet with a flowing undercurrent through them that I am glad they have been saved in time', adding that his arrangements would be 'something completely different from that found in the Lindeman collection, where one does not know what is the original and what is Lindeman'.[20] Grieg was therefore at pains to create a clear critical context for the set. To Frants Beyer on 2 September 1902 he wrote in greater detail:

> The past fourteen days I have been taken up with Knut Dahle's and Halvorsen's folk tunes. It interests me greatly, but it is a hellish work. Why? Well, because I have become more critical than before in the interests of adhering to the style. Here there is a completely different difficulty from that involved in dealing with Lindeman [for op. 17], namely the decision over what should be retained of the original violin notation with respect to the lower part. And now, since the original will be published alongside my arrangement, I will no doubt provoke the German critics. Incidentally, for this reason I have been thinking about writing a preface which describes my perspective. This will give a better understanding of what I have and have not intended and will hopefully disarm to some degree those who might wish to

i mig af Fryd. Men samtidig har jeg skjændt og brændt over ikke at være Felespiller. Hvor jeg dog hader dette Konservatorium i Leipzig! –

Men til Sagen: Dette "mærkelige" som Du siger med *Gis* i D Dur var det som gjorde mig vild og gal i Året 1871. Jeg stjal den naturligvis fluks i mine "Folkelivsbilleder". Denne Tone er Noget for Forskeren. Den forstørrede Kvart kan også høres i Bondens Sang. Det er Gjengangere fra en eller anden gammel Skala. Men hvilken? Ubegribeligt at Ingen hos os slår sig på national Musikforskning, da vi i vor Folkemusik har så rige Kilder for dem der har Øren at høre med, Hjerte at føle med og Forstand til at nedskrive.

Foreløbig står det for mig som en Synd at behandle Slåtterne for Klaver. Men den Synd kommer jeg dog før eller siden at begå. Den er for fristende. Du skal ha hjærtelig Tak for Dit Arbejde, hvorved Du har gjort mig en stor Glæde og det vil i Fremtiden vise sig, at Du har gjort mere end det.' Ibid., 372.

[20] 'De er så genuine og så sprættende yr og vild med rørende Understrøm indimellem at jeg er lykkelig over at de bleven reddet itide. . . . Det er noget Andet, end at få fåt i den Lindemanske Samling, hvor man ikke ved, hvad der er det oprindelige og hvad der er Lindeman.' Letter dated 15 September 1902, ibid., 460.

attack me. There is a pair among the dances that you will love.
How easy it would be to take the bloom off them! Indeed, here
it pays to have saved up your finest feelings.[21]

Grieg's correspondence around the time he was working on op. 72 points
to the uneasy generic status of the *Slåtter*. His whimsical suggestion to
Beyer, 'How easy it would be to take the bloom off them!', suggests that
Grieg understood the peasant dances as an exotic delicacy, as Dahlhaus's
reading of such folk materials in nineteenth-century music later implies.
But Grieg's reference to German music criticism might equally well signal a
conscious awareness of the *Slåtter*'s radicalism (which was as much rhythmic
as harmonic), and indicates that he was already considering their place
within a wider art-music marketplace. Significantly, the set was eventually
dedicated to the influential German music theorist and historian Hermann
Kretzschmar, suggesting that Grieg had ultimately conceived the set from
a cosmopolitan perspective. This dedication, and Grieg's unusually keen
desire to write a preface clarifying his compositional intentions, suggests
that he was aware of the potential ethnomusicological importance of op.
72. But it also indicates perhaps a sense of inferiority or peripheralisation, a
perceived need to explain and justify the basis for his aesthetic decisions in
the face of mainstream critical incomprehension. Hence, Grieg's desire to
'adhere to the style' within the work suggests both a concern with issues of
authenticity, and with the attempt to maintain a level of authorial control
that recalls the abstract structuralist thought evident in his earlier sets of
folk-music arrangements op. 17 and op. 66.

Authenticity and musical identity: the reception of the Slåtter, op. 72

The issues of intentionality raised by Grieg's correspondence above are
inevitably problematic. The extent to which Grieg had privileged insight
into his own compositional processes during his work on op. 72 is surely
questionable, as it is for any musical work. Rather, his comments foreshadow
the later critical reception of the set. Moreover, they point to the structural
tensions within the music, which were to provide the primary creative
driving forces in op. 72. In the covering letter with the manscript to his

---

[21] 'De sidste 14 Dage har jeg været oppe i Knut Dahlhes og Halvorsens Folkeviser. Det interesserer
mig svært, men det er et Helvedes Arbejde. Hvorfor? Jo, fordi jeg er bleven mere kritisk end før,
i Retning af at holde Stilen fast. Her er også en ganske anden Vanskelighed end ved at behandle
Lindeman, nemlig den at afgjøre, hvad der skal beholdes af den originale Violinoptegnelse med
Hensyn til Understemmen. Og nu, da Originalen skal foreligge trykt ved Siden af min Bearbejdelse,
vil jeg jo ligefrem udæske den tydske Kritik. Jeg har forresten tænkt mig i denne Anledning at skrive
et Forord, som betegner mit Standpunkt. Dette vil give mere Forståelse af, hvad jeg har villet og ikke
villet, og forhåbentlig for en Del afvæbne de Angrebslystne. Der er et Par blandt Dansene, som Du
vil bli glad i. Hvor let er det ikke at ta Duften af dem! Isandhed, her gjælder det at have opsparet sine
fineste Fornemmelser.' Grieg, *Brev til Frants Beyer*, 276–7.

publisher at Peters Edition, Hinrichsen, dated 28 February 1903, Grieg insisted that Halvorsen's transcriptions should be published alongside his arrangements, and wrote defensively: 'although my individual voice can clearly be heard in this piano arrangement – indeed, more clearly perhaps than many would wish – I can well understand that you would rather have had an original work from me'.[22] Furthermore, Grieg maintained that 'as the main focus of these pieces falls on their cultural-historical interest, I consider the preface as well as my notes and comments to be indispensable'. Grieg therefore seems to have been reluctant to promote the *Slåtter* on the basis of their structural or aesthetic qualities, or to present op. 72 as an autonomous work in its own right. His apparent cautiousness reflects not just reservations about the generic status of music but also his concerns about its stylistic and practical difficulties: fears that were partly fulfilled by the music's subsequent failure to find an immediately sympathetic critical response at home in Norway. To the Norwegian folklorist and historian Moltke Moe, for instance, Grieg wrote 'they sound so unatural, that I expect no understanding in Norway from this work', a remark which was to prove largely accurate, and added that 'in addition they are difficult to perform . . . but if a player can be found with a strong rhythmic and harmonic sense – and I could add: demonic sense! – then direct him to nos. 4, 6, 7, 10, 11, 14, 17, which are pearls for those that have ears to listen with'.[23]

Grieg's fears for the critical reception of the *Slåtter* initially appear to have been realised. Otto Winter Hjelm's review in *Aftenposten*, after Grieg's performance on 21 March 1906, for example, was essentially defensive despite its outwardly positive tone:

> To me Grieg seems to be most poetic in the older pieces, the 'Humoresque' from op. 6, the *Fire Albumblad*, op. 28, the 'Berceuse' from op. 38 and the *Holberg Suite*, op. 40, and among the audience it appeared to me that they were received with the greatest pleasure. I thought the later compositions, *Stemninger* ('Moods'), op. 73, and *Slåtter* , op. 72, held the attention less. It is now no more than fifty to sixty years since folk songs and folk dances came of age in the concert hall. And even if the arrangement for piano is made with such a sympathetic ear for the characteristic sound and accent as for example in the 'Peasant Dances' of op. 72, and even if they are played as vividly and 'nationally' as Grieg performed them this evening, it is quickly apparent from the audience that most of them would not put up with a whole

---

[22] Quoted in the Afterword to the Henle Edition, ed. Einar Steen-Nøkleberg (Munich: 1994), 63.

[23] 'Så unaturligt det klinger, så venter jeg ingen Forståelse i Norge af dette Værk. Tilmed er det vanskeligt at udføre . . . Men træffer De på en spiller med stærk rytmisk og harmonisk Sans – og jeg kunde tilføje: dæmonisk Sans! – så henvis ham til No 4, 6, 7, 10, 11, 14, 17 som er Perler for dem, der har Øren at høre med.' Letter dated 7 October 1903, *Brev*, I, 525.

evening of this kind.[24]

Winter Hjelm did concede that 'it is another matter for those that have a special affection for folk music. For them, the *Slåtter*, op. 72, in Grieg's arrangement are of great interest, not least as evidence of his ability to elicit acoustic effects from the piano which recall the Hardanger fiddle and peasant musicians.'[25] The implication, however, is that such specialist musical interest was relatively rare within the concert-hall audience, who preferred Grieg's more assimilable early works. Grieg's own diary entry for the evening records a similar impression, but he places even stronger emphasis on the sense of having moved beyond popular critical appreciation:

> What hurt me particularly was that the *Slåtter* didn't succeed as they should and ought to have done. I played them with all the affection and wizardry I possess. But – I have no-one at home where my development has led me, that is the difficulty. Here they pine continually for the standard of my youth, which on appropriate occasions they praise at the expense of my current position. But – I must not let myself be held back by it. I must simply be allowed to develop for as long as I live. That is my greatest wish. General understanding will come when the time is right.[26]

For Grieg, the *Slåtter* were clearly in a special category, since their perceived modernist difficulty apparently came into conflict with their folk character. As Trygve Trædal has commented, 'here one is confronted with the paradox that the *Slåtter* – for Norwegians – seem to have been too Norwegian, both for critics and the public'.[27] Grieg evidently sensed this paradox, for the first pianist to take up op. 72 succesfully was an Australian, Percy Grainger. Grieg

---

[24] 'Mest Digter synes mig Grieg at være i de ældre Stykker, Humoresken af op. 6, Albumsblade op. 28, Berceuse af op. 38 og Holberg-Suiten op. 40, og blandt Tilhørerne forekom det mig, at de modtages med størst Glæde. Mindre tror jeg at de senere Kompositioner, 'Stemninger' op. 73 og 'Slaatter' op. 72 tog Interessen fangen. Det er nu ikke mere som for 50–60 Aar siden, at Folkevisen og Folkedansen i Koncertsalen eller Salonen er paa Moden. Om end Bearbeidelsen for Klaver er gjort med en saa lydhør Sans for det karakteristiske i Klang og Accent som f. Ex. i 'Slaatter' af op. 72, og om de end spilles saa friskt og 'nationalt', som Grieg spillede dem iaftes, saa kan man dog snart se paa Tilhørene, at de fleste af dem ikke taaler meget paa én Aften af den Slags.' Quoted in Trygve Trædal, 'Harmonisk særtrekk i Griegs *Slåtter*, op. 72', hovedoppgave til historisk-filosofisk embetseksame (Oslo University, 1972), 9–10.

[25] 'Det er en anden Sag med dem, der har speciel Kjærlighed til Folkemusiken. For dem er Slaaterne op. 72 i Griegs Bearbeidelse af høi Interesse, ikke mindst som Vidne om hans Evne til at aflokke Klaveret Klangvirkninger, der minder om Hardaner-fele og Bondespillemænd.' Quoted in ibid.

[26] 'Hva der gjorde mig ondt var, at "Slaatterne" ikke slo ned, som de skulde og burde. Jeg spillede dem med al den Kjærlighed og Troldskab jeg ejede. Men – derhen min Udvikling nu har ført mig, har jeg ikke Folk herhjemme med, det er det Tunge. Her tæres det bestandig paa mit Ungdomsstandpunkt, som ved passede Leiligheder berømmes paa Bekostning af mit nuværelse. Men – det faar jeg ikke lade mig hindre af. Maatte jeg bare faa Lov til at udvikle mig saalænge jeg Lever. Det er mit høyeste Ønske. Den almene Forstaaelse faar da komme naar dens Tid er inde.'

[27] 'Og her blir man faktisk stående ved det paradoks at slåtterne – for Nordmenn – syntes å være for norske, både for Kritikere og publikum.' Trædal, 'Harmoniske særtrekk i Griegs *Slåtter*', 11.

wrote in his diary on 24 May 1906, 'I have never met anyone that *understands* me like him',[28] but his admiration was tempered by a sense of disappointment that the *Slåtter* had not met with greater critical understanding at a time when Norway finally seemed to have achieved a breakthrough in its search for cultural and political independence.

A recent exchange in the Bergen daily newspaper, *Bergens tidende*, in June 2002 suggests that the controversy surrounding op. 72 remains unresolved.[29] Whereas historically the reception of op. 72 has centred on the music's 'difficult' modernist character, however, more recent debates have focused on issues of authenticity, ownership and performance practice rather than questions of aesthetic orientation. Grieg's *Slåtter* lie at the heart of wider arguments about the current status and place of folk music in Norway. At one extreme, they are attacked as misappropriations of a pure folk source, a more or less cynical attempt to exploit the resources of a venerable local tradition through the creation of a hybrid musical form. On the other side of the debate, Grieg's arrangements have been praised as an open and innovative attempt to bring Norwegian folk music to a wider international audience, and as a means of laying the foundations for a new Norwegian musical style on the basis of a rich local tradition. In a review article entitled 'Folkemusikk som angår oss' ('Folk music which concerns us') following a folk-music concert held by Ole Bull Academy in Bergen, for example, Espen Selvik maintained that

> Folk music concerns us in fundamental ways. Rhythm, sound and melody 'take off' when the performance has nerve and engagement. This music is created and refined in our own geography, by our own soil. It is Norwegian music of which we should be proud. Ole Bull was one of the first who understood this, as was Edvard Grieg. Grieg's *Slåtter* have been on the festival programme many times, for example; one of the most inspired piano pieces ever written and based on our own folk music.[30]

It is significant that metaphors of landscape, geography and collective ownership once again figure strongly in such debates as markers of musical identity. In a response headed 'Når folkemusikarar slår på tromme' ('When folk musicians beat the drum') a few days later, Kjell Kjerland argued:

---

[28] 'Jeg har ikke truffet Nogen, der *forstaar* mig som ham.' Quoted in ibid., 10.
[29] I am indebted to Ragna Sofie Grung Moe at the Grieg Academy for first bringing this correspondence to my attention.
[30] 'Folkemusikk angår oss faktisk på fundamentalt vis. Rytmer, klanger og melodier gir «fot» når fremførelsen har nerve og engasjement. Denne musikken er skapt og foredlet i vår egen geografi, vårt eget jordsmonn. Det er norsk musikk som vi bør være stolt av. Ole Bull var en av de første som forsto dette, likeledes Edvard Grieg. Nå under Festspillene var eksempelvis Griegs «Slåtter» på programmet flere ganger, et av de mest geniale klaverstykker som noensinne er laget, og med basis i vår egen folkemusikk.' *Bergens tidende*, Saturday 15 June 2002, 58.

BT's reviewer takes the matter seriously and has provided an honest report except in one regard, when he calls Edvard Grieg's *Slåtter* 'one of the most inspired piano pieces ever written'.

For many years, the festival musicians were shipped over to Troldhaugen where the *Slåtter* were performed by a pianist of high standing. At the same concert there was also a *spelemann* who played the *Slått* in his own way. So the pianist presented art music, and the *spelemann* the 'primitive' point of departure. For my part, I believe that even Grieg himself recognised that in fact the opposite was the case. A *slått* for Hardanger fiddle can never be reproduced decently on a piano. It is the *slått* on the Hardanger fiddle, played by a decent performer, that represents perfection here, and occasionally the 'inspired'.

But then those who represent folk music have accepted such things every year: to cast themselves in the shadow of a famous performer. Just as those associated with the concert did last Friday.

Until we can get to grips with this, and folk musicians show that they have thought for themselves about what they stand for, things will continue in this way.[31]

Kjerland's model seeks to invert the top-down model implied by Grieg's preface to op. 72, in which he speaks of his Ibsenesque desire to 'raise these works of the people to an artistic level' ('et kunsterisk Niveau'). For Kjerland, such an attitude is patronising, and points to a sense of inferiority within the folk community itself. His polemic is therefore an attempt to regain critical and creative space for Norwegian folk music as a proper mode of musical communication in its own right. From this perspective, the debate over the status of the *Slåtter* can be seen as part of a wider post-colonial discourse, in which various perceived levels of cultural domination and oppression are contested within a musical context. The implication is that Grieg's transcriptions represent a colonising activity, an external attempt to assert ownership of musical materials that rightly belong in another milieu. Hence for Kjerland, Selvik's claim that Grieg's *Slåtter* are 'one of the most inspiried piano pieces ever written' not only supports such

[31] 'BT sin meldar tek emnet alvorleg og har gitt eit grett referat. Bortsett for i eitt høve. Naår han kallar Edvard Griegs «Slåtter»: «– et av de mest geniale klaverstykker som noensinne er laget.»

I fleire år hadde Festspillene tilskipingar på Troldhaugen der «Slåtter» var framført av ein pianist med høg status. På samme konserten var òg ein spelemann som spela slåtten på sitt vis. Pianisten presenterte då kunstmusikken, og spelemannen det «primitive» utgangspunktet. Eg for min del trur at endå Edvard Grieg var klar over at det eigentleg er det motsette som er tilfellet. Ein slått for hardingfele kan aldri attgjevast skikkeleg på eit piano. Det er slåtten på hardingfele, spela av ein skikkeleg utøvar som her representerer det fullkomne, og av og til det «geniale».

Men også slike ting har dei som representerer folkemusikken godteke i ale år: Å still seg i skuggen av utøvrar med status. Slik dei òg gjorde i samband med konserten sist fredag.

Før det blir teke fatt i dette, og folkemusikkutøvarane viser at dei sjølve har tru på det dei står for, vil det òg halda fram slik.' *Bergens tidende*, Wednesday 19 June 2002, 29.

colonial appropriation, but also denies Norwegian folk music its own sense of independence and originality. In a response the following weekend, the rector of the Ole Bull Academy, Jostein Mæland, sought to steer a middle way between these opposed positions by highlighting the isolationist trends in such debates, particularly the tendency for such fixed definitions as 'folk' or 'art' in music to become exclusive categories:

> So to Edvard Grieg and *Slåtter* and the 'primitive point of origin'. Over the years I've met with many great musicians, both pianists and *spelemenn*, in similar collaborations. Who could think of Buen, Rygg or Osa as representatives of the primitive point of departure? They have absolutely no grounds for placing themselves in the shadow of anyone, and do not do so.
>
>   No, I think rather that there are some in our milieu who bear a feeling of inferiority, and it is clear that all who are familiar with that part of Norwegian music realise that it is our national musical language and should be proud of it. But may it not be that as soon as an attempt is made to open new doors, the locksmiths arrive?[32]

Kjerland's final contribution to the exchange, 'Diskusjon om folkemusikk – eller om noko anna' ('Discussion of folk music – or of something else'), is in some senses a retreat from his earlier position: 'when I used the expression "primitive point of departure" I was trying to use irony'. But the basic thrust of his argument remains essentially the same:

> If there is anything that is primitive in this respect, it is the temptation to transfer Hardanger-fiddle dances to such a restricted instrument, in comparison with the starting point of the Hardanger fiddle, as the piano, whether upright or concert grand.
>
>   I still have such great respect for Edvard Grieg as composer and musician that I reckon he was clear about this.[33]

Though Kjerland reinforces his colonial reading of the *Slåtter*, in which

[32] 'Så til Edvard Grieg og slåttane og det «primitive utgangspunktet». Eg har gjennom åra opplevet mange store, både pianistar og spelemenn, i slikt samarbeid. Kven kan tjenka seg ein Buen, Rygg, Hamre eller Osa som representantar for det primitive utgangspunktet? Dei har så visst ikkje grunn til å stilla seg i skuggen for nokon og gjer det heller ikkje.

Nei, eg trur heller det er somme i miljøet som ber på ein mindreverdskjensle og det er leitt, all som er kjende med den delen av norsk musik veit at den er vårt nasjonale tonespråk og gør vera byrge av det. Men det må ikkje bli slik at straks ein freistar å opna nye dører, så kjem låsesmedane.' 'Ein folkemusikkjennar på avvegar', *Bergens tidende*, Saturday 22 June 2002, 37.

[33] 'Når eg brukar uttrykket «det primitive utgangspunktet», så prøver eg å bruka ironi. . . . Om det i dette høvet er noko som er «primitivt», så er det freistnaden på å overføra hardingfelaslåttar til eit så avgrensa instrument, i høve til utgangspunktet hardingfele, som piano, klaver, eller for den del flygel.

Eg har endå så stor respekt for komponisten og musikaren Edvard Grieg at eg reknar med at dette var han klar over.' *Bergens tidende*, Tuesdag 25 June 2002, 23.

Grieg's transcription constitutes an attempt to appropriate or control an original folk source, he subtly shifts attention away from the broader ideological issues raised by op. 72 and their implications for the perceived status of folk versus art music. At the same time, his discussion leads towards a narrower definition of authenticity, one that is premised primarily on the piano's inability to recreate the characteristic timbre of the Hardanger fiddle itself. Although in this limited sense, Grieg's *Slåtter* are arguably inauthentic, closer examination of the dances themselves can encourage a keener critical appreciation of their individual qualities. It also suggests that authenticity and identity are more flexible concepts than the exchanges in *Bergens tidende* initially allow. The apparent contradiction between the local and the universal suggested by the folk/art polarisation in the critical reception of the *Slåtter* is not necessarily a fatal one, but rather a creative tension (as in the *19 norske Folkeviser*), which ultimately enriches the discursive character of the set.

Modernism and Norwegian musical style: structural play in the Slåtter, *op. 72*

The advent of modern recording technology has enabled scholars to undertake a detailed comparison of Grieg's arrangements with the dances in their original form. Fragments of the 'Grieg Slåtter' were recorded on wax cylinders by Knut Dahle in 1910 and 1912, and a more complete version on gramophone exists by Knut Dahle's grandson, Johannes Dahle (1890–1980) which dates from from the early 1950s.[34] By using the recordings in comparison with Halvorsen's transcriptions, it has been relatively easy to identify precisely how much of the original tune has been altered in Grieg's arrangement. Contemporary folk fiddler Sven Nyhus has helped prepare an edition of Grieg's arrangements that attempts to mediate between the various different versions of the tunes, some of the implications of which are discussed below.[35] In transferring music from one medium (the fiddle) to another (the piano) with an entirely different method of sound production, Grieg was inevitably unable to retain many of the idiomatic characteristics of the original instrument, a loss that lies at the heart of Kjerland's critique. As various writers, including Nyhus, Pandora Hopkins and Ståle Kleiberg,[36] have observed, this loss involves timbral features such as the ringing sound of the Hardanger fiddle's sympathetic strings, as well as the complex cross-beat bowings and the microtonal tunings that are associated with the fiddle

[34] The recordings have recently been reissued on CD and remastered by Hardanger fiddler Sven Nyhus (Musikk-Husets forlag M.H. 2642-CD, 1993).

[35] *Edvard Grieg: Slåtter op. 72 for klaver*, gjennomgått og bearbeidet av Geir Henning Braaten og Sven Nyhus (Oslo: Musikk-Husets forlag, 2001).

[36] Pandora Hopkins, *Aural Thinking in Norway: Performance and Communication with the Hardingfele* (New York: Human Sciences Press, 1986); and Ståle Kleiberg, 'Grieg's *Slåtter*, op. 72: Change of Musical Style or New Concept of Nationality?', *Journal of the Royal Musical Association* 121 (1996), 46–57.

repertoire. Kleiberg has drawn attention to particular instances where Grieg appears to model the sound of the Hardanger fiddle, notably the resonant compound-fifth sonorities at the climax of the eleventh dance, 'Knut Luråsens Halling II' (bars 45–52).[37] Even here, however, the piano can only approximate or evoke the sound of the original instrument. Other aspects of performance practice associated with the fiddle repertoire are even harder to try and recreate. The fiddler's habit of tapping the feet (often apparently against the accentual pattern of the dance melody so as to create an additional level of rhythmic complexity) is virtually impossible for a pianist to reproduce, even though it could be argued that Grieg's addition of a lower part serves as an appropriate contrapuntal substitute.[38] Similarly, though Grieg partially identified the microtonal colouring in the melodies as a modal inflection, the actual degree of pitch variation used by the fiddlers cannot be recreated on a fixed-tempered instrument. It is equally difficult for the piano to recreate the effect of different tunings or scordatura (a detail which Grieg was nevertheless eager for Halvorsen to record). This has implications not just for the music's sound world but also its function and affect. As Pandora Hopkins has noted, 'particular tunings are still considered appropriate to particular times of day and situations. Troll tuning (*Trollstilt*) is considered appropriate to the time between midnight and dawn, and is used in *nøring slåtter* (special *slåtts* played to bridal guests before they rise from bed in the morning.'[39] Most importantly of all, perhaps, the very act of notation compromises the improvisatory nature of the fiddle repertoire. Most of the *slåtter* are dance tunes, and consist of open, endlessly variable melodic fragments. Though, as close reading below suggests, this sense of spontaneous invention is partly evoked by Grieg's avoidance of strict repetition in favour of a continual redecoration of tiny melodic figures or progressions, this does not constitute 'improvisation' in the sense understood by the *spelemenn* themselves.

Grieg openly acknowledged the constructed nature of his musical syntax in the *Slåtter*. In spite of the reservations outlined above, however, it would be a mistake to equate this solely with a process of artificialisation. Rather, Grieg's concern with authenticity appears not to have been directed towards a futile attempt to reproduce the *Slåtter* on the piano in their original form, but with capturing some sense of their mode of utterance. In a letter to Gerhard Schjelderup concerning the broader status of Norwegian folk music, he wrote:

---

[37] Kleiberg, 'Grieg's *Slåtter*', 51–3.
[38] The tapping is intermittently audible during the dances recorded for the Norske folkemusikksamling in 1953 by Johannes Dahle included on the Musikk-Huset disc, and can also be heard on Knut Buen's modern recording of the 'Grieg Slåtter' on Simax PSC 1040 (Oslo: Pro Musica, 1988).
[39] Pandora Hopkins, *Aural Thinking in Norway*, 137.

'To treat them so that they can even be used in concerts', as you say, is precisely what Johan Svendsen has done with such mastery in his 'Rhapsodies', and which I have also attempted in my 'Norwegian Dances'. To fuse the folk tune in this manner together with one's own individuality and then having gone through that process contributing to the work of art. I have also published folk songs in their original form, but harmonised them according to my own inclination. This treatment is only for 'connoisseurs' and dare not expect wider distribution. If on the other hand you harmonise or otherwise treat folk songs with the goal of getting them disseminated among the people, then you must hold back the 'oysters and caviar' and be content with 'rye bread and butter'. One must let go of heaven and come down to earth. Such publications have their greater justification when they are sensibly and conciously organised, and not as chaotic and unpractical as Lindeman's collection.[40]

Grieg's comments here suggest that his arrangements should not necessarily be understood as 'dressing up', or an attempt to elevate the melodies 'to an artistic level', as his preface in op. 72 claimed, so much as a 'stripping down' or essentialisation. By adopting the category of *Heimatkunst* introduced in the preceding chapter, the *Slåtter* can be understood as a search for origins, the uncovering of a basic means of expression or musical identity. Hence, the charge of 'inauthenticity' the *Slåtter* have often attracted in folk-music circles is in some senses misjudged, since the *Slåtter*'s proper sense of authenticity is as much discursive as ethnic. Indeed, in this sense they exemplify Hutchinson's notion of cultural nationalism as a progressive, regenerative force, directed towards an imaginative transformation of national identity in the light of a synthetic (or artifically constructed) folk modernism.

The problem remains, however, that it is unclear which audience Grieg's 'rye bread and butter' was intended for precisely in op. 72. The second dance in the set, 'Jon Vestafes Springdans' ('Jon Vestafe's Leaping Dance'), illustrates the issues raised by this question vividly (Ex. 4.1). Grieg's arrangement can be understood as a physical narrative, similar in concept and design

---

[40] '«At behandle dem så, at de endog kan benyttes til Koncertbrug,» som De siger, er det netop Johan Svendsen med så stort Mesterskab i sine "Rhapsodier" har gjort og som jeg også har forsøgt i mine "Norske Danse". På denne Måde smelter Folkevisen sammen med den egne Individualitet og blir efter den Proces den har gjennemgåt, medvirkende i Kunstværket. Jeg har også udgivet Folkeviser i sin oprindelige Skikkelse, men harmoniseret dem efter min egen Tilbøjelighed. Denne Behandling er dog kun for «Feinschmeckere» og tør ikke påregne større Udbredelse. Vil De derimod harmonisere eller idethele behandle Folkeviser, med det Formål, at få dem spredet ud blandt Folket, da gjelder det at holde inde med «Østers og Kaviar» og tage fat med «Rugbrød og Smør». Man får da give Slip på Himmelen og blive ved Jorden. Sådanne Udgaveer har også sin store Berettigelse når de er klogt og bevidst tilrettelagt og ikke så femkantet og upraktisk som Lindemans Samling.' Letter dated 26 October 1905, *Brev*, I, 627.

to that of the *springar* that opens the op. 17 set (discussed at the end of Chapter 1 above) but here on a much more expansive scale. The dance consists of three strophes (Halvorsen's transcription indicates only a single strophe), each of which has a different registral, dynamic and rhythmic character (Halvorsen's transcription includes no dynamic or rhythmic indications other than an initial *forte* marking). The dance begins with a two-bar melodic cell that is repeated and then rhythmically varied (so as to produce a larger two x four-bar phrase). In the first two strophes this variation offers Grieg an opportunity to alter the left-hand accompanimental figuration from the motoric opening pattern (with its characteristic swung *springar* leap and accent on the final beat of the bar) to a more neutral off-beat quaver syncopation. After a transitional four-bar phrase (two x two-bar units) which lands on the dominant (with further leaps in the left hand), a second two-bar melodic cell, closely based on the two preceding phrases, is announced, repeated and varied. This time, the left-hand figuration is more cumulative: a rising quaver figure with pedal that suggest an increase in dynamic and rhythmic momentum. The strophe then concludes with a final two-bar closing unit, repeated three times (plus a final two-bar tag), which is displaced through three different registral levels. In the first strophe, this closing phrase has the character of abatement, or of a weakening in tension, an effect reinforced by the decreasing dynamic level and descending register (as well as the falling chromatic voice-leading in the left hand). The second strophe is essentially an echo strophe, like the corresponding strophe in op. 17/1, of contrasting dynamic and registral character. Here, however, Grieg reverses the function of the final closing phrase (bars 51–60) so that it now serves a sharply cumulative purpose. The left-hand accompaniment is inverted so that it rises, rather than falls, and the dynamic level begins a relatively swift ascent from *pianissimo* (bar 49) to *fortissimo* at the beginning of the third and final strophe. There is therefore a significant shift of structural momentum, away from a static (or circular) rise and fall in musical tension in the first strophe to a more strongly end-oriented design in the second and third strophes. Grieg marks the final strophe *marcato*, and the contrast with the previous two strophes is not merely dynamic (and registral) but also rhythmic. The left-hand accompaniment midway through the first phrase (bar 65) changes from a three-crotchet pattern to three accented quavers on strong metrical beats. The effect is to create the impression of a momentary change of metre, from the dance's prevailing triple time to a Stravinskian one-beat bar (1/4). The return of the motoric *springar* rhythm in bar 69 reasserts the dance's proper triple-time measure. The sense of cumulative momentum is only intensified, however, so that the closing section (bars 81 ff.), with its dramatic octave leaps in both hands, contains the most extravagently physical music in the whole number. This formal

Example 4.1. Grieg, Jon Vestafes Springdans, op. 72/2

trajectory is summarised and gathered up by the *stretto* in the final four bars. A momentary lull in dynamic level is followed by a vertiginous expansion from the centre of the instrument to its extreme outer reaches, until the music figuratively drops of the end of the keyboard. The final chord is both the loudest point of the dance and its widest single registral span.

The formal trajectory of 'Jon Vestafes Springdans', as of the 'Jølstring', another of the dances from the op. 17 set analysed above in Chapter 1, suggests a strongly teleological narrative that lends itself readily to metaphors of liberation and release. Exactly how such metaphors should be interpreted programmatically remains a moot point. For example, they might suggest an evolutionary progression from an imagined folk simplicity (the initial strophe) towards aesthetic fulfilment or completion in an art-music context (the virtuosity of the final strophe). This implies an essentially colonial reading of the music's supposed folk source that current musicians such as Kjerland would surely contest. But at the same time, the dance could also suggest the gradual uncovering and celebration of an essentialised folk identity, the presentation of a constructed western Norwegian musical style in its 'raw' state. In this sense, the final strophe becomes the apotheosis of Grieg's musical regionalism. The fact that such diametrically opposed readings can be entertained with equal justification ultimately underlines the music's referential richness.

'Jon Vestafes Springdans' also illustrates in greater detail why the critical reception of the *Slåtter* has been more complex than Grieg initially assumed. The dance demands a level of keyboard athleticism that is challenging for both player and listener alike. The difficulty is not so much a matter of velocity, tone or voicing, as physical strength, stamina and rhythmic precision (notably the ability to maintain the sense of cumulative growth from the middle of the second strophe right through until the very final bar). Other dances in the set are equally challenging. The seventh number, 'Røtnams-Knut, Halling', for example, has a ternary structure rather than the strongly goal-directed form of 'Jon Vestafes Springdans', but the outer sections unwind their own teleological physical narrative from the relative stability of the initial statement to a transformed restatement that makes considerable demands upon the pianist. The impetus for this progression is provided by the dance tune, which is associated with a local rhyme celebrating the athletic prowess of Røtnams-Knut himself.[41] In this way, local detail becomes abstracted in Grieg's setting so that it assumes a more abstract formal quality. Another feature of the *Slåtter* that may have been difficult for contemporary audiences to assimilate is the extreme diatonicism

---

[41] The rhyme exists in various different forms. The version quoted by Carl O. Gram Gjesdal runs as follows: 'Røitnæms Knut æ friskø o mjuk,/ dæ finst inkje ein, so kast'an ut' ('Røtnams-Knut is so lively and strong/ That no-one can take him on') (Simax CD PSC 1102, 9).

of their harmonic language. In a letter to Johan Halvorsen dated 3 February 1900, the year before work on the *Slåtter* began, Grieg had written from Copenhagen: 'my thoughts although I am abroad are only about Norway and Norwegians, about all our youthful combativeness up there. Yes, it is like the music of hard triads compared to all the soft-sweet seventh chords down here. Up there the struggle concerns spiritual existence.'[42] The *Slåtter* are so saturated in 'hard triads', however, that if they are performed in concert as a complete set, the effect can easily become over-bright: compared with other large-scale works, the lack of chromatic harmonic variety must have seemed strikingly austere. Indeed, this is partly what Otto Winter Hjelm may have alluded to when he observed that audiences would struggle to endure 'a whole evening of this kind'. But if it was difficult to conceive of the *Slåtter* as a straightforward concert work, they must have seemed equally unsuited to the intimate domestic use for which the majority of *Lyric Pieces* had been intended. This is a question of presentation as much as scale and content. The folk material in 'Jon Vestafes Springdans' is arguably presented in a more brutal, primitivist kind than in either the earlier op. 17 or op. 66 sets. As Kleiberg concludes, it is hard to see how the *Slåtter* can ever have been intended as a straightforwardly 'popular' work, whatever Grieg may have written in his preface. Rather, they demand their own innovative sense of musical space. Hence, Kleiberg argues that:

> Grieg's way of treating the original material is to build on the harmonic resources of the Hardanger fiddle. He does not, then, use the surface details of folk music as a kind of exotic spice to an otherwise conventional German/Romantic musical idiom. On the contrary it is the basic structures of the original material which form the starting point for his piano versions. This represents a new attitude to the application of folk-music material in art music. The folk material is now, to a far greater extent, treated on its own terms. Should this result in music which is rich in dissonance and less accessible, so be it. It is perhaps more important to create an authentic art than an art which may function as a national symbol.[43]

Kleiberg argues persuasively for a more discursive sense of authenticity than the narrow positions adopted by some commentators in the debate. Nevertheless, 'Jon Vestafes Springdans' draws attention to a specific rhythmic problem that remains difficult to resolve for many scholars. Pianist Einar Steen-Nøkleberg summarises the issue concisely in the notes accompanying

---

[42] 'Mine Tanker kredser trods al Udlændighed bare om Norge og Nordmænd, om al vor unge Stridbarhed deroppe. Ja, den er som musik af hårde Treklange sammenlignet med alle de blødesøde Septimakkorder hernede. Deroppe gjælder Kampen åndelig Ekistents.' *Brev*, I, 364.
[43] Kleiberg, 'Grieg's *Slåtter*', 57.

his edition of op. 72, when he observes that, in Norwegian folk music, 'the Springdans has three beats with identical subdivisions, although the length of the beats and the distribution of accents varies from region to region. In the case of the Telemark Jumping Dance the principal accent occurs on the second [crotchet], the final [crotchet] being somewhat shorter in duration.' Indeed, Bjørndal provides anecdotal evidence that Grieg struggled with precisely this rhythmic characteristic when he attempted to transcribe Hardanger fiddle music directly himself.[44] The problem is similar to other European dance types such as the waltz or mazurka, but, according to Norwegian scholars, the degree of rhythmic variation is much greater. Steen-Nøkleberg concludes that, 'as such nuances and irregularities cannot by their very nature be captured in musical notation it is in this area that the greatest discrepancies are to be found between the fiddle versions (still played today) and their adaptation by Halvorsen and Grieg'.[45] For other musicians, such as Sven Nyhus, Geir Henning Braaten and particularly Jan-Petter Blom,[46] the issue is even more complex. Nyhus and Henning Braaten identify two different basic dance types: an iambic form and a trochaic form, but note that 'one should not, however, consider the asymmetric pattern of [the *springar*] rhythm as a rigid one. Indeed, it may vary from one locality to another, this particular player may play this particular tune in this particular way at this particular social event.'[47] In other words, the *springar* rhythm potentially becomes an infinitely variable pattern that contradicts any fixed notion of a single 'correct' style of performance. Indeed, in this sense the rhythmic pattern of any single dance could be described as authentic only in so far as it obeys a fundamental rule that no two performances should be the same. To the extent that the Halvorsen's transcriptions (and therefore Grieg's arrangements) attempt to fix one particular performance in notated form, they are necessarily 'inauthentic'. But, in the same respect, so is every other attempt to transcribe or reproduce the melodies, whether in transcription or in recording.

The proposed solution offered by Nyhus and Henning Braaten is a dramatic rebarring of 'Jon Vestafes Springdans' (Ex. 4.2). The bar line is shifted so that the piece begins with an anacrusis (rather than on a strong beat). As a result, the crucial accent previously on the third beat of the bar in the left hand's initial *springar* pattern is now pushed forward on to the second

---

[44] Bjørndal, 'Grieg og folkemusikken', 14.

[45] *Edvard Grieg: Slåtter*, op. 72, ed. Einar Steen-Nøkleberg (Munich: Henle, 1994), 2.

[46] Jan-Petter Blom has written extensively on the structure of dance steps and Norwegian folk music. See, for example, his essay 'The Dancing Fiddle: On the Expression of Rhythm in Hardingfele Slåtter', in *Norsk folkemusikk serie I, Hardingfeleslåttar*. Band 7, Springar i 3/4 takt, ed. Jan-Petter Blom, Sven Nyhus and Reidar Sevag (Oslo: Universitetsforlaget, 1981), 305–21.

[47] *Edvard Grieg: Slåtter op. 72 for klaver*, gjennomgått og bearbeidet av Geir Henning Braaten og Sven Nyhus (Oslo: Musikk-Husets forlag, 2001), 4.

Example 4.2. Grieg: 'Jon Vestafes Springdans', op. 72/2, edited by Geir Henning Braaten and Sven Nyhus (showing metrical realignment of Springar rhythm)

beat. This also involves more substantial changes in layout: a crotchet rest is added to bar 14 (and at the corresponding point in the second strophe, bar 42), so that the following phrase begins on a strong beat. In order for the next strophe to begin at the 'correct' metrical point, however, a crotchet beat is then excised from bars 30 and 60, an effect that ultimately serves to reinforce a sense of asymmetrical phrase rhythm. Henning Braaten and Nyhus argue that 'a conventional notation [of a *springar*] will never reflect the true shape of asymmetric rhythms. The correct position of the bar, on the other hand, will provide essential information about which beats are to be stressed, and which unstressed.'[48] Their edition therefore rests on a distinction between levels of metrical organisation, namely the bar versus the individual beat. But the notion that the bar can be placed in a 'correct' position is surely contestable given the flexible nature of the rhythmic articulation in individual performances described above. A more positive reading of op. 72 suggests that Grieg's arrangement creates an additional layer of rhythmic counterpoint with the dance in its traditional Dahle-Telemark form. Grieg's aim was not necessarily to attain accuracy in respect of every single musical parameter, but to capture the sense of physical movement or tension within the dance as a physical gesture. Certainly, this is a more attractive way of accounting for the structural prominence that subtle variations in rhythmic articulation begin to gain in other dances from the set.

Similar problems of rhythm, structure and authenticity are involved in the thirteenth dance, the *springar* 'Håvar Gibøens Draum ved Oterholtsbrua' ('Håvar Gibøen's Dream on the Oterholt Bridge') (Ex. 4.3). Nyhus and Henning Braaten once again propose a rebarring, similar to that in 'Jon Vestafes Springdans', so that the whole dance is shifted forward by a crotchet beat. This has the effect of emphasising the syncopated character of the opening left-hand accompaniment, and means that the right hand's initial entry starts with a kick on an accented final beat of the bar (a metrical change which reinforces the angular quality of the g$\sharp^2$). Unlike 'Jon Vestafes Springdans', there is no need to provide further 'corrective' alterations later in the music: the dance rather finishes somewhat awkwardly half-way through the final bar. But the principal reason underlying their proposed change is the perceived need to reinterpret the metrical function of the triplet figures that predominate in the melody. The editors argue that this figure usually serves as an anacrusis in Norwegian folk music. Halvorsen and Grieg, they maintain, have effectively misunderstood this characteristic aspect of the dance's rhythmic syntax, just as they had distorted the asymmetrical pattern of the *springar* rhythm in the earlier number. This criticism, however, is not entirely justified. As

[48] Ibid.

the following analysis seeks to demonstrate, Grieg's arrangement does in fact reveal a sensitivity to precisely the rhythmic and meterical nuances that Nyhus and Henning Braaten describe. Indeed, adapting a thematic-rhythmic approach developed by Keliberg and others, Grieg's arrangement can be heard as an attempt to develop the structural implications of certain kinds of rhythmic figuration, and that levels of metrical dissonance provide a foundation for the organisation of other musical parameters.

On first hearing, 'Håvar Gibøens Draum ved Oterholtsbrua' sounds through-composed rather than strophic as in 'Jon Vestafes Springdans'. Closer listening, however, reveals that the dance falls into two broad halves, bars 1–41 and 42–61, a division also reflected in Halvorsen's transcription. Like 'Jon Vestafes Springdans', the dance is almost exclusively built from two-bar units, which are continually repeated and varied as the dance progresses. The first exception to this rule is bar 16, which elides two bars to create a metrical 'jolt' that is subsequently corrected by bar 22. Throughout bars 16–21, however, the effect is of a shifted first hypermetrical bar,[49] which is reinforced internally by a displaced accent on the second, rather than the third, beat of each bar in the left hand (a retrograde that produces the rhythmic pattern crotchet–minim, rather than the prevailing minim–crotchet). The other exceptions to the two-bar convention are the four-bar units in bars 31–4 and 35–8, which are followed, exceptionally, by a three-bar unit (bars 39–41) that articulates the end of the first large-scale structural phrase. The rest of the dance is entirely in two-bar segments, though it is possible to hear larger divisions within this phrase: the *a tempo*, *marcato* direction in bar 54 marks just such a point, and is of formal importance since it also marks the dynamic climax of the dance.

A glance at the harmonic structure of the dance suggests that it also broadly supports this bipartite formal division. The strong sense of cadential arrival in bar 41 inevitably evokes the feeling of an antecedent phrase, particularly given the descending chromatic bass line in bars 31–8 that seems to drive towards a firm cadence on the dominant. Furthermore, the prominent melodic emphasis on a 'corrective' g♮ in bar 42, at the beginning of the next phrase might have suggested to Grieg some sort of consequent or tonic response, the legacy of a familiar diatonic practice in which such subdominant inflections are conventionally used to suggest closure.

Kleiberg, however, downplays such harmonic evidence and argues that the *Slåtter* are essentially thematic structures. He proposes a form of motivic

---

[49] Throughout this study, the term 'hypermetre' is used to define a higher level of phrase organisation, similar to that defined in William Rothstein's *Phrase Rhythm in Tonal Music* (New York: Schirmer, 1989). However, whereas Rothstein's model relies principally on the rate of harmonic change, my use of hypermetre takes other parameters into account, especially the grouping of foreground rhythms as emphasised by scoring and accentuation.

Example 4.3. Grieg, 'Håvar Giboens draum ved Oterholtsbrua', op. 72/13

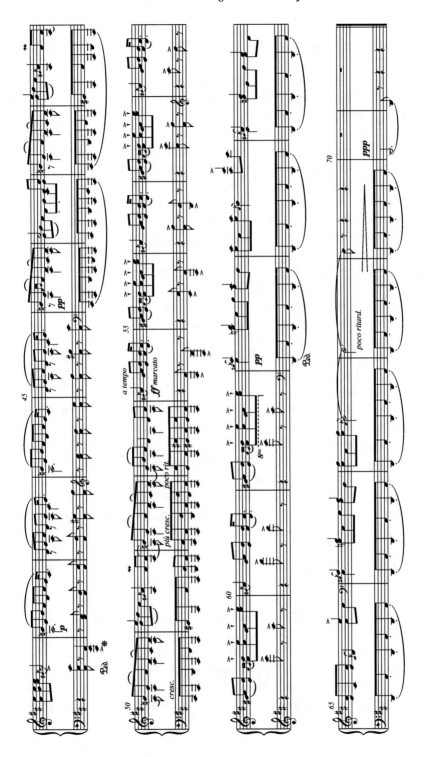

analysis that he calls 'budding', named for a process developed by the mid-twentieth century Norwegian composer Harald Sæverud, to illustrate how Grieg permutates thematic cells in the opening bars of op. 72/13. A similar approach is also advocated by Peer Findeisen.[50] Ex. 4.4 presents an analysis of the thematic structure of the first phrase based on these models. The opening two bars function simply as a rhythmic introduction that initiates the basic accentual pattern of the dance (minim–crotchet or long–short) and creates the momentum that the right hand 'kicks' against. Grieg therefore creates a small-scale rhythmic counterpoint between the two hands that prefigures some of the more complex rhythmic permutation later in the piece. The motivic cell presented in bars 3–4 is little more than a decorated three-note descent with a piquant Lydian appoggiatura: an example of the 'fixed' modal variance in Grieg's arrangements discussed above. Throughout op. 72, this Lydian inflection functions as a *hyperconsonance*, a nominally dissonant note that through reiteration becomes consonant and ultimately serves to heighten the consonant (in this case 'sharp-side') effect. This two bar unit is subsequently repeated three times, to create a four-unit block that is underpinned by a descending tetrachord in the left hand. The purpose of this bass line, as in op. 17/1, is to generate linear momentum. To this end it is accompanied by a dynamic rise from *piano* to *forte*, that anticipates the dynamic shape of the whole *slått*. As we shall see, it is this dynamic rise that motivates the sudden explosion of energy in the second phrase.

Bar 11 (marked by a double barline in Halvorsen's transcription) begins as though it is to be a varied second strophe. Grieg marks a change of dynamic level back to *piano* (though no such indication is marked by Halvorsen), and, crucially, a change of articulation. As Ex. 4.4 shows, the opening motivic cell is altered so that a reconfigured version of the four-quaver figure in the first bar is transferred to the end of the second, and the triplet figure begins to sound more like an anacrusis. Bar 16 is disruptive precisely because it cuts across the pattern of four two-bar units that bars 3–10 had apparently established. The motivic cell is reworked again so that the triplet figure really does begin to function as an anacrusis, creating the momentary impression of a downbeat on the second beat of each bar. The change of rhythmic articulation (the appearance of dotted figuration) noted by Halvorsen in bar 19 suggests a gradual heightening of musical intensity, similar to that in 'Jon Vestafes Springdans'. Bar 23 subsequently marks a point of relative relaxation, reinforced by the rich arpeggiated figuration in the left hand. Though bars 23–4 obviously refer back closely to the opening motivic cell, they also reorder the two-bar unit, so as to suggest a greater sense of forward progression. Bar 27 is in some senses even closer to the

---

[50] Kleiberg, 'Grieg's *Slåtter*', 49–50, and Findeisen, *Instrumentale Folklorestilieserung*, especially 127–8.

Example 4.4. Grieg: 'Håvar Gibøens draum ved Oterholtsbrua',
op. 72/13: thematic 'budding' chart

melodic profile of the opening, but any hint of return is dispelled by the sudden *forte* dynamic (again, a marking that is not indicated in Halvorsen's transcription). Bar 27 also brings the potential metrical conflict between the two hands explicitly into play for the first time so that, as in op. 17/1, the left hand articulates a distinct 2/4 against the 3/4 of the right. This metrical counterpoint is intensified by the sudden stretching of the hypermetre, and the new melodic impulse in bar 33 that *rises* in the dotted rhythm of bar 19.[51] Hitherto, the melodic emphasis has been predominantly upon descent. Bars 33–4 are also metrically important, because they articulate a 4+2/4 metre that cuts across the prevailing triple/duple metrical pattern.[52] This could perhaps be heard as an attempt to resolve the rhythmic conflict of the preceding bars, in which it is only partially successful. The effectiveness of bars 35–8, as well as of the following three-bar unit, is compromised by the thumping left-hand chords on the final beat of bars 38 and 41, which hit the dance's lowest register[53] and threaten to throw the music entirely off balance.

The beginning of the second phrase, bar 42, is marked by a return to the dynamic level of the first, and an extended version of the opening motivic cell, which, as Ex. 4.4 shows, falls from g♮ to c♯. However, by far the most important thematic impulse in the second phrase is the rising bass line, heard in syncopated contrary motion with the right hand from bar 42 onwards. The rising bass figure is in fact an augmentation of the prominent quaver ascent in bar 39, and is the first example of genuinely thematic left-hand behaviour in the dance. From here on, the left hand is significant because it has an insistently cumulative dynamic effect, despite the temporary drop to *pianissimo* in bar 46, which is dramatically reinforced by the octave doubling in bars 51–3. So great is the impact of this figure, in fact, that it succeeds in changing the whole nature of the dance from a thematically defined structure to a registrally defined one, whose logical endpoint is the *fortissimo marcato* section beginning at bar 54. This climax is in many senses the most obviously 'inauthentic' passage in the whole dance, Grieg's point of furthest departure from the Hardanger-fiddle original as transcribed by Halvorsen. The registral leaps, covering virtually the whole range of the modern instrument from D1 to e⁴ (a distance of over six octaves), far exceed the range of a fiddle. Though such widely spaced textures are hardly uncommon in nineteenth-century piano music, in the context of this particular work the climax can certainly be heard as an

---

[51] Indeed, it might be possible to hear bar 33 as a free inversion of bar 19.

[52] The basis for my reading is a comparison of the harmonic movement in bars 35–8 and 39–41, with the melodic contours of each unit and the placement of Grieg's accents. Though by no means definitive, this seems like the best analysis given the parameters set up by the rest of the dance.

[53] The actual lowest note is the D1 in bar 54 that launches the spectacular registral leaps of the *marcato* section.

exceptional event. At the same time, however, bars 54–61 are also the most 'authentic' passage in the dance, since they are easily the most dissonant, the most physical and the most metrically lop-sided music in the piece, precisely those characteristics that Grieg himself had identified as defining features of the Hardanger repertoire. What makes bars 54–61 special is that the whole passage, in terms of dynamics, articulation, register and pitch content, seems to designed to intensify, and revel in, the music's apparent primitivism. The climax, like the closing bars of 'Jon Vestafes Springdans', reveal the dance in its rawest state. They also define the dance's outer structural limits: beyond the stratospheric leap in bar 61, there is nowhere for the pianist left to go, except off the end of the keyboard. The postlude is then heard simply as a 'warming down' after such exertion, complete with residues of earlier boisterousness such as the accented final beats of each two-bar unit (a detail that is also recorded by Halvorsen). Closer examination suggests that the postlude is also motivated structurally, since it is a symmetrical registral gesture that mirrors the ascent of the previous bars, much as bars 33–4 had mirrored (in less dramatic fashion) the descending melodic contour of bars 31–2. Just as the dance had risen through four different registers in bars 54–61, so the postlude sinks through three, content to leave the final bass tessitura untouched. To emphasise this sense of balance and resolution, the left-hand ostinato becomes a deliberately unaccented metrical layer that liquidates the irregularity of the previous music. The very final two bars echo the first, but ameliorate rather than catalyse the momentum of the music. Closure is achieved not so much through harmonic or motivic means, as through sheer physical enervation.

The most spectacular feature of 'Håvar Gibøens Draum ved Oterholtsbrua' is undoubtedly the leaping passage in bars 54–61. It is here, perhaps literally, that we rediscover the dance steps that Grieg's piano arrangements had supposedly left behind (a *springar* is, after all, a 'leaping dance', and a suitably lively performance of op. 72/13 should be equally spectacular in its own fashion). But here is also the crux of the syntactical conflict that underlies op. 72. We hear bars 54–61 as dissonant, since the formal shape of the dance suggests an intensification–release trajectory almost in the manner of conventional diatonic practice. Simultaneously, however, bars 54–61 are also the most consonant part of the whole dance, since they are the closest Grieg comes to the spirit, if not the letter, of his folk 'original'. The function of these bars is therefore contradictory: dissonant on the one hand, and consonant on the other.

The binary oppositions that underpin op. 72/13 are intensified in one of the largest and most complex dances in the set, 'Knut Luråsens Halling II', op. 72/11 (Ex. 4.5). This dance articulates two large-scale formal shapes.

Example 4.5. Grieg: 'Knut Luråsens halling II', op. 72/11

The first is the dynamic, metrical and registral arch, which, like op. 72/13, begins in a state of relative repose, reaches a point of maximum volume, registral span and metrical complexity in bars 49–53, and then gradually returns to the relatively quiet and registrally restricted state of the opening. The second formal shape is the clear strophic structure, articulated by tempo and thematic shape, which divides the piece in three at bars 24 and 54. This fundamental formal dualism is echoed by the metrical conflict that runs throughout the entire dance, and which arguably constitutes its primary structural parameter.

The single opening introductory bar establishes the dance's basic duple pulse. As in op. 72/13, the dance begins with a simple melodic idea that serves as a motivic cell (bars 2–3). In this case, it consists of a graceful arch, supported by dynamic hairpins (again not indicated in Halvorsen's transcription), that models in miniature the dynamic shape of the whole dance. However, the melody as notated by Halvorsen also opens up register as a potential field of musical play via the octave transposition of the initial a^1; the structural high point of the melodic curve (a^2) is decorated by both upper and lower auxiliaries and an accented mordent figure (here Grieg alters Halvorsen's notation, where no such accent is indicated on this beat). More important for the long-term development of the dance than the thematic contour, however, is the metrical shape of the two-bar unit, which articulates a bar of 3/4 against the duple beat of the accompaniment, followed by a bar of 6/8 where the hands move more smoothly together.[54] The first change in this pattern of metrical alternation takes place at bar 18, over midway through the first strophe. The articulation, supported by both the raised dynamic level and the expression marking *scherzando*, engenders the first change in accompanimental figuration. More important, however, is that the music articulates a definitive 3/4, as though seeking to regularise the instability of the opening bars. The resolutory effect of bar 18 is compromised, however, first by the syncopation in bar 19, as though the two hands are genuinely unable to play in time together, and then dramatically by the 3/8 bar in bar 20. This is the first interruption in the series of stable two-bar units that had apparently been established at the outset. It is also the most severe metrical 'jolt' to have shaken the dance. Grieg's placement of a *fortepiano* accent on the final beat of bar 19 creates the feeling of a 4/8 bar, despite Halvorsen's bar line, so that the complete three-bar unit in bars 18–20 is in effect a telescoped 3/4–5/8–4/8 structure that hurries towards the leap at the beginning of bar 21. The metrical effect is varied again upon the

---

[54] At this stage, the rhythmic effect probably sounds like a syncopation. However, in the context of the dance as a whole, in which there is genuinely a sense of different metrical lines running concurrently at places such as bars 45–53, it seems reasonable to hear the opening bars as an embryonic version of later metrical conflict.

repetition of this three-bar unit, since the final beat of bar 23 functions as an anacrusis that leads smoothly into the beginning of the second strophe.

The second strophe begins with a texturally filled-out version of the opening, and is both a point of relative musical relaxation and an intensification. The leaping fifths in the left hand, for example, prefigure the more athletic accompanimental figuration to come, and locally strengthen the 6/8–3/4 conflict in bar 24. Indeed, the potential dynamism of the second strophe is swiftly realised by the dynamic surge in bar 26. Following the convention of the first strophe, bar 26 should have been a straightforward variation of bars 24–5, but instead it quickly becomes the beginning of a new 2½ bar unit. This is reminiscent of the earlier metrical jolt at bars 18–20 but, in Grieg's arrangement, it has greater disruptive effect. The leaping fifths in the left hand, for example, introduced unassumingly in bar 24, assert their strident 3/4 metre with a seemingly new-found energy. Accordingly, the sudden drop to *pianissimo* in bar 32 is the most drastic dynamic change so far in the dance, and begins the ascent to the central climax of the dance. The melody's compass is reduced from over an octave to barely a fourth, but Grieg brings a number of new factors into play in bar 32, most crucially the 2/4 octave leaps in the left hand. Bar 32 also initiates a broad nine-bar melodic unit, 2+2+2+3 bars, that, in Grieg's arrangement rises to *fortissimo* just as the music slips momentarily back into the 6/8 of the opening.

Within the formal context of the second strophe, bars 41–4 can be understood as a tranquil window, a brief respite before the onslaught of the central climax. But they are also one of the most magical moments in the whole of op. 72. Halvorsen's transcription provides an initial impetus: the drop to piano is followed by a fortissimo marking in the next phrase (an unusually wide dynamic range). For Grieg this means that, for virtually the first time in the piece, the two hands work together co-operatively as a duet: the upper parts articulate a clear 3/4+6/8 metre, while the syncopated first bar of the bass acts a reminder of the growing rhythmic complexity that has dominated the progress of the dance. To mark this brief sense of metrical consonance, Grieg brings the tiny mordent on the very last beat of each second bar into the very heart of the keyboard texture. However, the sense of intimacy conveyed by bars 41–4 is swept away by the central climax, which consists of two four-bar blocks, rising from *forte animato* to *fortissimo feroce* in bar 49. The motivic cell from the opening is here relegated to an inner part, covered by an inverted pedal in the right hand and almost swamped by the dramatic swinging seventh-clusters in the left. Though the central climax is an exceptional textural event, its most striking characteristic is its systematic rhythmic complexity, which surpasses anything in the second or thirteenth dances, or indeed elsewhere in the set. The left hand articulates a martial syncopated 2/4, which had been planted as early as bar 32. The inner parts in the right hand follow the pattern set up in the previous four bars, and articulate 3/4+6/8. The placing of the accents in the inverted pedal, however, suggest something much broader: the minim tread of 3/2, so that each bar in the top of the right hand coincides with every two bars in the lower parts. Consequently, there are at least four different metrical streams running concurrently through bars 45–53 (Ex. 4.6). The result is a *polymetric stratification* of a kind more readily associated with later modernist figures such as Stravinsky. As noted above, Kleiberg presents this passage as a prototypical example of Grieg modelling the distinctive sound of the Hardanger fiddle's sympathetic strings. But bars 45–53 can equally be heard another way, as serving a more strictly structural purpose whose function is ultimately far removed from any literal sense of authenticity.

Example 4.6. Grieg: 'Knut Luråsens halling II', op. 72/11, bb. 45 to 52, simplified metrical structure

As with bars 54–61 in 'Håvar Gibøens Draum ved Oterholtsbrua', the central climax in 'Knut Luråsens Halling II' creates a point of no-return. Consequently, bar 53 leads both registrally and metrically back to the *dolce tranquillo* beginning of the third strophe, a gesture which explicitly recalls the earlier moment of transition in bar 23 (and which is suggested in Halvorsen's transcription by a return to a *piano* dynamic level). The third strophe also begins to reimpose the normative pattern of two-bar units plus two-bar echoes, but, as in op. 72/13, the music still maintains residues of earlier disruptive gestures. The intrusion of an elided 3/8 bar at bar 61, so that bars 58–63 consist of two three-bar units welded together by the second half of bar 60, takes place at just the point where the first strophe had also broken away at bar 18, a detail in Halvorsen's notation which gains added significance in Grieg's arrangement. The retrospective feel of the third strophe is intensified by the intrusion of C♮s from bar 63 onwards. Though the modal variance of the fourth scale degree is relatively common in op. 72, as noted previously, a modally altered seventh degree is much more exceptional. In the context of Grieg's arrangements, if not the fiddle dances themselves, the C♮s constitute a striking 'blue note'. One speculative possibility is that Grieg simply misread Halvorsen's transcription of the dance at this point (though he seems to have understood the notation perfectly well elsewhere). As Grieg had instructed, Halvorsen had transcribed the music with a *scordatura* indicated at the top of the page, so that the notes played on the bottom string of the violin sound a tone higher. In this case, the notated c♮¹ would sound d¹, a reading which Johannes Dahle's recorded version of the *slått* confirms. As Nyhus and others have suggested, it could equally well be argued that Grieg's C♮s represent a response to the variable tuning characteristic of the Hardanger repertoire, in which notes at the lower end of the violin's range tend to be played slightly flatter than those higher up the instrument. On balance, however, it is hard not to hear this sudden flat-side inflection, in the context of the *Slåtter*'s harmonic language, as a further remnant of diatonic tonal procedure. This reading seems especially convincing since the figuration, from bar 68 onwards, may also have suggested distant horn calls, one of the most poignant syntactical devices in diatonic music. Even given the radical metrical language of the dance, Grieg appears to have been thinking diatonically, such a flatside step is necessary after the excessive sharpness of the preceding music. The C♮s also point to the underlying tension between tonal and other forms of organisation that underpin the set, a conflict which persists until the sforzando suspension in the prepenultimate bar. The final word, however, is given to metre and register. The postlude perpetuates the rocking left-hand figure from bar 64, ameliorating the metrical conflict of the previous bars. As in 'Håvar Gibøens Draum ved Oterholtsbrua', the right hand gathers together the registral space of the dance by descending through each tessitura in turn. The accents over Halvorsen's slurs in the bar 76 create a dragging 3/4 in the right hand against a static chordal accompaniment, but the final bar itself seems to settle on 6/8, and the dance eventually winds down and achieves closure with a satisfying sense of symmetrical balance.

In an important essay entitled 'What is Folk Music?' in the collection *Fanitullen* edited by Nyhus and Bjørn Aksdal,[55] Jan-Petter Blom has provided an insightful summary of the development of nationalism, Norwegian folk music and regional identity in both a local and a wider international context. Blom argues for the importance of a Nordic nationalist movement (*Norskdomsbevegelsen*) that, 'in distinction from the urban national Romanticism, was a cultural-political force with support in rural milieux. Grundtvigianism and the Free Youth Movement were also characterised by the same thoughts, but saw national culture more as a means towards the liberation of the individual.'[56] For Blom, this tension between urban

---

[55] Jan-Petter Blom, 'Hva er folkemusikk?', in Bjørn Aksdal and Sven Nyhus (eds), *Fanitullen: innføring i norsk og samisk folkemusikk* (Oslo: Universitetsforlaget, 1993), 7–14.
[56] 'Norskdomsbevegelsen ble til forskjell fra den borgelige nasjonalromantikken, en kulturpolitisk

and rural contexts, and collective and individual identities, is basic to an understanding of the formation of a Norwegian musical identity. Indeed, in many senses it maps directly onto the broader models of nationalism proposed by historians such as Anderson, Smith and Hutchinson discussed in Chapter 1 above. Blom continues:

> The folk musicians' movement that seriously took off in the 1920s adopted the Nordic movement's world-view and the scholarly understanding of folk music's unique national character. Expressions such as 'the national music' and 'the national performance' were therefore useful at this time.
>
> After the war the national project receded further and further into the background in place of a regionalism that emphasised the local and regional characteristics in the traditional material. In the folk-music milieu they therefore spoke often of 'dialects' in connection with local characteristics in music and dance.[57]

Blom's analysis provides a useful model for understanding and interpreting the genesis and critical reception of Grieg's *Slåtter*. Grieg himself acknowledged a tension between different musical cultures, the mainstream Austro-German tradition of which he was essentially a product, and the local Norwegian folk tradition to which he felt he more properly 'belonged', in an interview in the conservative Leipzig magazine *Signale für die musikalische Welt* in 1907:

> I was educated in the German school. I have studied in Leipzig and musically speaking am completely German. But then I went to Copenhagen and got acquainted with Gade and Hartmann. It then struck me that I could only develop myself further on a national foundation. It was our Norwegian folk tunes which showed me the way.[58]

Blom stresses that, 'in all modern societies, the concept of folk music appears to be connected to historically rooted values such as traditionalism and local or ethnic/national identity. These values say something about what is being controlled and by whom.'[59] Such questions of ownership and identity are

kraft med støtte i bygdemiljøene. Gruntvigianismen og den 'frilynte ungdomsbevegelsen' var også preget av de samme tankene, men så den nasjonale kulturen mer som middel til frigjøringen av individet.' Ibid., 12–13.

[57] 'Spelemannsbevegelsen som for alvor tok av i 1920-årene, adopterte norskdomsbevegelsens verdisyn og forskernes oppfatning av folkemusikkens unike nasjonale karakter. Uttryk som 'den nasjonale musikken' og 'det nasjonale spelet' var derfor vanlige på denne tiden.

I efterkrigsårene har det nasjonale prosjektet mer og mer kommet i bakgrunnen til fordel for en regionalisme som betoner de lokale og regionale særdrag i tradisjonsmaterialet. I folkemusikmiljøet snakkes det derfor ofte om 'dialekter' i forbindelser med lokale særdrag i musikk og dans.' Ibid.

[58] Quoted in Benestad and Schjelderup-Ebbe, *Edvard Grieg*, 334.

[59] 'I alle moderne samfunn synes folkemusikkbegrepet å være knyttet til historisk forankrede verdier som tradisjonalitet og lokal eller etnisk/nasjonal identitet. Disse verdiene sier noe om hva som skal kontrolleres og av hvem.' Blom, 'Hva er folkemusikk?', 14.

fundamental to any musical evocation of place. But Blom's account only tells part of the story since, as closer reading has suggested, the conflict between these different musical worlds also forms a compelling structural narrative within Grieg's music. Hence, the sense of place evoked by op. 72 need not necessarily correspond with an actual location but can be understood as an abstract formal idea or proposition, a meeting point of particular musical parameters or patterns (rhythmic, metrical, motivic, dynamic or registral). Questions of authenticity are therefore ultimately subordinate to, or at least run in parallel with, the sense of dialogue between different levels of musical experience that the *Slåtter* articulate. Unravelling the various strands of musical thought bound up in op. 72 has ensured that the collection continues to provoke and sustain a striking degree of controversy. In the process, the set remains one of Grieg's most challenging and influential works, creating a critical musical legacy that the following chapter will consider.

CHAPTER FIVE

Distant Landscapes:
The Influence of Grieg's Folk-Music Arrangements

The critical controversy that continues to surround the musical status and cultural value of Grieg's *Slåtter* underlines the extent to which his folk-music arrangements resist easy interpretative containment. In spite of the music's energetic emphasis on achieving a sense of structural unity and symmetry (often of an innovative formal kind involving metrical and rhythmic elements alongside more conventionally diatonic means), many of the numbers from both op. 66 and op. 72 can also be heard as open or unstable. They articulate different and sometimes opposed musical discourses: urban, rural, local, cosmopolitan, modernist, nostalgic and retrospective. It is the tension between these competing musical styles or voices that, previous chapters have argued, points towards their relationship with the idea of landscape. The simultaneous creation or evocation of various levels of temporal or spatial organisation within a given framework that the music suggests results in the perception of multiple figures and ground. The music operates discursively within such parameters. Furthermore, the manner in which it negotiates these different levels of perception implies a deeper, more abstract, notion of landscape than purely visual means of representation would normally suggest.

This emphasis on musical depth, openness and complexity is not intended simply to displace one set of analytical paradigms and substitute it with another. Critical discourses of fragmentation and disunity are no less ideological than those of symmetry or balance, though they might at first seem to serve different interpretative purposes. Rather, the aim is to stress that Grieg's folk-song arrangements are not as straightforward as they can immediately appear, and that they support and demand some level of analytical engagement in order to be understood fully. One way in which this critical reappraisal can be achieved is to consider their compositional influence on music written after Grieg's death in 1907. Though the folk-music arrangements have never established the same kind of popularity in the concert hall as that enjoyed by Grieg's Piano Concerto or the *Peer Gynt* suites, close examination suggests that they have nevertheless had a significant impact on twentieth-century music. Regrettably, in this final chapter, there is only space to consider two individual case studies: David Monrad Johansen, best known outside Norway for his biography of Grieg but a substantial composer in his own right, and Percy Grainger, whose well-known assocation with Grieg during the final years of Grieg's life provided him with a particularly close insight into Grieg's music, most notably the *Slåtter*. Though a comprehensive account of Grieg's musical influence requires a full-length study (and is therefore beyond the limits of the current project), brief discussion of Grainger and Monrad Johansen serves to illustrate some of the strategies composers developed in order to process and assimilate Grieg's work. In addition, it introduces the historical contexts in which Grieg's folk-music arrangements were subsequently played and understood, the implications of which, as the example of op. 72 suggests, continue to dominate the critical reception of Grieg's work.

A series of important musicological discussions in the early 1990s, conducted in the context of a broader disciplinary re-evaluation of historical and analytical methodology, argued that musical influence is both a positive and a negative phenomenon.[1] It can catalyse or inspire composers, or inhibit and restrict them. In practice, influence usually needs to be understood as a complex mix of the two: it is rarely solely positive or negative in effect, but is rather an unstable creative dynamic. Kevin Korsyn is one of the leading scholars to have adopted this more multivalent view of musical influence.[2] For Korsyn, the question of musical influence is allied to a broader concern with 'analysing pieces as "relational events" rather than "closed and static entities"'.[3] This task is motivated not merely by a desire to reflect the performative character of musical works, but also by a commitment to an intertextual view of music history. This in turn poses particular challenges to the conceptual basis for writing a history of musical influence. As Carl Dahlhaus has argued, 'music history either fails as history by being a

---

[1] In addition to the essays by Kevin Korsyn noted, below, relevant discussions include Joseph N. Straus, *Remaking the Past: Musical Modernism and the Influence of the Tonal Tradition* (Cambridge, Mass.: Harvard University Press, 1990); Richard Taruskin's review article of Korsyn's essay and Straus's book in the *Journal of the American Musicological Society* 46/1 (Spring 1993), 114–38; Lloyd Whitesell's 'Men with a Past: Music and the "Anxiety of Influence"', *Nineteenth-Century Music* 18/2 (Fall 1994), 152–67; and Robert Knapp, 'Brahms and the Anxiety of Allusion', *Journal of Musicological Research* 18/1 (1998), 1–30.

[2] The two principal essays discussed here are 'Towards a New Poetics of Musical Influence', *Music Analysis* 10/1–2 (1991), 3–73, and 'Beyond Privileged Contexts: Intertextuality, Influence and Dialogue', in *Rethinking Music*, ed. Nicholas Cook and Mark Everist (London: Oxford University Press, 1999), 55–72. See also Korsyn's discussion of Brahms scholarship, 'Brahms Research and Aesthetic Ideology', *Music Analysis* 12/1 (1993), 89–103, and Martin Scherzinger's review, 'The "New Poetics" of Musical Influence: A Response to Kevin Korsyn', *Music Analysis* 13/2–3 (1994), 298–309.

[3] Korsyn, 'Towards a New Poetics', 3.

collection of structural analyses of separate works, or as a history of art by reverting from musical works to occurrences in social or intellectual history cobbled together in order to impart cohesion to an historical narrative'. The potential difficulty with music history, Dahlhaus explains, is that 'on the one side it is flanked by the dictates of "aesthetic autonomy", on the other by a theory of history that clings to the concept of "continuity"'.[4] Influence cannot therefore be understood simply as a process of transference or borrowing from one work to another, and from one composer to another, in strict chronological sequence, since the appearance of discrete musical works upon which such a view relies is, as Dahlhaus suggests, ultimately illusory. Influence, once it is conceived within an intertextual context, becomes a more discursive process.

In an attempt to address such concerns over the nature of musical influence in an intertextual domain, Korsyn turns to the work of a literary theorist, Harold Bloom, in search of a critical model that offers the possibility of combining close reading with a more fluid, discontinuous view of historical process. Bloom's work has now been so widely adopted in musicology that it scarcely needs introduction, though its application remains controversial given the strongly canonic thrust of Bloom's writing. As Korsyn summarises,

> Bloom replaces the mimetic view of influence with a new notion of 'antithetical influence', conceiving influence as 'discontinuous relations between past and present literary texts'. Influence becomes something poets actively resist, rather than something they passively receive, and poetry becomes a pyschic battlefield, an Oedipal struggle against one's own poetic fathers, in which poems seek to repress and exclude other poems.[5]

In other words, influence becomes a state of anxiety, an urge to clear creative space, the response to a sense of inherited tradition that appears to permit no room for individual expression. Though this model might appear to place the notion of authorial intention problematically at the centre of historical interpretation, such fears are surely allayed by the discursive nature of musical works themselves. Just as the idea of a closed, discrete musical work is no longer sustainable, the authorial figure of the composer cannot remain a privileged category. Hence, Korsyn glosses Bloom's theory by stating that 'the meaning of a composition can only be another composition, a composition not itself, and *not* the meaning of the other piece, but the otherness of the other piece, manifested not only through the presence of

---

[4] Carl Dahlhaus, *Foundations of Music History*, trans. J. Bradford Robinson (Cambridge: Cambridge University Press, 1983), 19–20.
[5] Korsyn, 'Towards a New Poetics', 8.

the precursor-piece, but also through the precise figuration of its absence'.[6] Bloom's various categories of 'misreading', through which he models such processes of antithetical influence, therefore constitute an analytical tool in the broadest sense, not merely a means of tracing compositional genesis or intention but a wider theory of musical rhetoric.

Two of Bloom's categories, as summarised by Korsyn, seem particularly relevant for the music discussed in this chapter. The category of *tessera*, or antithetical completion, describes David Monrad Johansen's relationship with Grieg, while that of *apophrades*, or transumption, is more appropriate to Percy Grainger. But Bloom's theory potentially also offers an additional perspective on the broader formation of a national musical style. The idea of national identity itself could be conceived as a state of anxiety, an Oedipal struggle for independence and self-determination allied to the fear of abandonment or annihilation by external forces (imaginary or real). Hence the tension between cultural and political forms of nationalism, and between mainstream and peripheral national discourses, identified by writers such as John Hutchinson (Chapter 1), assumes a more anxious edge. Korsyn suggests that, according to Bloom, 'the poet's preoccupation with selfhood is the anxiety that his precursors have not left him room to become a self, to speak with his own poetic voice. Self-conciousness manifests itself as text-consciousness, because "the poet's conception of himself necessarily is his poem's conception of itself".'[7] This model is also potentially applicable at a higher level to certain forms of nationhood. The promotion of the idea of a national musical style, as a cultural nationalist project in Norway at the end of the nineteenth century, can be seen as an assertion of otherness or difference in antithetical dialogue with another larger 'parent' tradition (whether Danish, German or more broadly European). 'Text-consciousness', in Korsyn's definition, becomes equivalent to a form of national consciousness. Bloom's categories of misreading, when applied to individual composers or more generally to the notion of a Norwegian musical style, can therefore represent strategies for promoting both a sense of collective identity and an acute awareness of creative individuality. It thus points to both a larger context (Norway's relationship with a European musical tradition), and to the more localised level of individual influence, a dialogue that ultimately underpins many nationalist discourses.

The 'lone evening star': Grieg's influence on David Monrad Johansen

These tensions, between collective and individual modes of musical utterance, and the antithetical relationship with a sense of inherited tradition, are

---

[6] Ibid., 14.
[7] Ibid., 7.

fundamental to the work of David Monrad Johansen. Monrad Johansen's writings from the 1920s and 1930s, during which time he was music critic for the national newspaper *Aftenposten*, repeatedly centre on the topic of Norwegian musical development. As Ståle Kleiberg has explained, Monrad Johansen's definition of Norwegian cultural identity was strongly influenced by the work of Arne Garborg, whose views on the interrelationship between music, language and political self-determination were discussed in Chapter 3.[8] Garborg defined nationalism not in terms of physical geographical boundaries, but in terms of a sense of collective cultural identification that found its most natural expression in language.[9] For Garborg, as we have seen, the formation of a synthesised Norwegian language (*nynorsk*) from various rural dialect forms, as opposed to the Danish-Norwegian language of the urban middle-classes, was fundamental to the articulation of this collective Norwegian identity. Like Garborg, Monrad Johansen believed that Norway had been oppressed by Danish occupation. He saw national culture properly as a form of *Heimatkunst*, and only through the formation of a distinctively Norwegian musical style could Norway achieve full political self-determination. Failure to do so would result in a musical equivalent of what Garborg described as self-translation (*selvoversettelse*), a form of self-imposed oppression. Like Garborg's argument for *landsmål*, this Norwegian musical style must in turn be based on the individual qualities of the Norwegian language, landscape and topography in order to be authentic. Hence, in article on Norwegian musical history from 1936, Monrad Johansen proclaimed:

> Though we had won our political independence in 1814 [through liberation from Danish rule], we had to lead a bitter fight for the next hundred years in order to be able to enjoy the fruits of it. But this led towards another battle for self-determination, another battle for freedom, which concerned perhaps equally great values, and that was the people's cultural liberation. It was the battle to create a national culture sprung from the people's own culture and built upon it, such as we can observe in every healthy and vigorous nation.[10]

[8] Ståle Kleiberg, 'David Monrad Johansens musikksyn i mellomkrigstida, sett i lys av Arne Garborgs nasjonalitetsbegrep', *Studia Musicologica Norvegica* 10 (1984), 143–53, and 'Following Grieg: David Monrad Johansen's Musical Style in the Early Twenties, and His Concept of a National Music', in *Musical Constructions of Nationalism: Essays on the History and Ideology of European Musical Culture, 1800–1945*, ed. Harry White and Michael Murphy (Cork: Cork University Press, 2001), 142–62.

[9] Kleiberg, 'David Monrad Johansens musikksyn', 144.

[10] 'Vi hadde i 1814 vunnet vår politiske selvstendighet, den vi forresten i nesten hundre år ennu måtte føre en forbitret kamp for helt å kunne nyte fruktene av. Men det gjensto en annen selvstendighetskamp, en annen frihetskamp som gjalt kanskje vel så store verdier, og det var folkets kulturelle frigjørelse. Det var kampen for å skape en rikskultur utsprunget av folkets egen kultur og bygget på denne, slik vi kan iakkta det i enhver sunn og levedyktig nasjon.' 'Trekk av den norske musikks historie', *Allers Familie Journal*, 47 (21 November 1936), reproduced in Bjarne Kortsen (ed.),

Kleiberg notes that, as for Garborg, Monrad Johansen did not see the national and the international as necessarily opposed. Rather, he held out an optimistic vision of Norway taking its rightful place as an independent, culturally self-determined nation among a fellow community of nations.[11] Cultural independence, Monrad Johansen believed, was the natural condition of the nation state. Kleiberg sees Monrad Johansen's philosophical world-view therefore as being at odds with his later political decision to support the Quisling government during the German occupation of Norway in the Second World War. From an outside perspective, Monrad Johansen's position certainly seems strange given his apparent commitment to the idea of mutual international understanding and respect. But Monrad Johansen's vision of cultural independence also reveals a more anxious and double-edged character, as Bloom's model of influence suggests. Though he held out the possibility of creative liberation, Monrad Johansen's notion of collective national identity was as much exclusive as inclusive. Furthermore, metaphors of landscape, language and cultural purity inevitably assumed a far darker significance in the 1930s than they had done for Garborg in 1877 or Walter Niemann in 1908. In an article entitled 'Nordic Music at the Cross Roads' written for *Aftenposten* in 1936, Monrad Johansen asks:

> Should we perhaps follow in the footsteps of the painters and the poets and appoint geniuses both in the east and the west? No, the question is too serious for that, Nordic music carries too many obligations for that.
>
> But it cannot be denied that a dark cloud broods over the Nordic lands today. An attentive glance can surely discern a lightening here and there, but only farthest in the north, across the land with the desolate forests and the thousand lakes, sparkles a lone evening star in striking brilliance. May it be followed by many! May we soon set eyes upon the dawning morning star that heralds the day and inspires deeds and work![12]

Kleiberg suggests that what motivated Monrad Johansen's pessimistic attitude was a strongly anti-establishment aesthetic, a reaction to what he perceived as the negative chauvinistic trends in continental European music.[13]

Musikkritikeren og skribenten David Monrad Johansen (Bergen: Bjarne Kortsen, 1979), 2–12, here 3.

[11] Kleiberg, 'David Monrad Johansens musikksyn', 146.

[12] 'Vil man kanskje at vi skal følge i malernes og dikternes fotspor og utnevne genier både i øst og vest? Nei, dertil er spørsmålet for alvorlig, dertil innebærer nordisk tonekunst for store forpliktelser. Men der ruger mørke over de nordiske land idag, det står ikke til å nekte. En opmerksom iakttager kan visstnok hist og her øine en lysning, men bare lengst i nord, over landet med de øde skoger og de tusen sjøer funkler en ensom aftenstjerne i betagende glans. Måtte den følges av flere! Måtte vi snart få øie på den demrende morgenstjerne som bebuder dagen og maner til dåd og arbeide!' 'Nordisk Musikk på Skilleveien', *Aftenposten*, 27 October 1936, reproduced in Kortsen, *Musikkritikeren*, 154–7, here 157.

[13] Kleiberg, 'David Monrad Johansens musikksyn', 150.

His argument was therefore directed towards a sense of national renewal, rather that simply reversal or regression. But it is tempting to interpret his defensiveness additionally as in some senses a Bloomian anxiety, the creative fear of individual self-censure or oppression elevated to the level of collective national discourse.

Like Garborg, Monrad Johansen believed that a true Norwegian identity should be formed on the basis of its folk culture. Indeed, Monrad Johansen clung to an early-nineteenth-century Romantic view that 'the difference between art music and folk music lies in proportion, it is one of degree, not of kind, the one is an organic development of the other'.[14] In an earlier essay entitled 'National Values in Our Music' (1924), he had attempted to identify the fundamental elements of Norwegian folk music, much as Garborg and others had done for the dialect language, which could form the basis for the Norwegian art music of the future.[15] Like earlier nineteenth-century folklorists, Monrad Johansen pointed to the music's modal instability as its most pervasive feature, describing the raised (Lydian) fourth as 'the most characteristic expression of Norwegian temperament, Norwegian feeling'.[16] He also drew attention to the prominence of the perfect fifth, and the music's rhythmic liveliness and its 'resistance to regularity, the schematic and a reckless desire for freedom'.[17] It was these qualities which Monrad Johansen perceived not only in folk music, but also in the Norwegian national character and topography. To him they suggested something ancient: the medieval literature of the sagas, whose 'clarity and precision' ('klarhet og knapphet') he admired in the work of truly Nordic composers such as Grieg and Christian Sinding. This he believed was the standard by which all Norwegian art music should be judged.[18] Grieg was therefore a central figure for Monrad Johansen, since Grieg was the creative father figure who had succeeding in assimilating these authentic folk-music qualities into his compositional style for the first time. In his Grieg biography of 1934, Monrad Johansen wrote:

> He has awakened in Norwegians the consciousness that as a
> nation they too are capable of creating for themselves a strong,
> clear-cut individuality. He has set in motion forces which will
> not easily be checked. He has stimulated the flow of blood in

[14] 'Forksjellen mellem kunstmusikk og folkemusikk ligger i *graden*, det er en gradsforskell, men ingen vesensforskjell, det ene er en organisk utvikling av det annet.' 'Trekk av den norske musikks historie', 2.

[15] 'Nasjonale Verdier i vår Musikk', first read as a lecture held at the Kristiania Musikklærerforening, 22 May 1924 and the Musikklærernes Landsmøte, 4 July 1924 and published in *Aftenposten*, 5–9 July 1924; reproduced in Kortsen, *Musikkritikeren*, 33–46.

[16] 'det mest karakteristiske utslag av norsk lynne, norsk følemåte', 'Nasjonale Verdier', 36.

[17] 'en uvilje mot det regelrette, det skematiske og en hensynsløs trang til frihet', 'Nasjonale Verdier', 40.

[18] 'Nasjonale Verdier', 41.

a people who were sickening because violence had been done to their natural functions. He has made it possible for fresh blood to flow out once more from the heart through their whole organism. This connection with the heart of the people is precisely what was lacking in the Norwegian-Danish culture – that heart of the people which is the fountain of life and the origin of art.

If today these things seem more obvious, more natural, and the real facts of the case are more apparent; if Norwegians feel their hard fate more plainly and therefore find it easier to devise remedies; if the day is perhaps not far off when the Norwegian people will again have conquered their land and will have a national culture which has sprung from a folk culture as in every sound and truly living country, true to Edvard Grieg, is due the deepest gratitude.[19]

Grieg's legacy as the reinvigorator of Norwegian musical culture was in danger of being squandered, Monrad Johansen believed. But, given this weight of critical responsibility, his relationship with Grieg's music, particularly his folk-song arrangements, starts to become increasingly strained and difficult.

Kleiberg examines many of the contradictions in Monrad Johansen's writings, and rightly points to a discrepancy between his music criticism and his compositional practice. Furthermore, Kleiberg also perceives tensions between Garborg's and Monrad Johansen's approaches to the formation of a Norwegian cultural identity. He notes that, for example, 'Garborg's choice of the folk language as the starting point for a written and literary language was a political choice',[20] defined by its immediate historical context, but questions whether Monrad Johansen's decision to promote folk music as the basis for a Norwegian art music was motivated by precisely the same concerns. 'Though he speaks rightly of self-translation in the Garborg sense', Kleiberg suggests, 'what he identifies as typical of Norwegian musical feeling are general musical principles that cannot be regarded as the unique characteristics of Norwegian folk music'.[21] The modal instability, raised fourths and rhythmic character that Monrad Johansen claimed embodied 'Norwegian temperament, Norwegian feeling', were little more than general features of European folk music, whose real significance did not extend beyond their exotic quality. Hence, Kleiberg concludes, 'he does not seek the culture's fundamental utterance like Garborg did with

---

[19] David Monrad Johansen, *Edvard Grieg*, trans. Madge Robertson (New York: Tudor, 1945), 6.
[20] 'Garborgs valg av folkemålet som utgangspunkt for et skrift og litteraturspråk, er et politisk valg.' Kleiberg, 'David Monrad Johansens musikksyn', 147.
[21] 'Han snakker riktignok om selvoversettelse i Garborgsk forstand, men det han peker på som typisk for norsk tonefølelse, er allmene musikalske prinsipper som umulig kan si noe vesentlig om særegenhetene i norsk folkemusikk.' Ibid., 147.

linguistic research'. Rather, 'what Monrad Johansen seeks is a musical language that can become a national symbol'.[22] Though he claimed to be resistant to a process of assimilation or 'Norwegianisation', in which perceived folk characteristics were merely grafted on to a pre-determined art music framework to produce a stylistic hybrid, this was precisely the basis of Monrad Johansen's own compositional practice.

This process of assimilation can be seen as part of Monrad Johansen's engagement with Grieg's compositional legacy. The creation of structural musical discourse that draws on elements of Norwegian folk music, landscape and linguistic character was what Grieg was perceived to have achieved in works such as the *Slåtter*, which Monrad Johansen particularly admired. Nevertheless, Kleiberg maintains that it was only through his encounter with contemporary French music that enabled Monrad Johansen to develop his own individual compositional style. In his analysis of Monrad Johansen's Suite no. 1 for piano, *Nordlandsbilleder* ('Pictures from the Northland'), for example, Kleiberg draws attention to the use of whole tone and octatonic scale collections as structural devices, a technique that Kleiberg argues he derived from Debussy's late piano works such as the *Études* and *En blanc et noir*. If this is the case, it would complete a circular chain of influence: Debussy's enthusiasm for Grieg is well known, despite his grudging review in *Gil Blas* of Grieg's Paris concert in 1903.[23] Furthermore, it is possible to identify direct examples of Griegian syntax in Debussy's own work: compare the opening of the *Holberg Suite* (piano version) with that of 'Gradus ad Parnassum' from *Children's Corner*, for example, or the 'Notturno' ('Nocturne') from the op. 54 *Lyric Pieces* with 'Clair de Lune' from the *Suite Bergamasque*. Whether such references are intentional or not is arguably of lesser importance here than the principle of intertextual allusion that they exemplify. Monrad Johansen's use of Debussyan elements in his own piano works could therefore be reinterpreted as a Bloomian gesture, an antithetical swerve that deconstructs, and ultimately reinforces, his relationship with Grieg's music. In this sense his music can be seen as a form of antithetical completion, the realisation of a supposedly 'unfinished' creative project through an intentional act of discontinuity (turning to Debussy's music as a compositional model), which ultimately seeks to create a sense of new critical space.

A brief analysis of two numbers from the *Prillar-Guri* Suite no. 3, op. 12 (1923), and the first movement from the later *Nordlandske danser*, op.

[22] 'Han søker . . . ikke kulturens basisuttrykk slik Garborg med språkvitenskapelig gjør. Det Monrad Johansen søker, er et tonespråk som kan bli et nasjonalt symbol.' Ibid., 148.
[23] See, for example, Christian Goulbault, 'Grieg et la critique musicale français', in *Grieg et Paris: romantisme, symbolisme et modernisme franco-norvégiens*, ed. Harald Herresthal and Danièle Pistone (Caen: Presses Université de Caen, 1996), 139–49, especially 146–8.

30 (1958), however, reveals ways in which this process of antithetical allusion can work without explicitly referring to Debussy as an alternative compositional starting point. All three pieces illustrate, to varying degrees, Monrad Johansen's application of figures which he regarded as archetypal characteristics of Norwegian folk music: modal instability, a predominance of sharpened fourths and perfect fifths, and a marked rhythmic liveliness (though the music rarely suggests the kind of intense metrical irregularity found in Hardanger-fiddle music). In terms of genre alone, the pieces also invoke Grieg's folk-music arrangements as models. The first movement of the *Prillar-Guri* suite, for example, from which the set takes its name, is clearly indebted to the *Slåtter* (Ex. 5.1). The leaping left-hand figure with its prominent perfect fifths in the opening bars has a similar brutalist quality to the accompaniment in 'Røtnams-Knut Halling', a correspondance strengthened by the music's registral and dynamic intensification (*fortissimo marcato*) in the reprise section from bar 65. The second part of the opening phrase (bars 9–17) is a linear descending idea whose purpose is principally to generate momentum, a voice-leading device also exploited by Grieg in many of his arrangements (compare, for example, bars 23–9 in 'Jon Vestafes Springdans', or bars 28–35 in the 'Springdans'). Monrad Johansen's coda combines elements from both parts of the opening phrase, though chromatic descent is now associated with closure. The final bars also highlight an important difference between Monrad Johansen's musical syntax and his Griegian precursor. Parameters promoted by Grieg such as register and dynamics that serve to create a strongly cumulative or arch-like sense of large-scale formal structure are here used only at a secondary level. The emphasis rather is almost exclusively on linear contrapuntal behaviour. Local voice-leading articulation therefore takes precedence over other forms of structural organisation.

The fourth dance from the *Prillar-Guri* set, 'Lokk', demonstrates another significant difference between Grieg's musical practice and that of Monrad Johansen. Grieg's settings of *lokks* in op. 66, discussed in Chapter 2 above, dwell on the poignant tension between their diatonic setting and the tunes's open, non-diatonic modal quality. The longing for structural closure is expressed by the use of descending chromatic lines that initially support functional cadential articulation but ultimately deny any fixed sense of diatonic stability. The use of registral displacement often heightens this effect, so that the feeling of temporal progression conventionally associated with the diatonic field is replaced by a stronger sense of spatiousness. Monrad Johansen's 'Lokk' manipulates time and space in a similar way, with echo effects and much cross-beat slurring to suggest metrical freedom (Ex. 5.2). The whole number is built upon two basic ideas: an opening improvisatory call that revolves around a single cadential pattern, and a contrasting *lalling* that

Example 5.1. Monrad Johansen: Prillar-Guri, op. 12/1

Example 5.2. Monrad Johansen, 'Lokk', op. 12/4

Example 5.3. Monrad Johansen: Nordlandske Danser, op. 30/1.
Opening and elision (third strophe)

sounds initially more distanced (it is marked *dolce*) and introduces a change of mode from minor to major. Despite this modal shift, however, there is little sustained sense of diatonic context. Unlike Grieg's lokks, the harmonic background for Monrad Johansen's setting is formed by the superimposed fourths of the opening left-hand accompaniment. The music therefore has a quartic, rather than triadic, basis. These fourths can be understood partly as a response to Monrad Johansen's abstraction of Norwegian folk music (an inversion of the perfect fifths that he heard as an archetypal characteristic of the folk tunes). But they can also be understood as a sustained attempt to avoid intervals with strongly diatonic associations in favour of a more modernist-sounding harmonic language. In that sense, the interval loses its local 'folk' character and becomes a more cosmopolitan and generalised musical symbol, whose origin points to Schoenberg, Hindemith or Bartók as easily as Grieg.

The first of the set of *Nordlandske danser* reinforces this impression. The dance is an energetic *springar*, a lively triple time dance similar to those found in Grieg's op. 17 and op. 72 collections. Structurally, the dance divides into three strophes (the second and third are virtually identical). Unlike the comparable numbers from Grieg's op. 72, however, there is little sense of large-scale structural progression across the three sections. Though there is some feeling of dynamic intensification in the second and third strophes, the dance finishes at the *pianissimo* level with which it began. The piece is more remarkable perhaps for its juxtaposition of quartic and chromatic harmonic systems. The opening left-hand accompaniment reveals a tight interlocking of (027) trichords, usually expressed as chains of rising or falling fourths (Ex. 5.3). This is contrasted with a more linear passage (bars 13–22) that articulates a neo-Bachian chromatic counterpoint. These two idioms (vertical fourth-based and horizontal chromatic) are rarely brought together: the only true moment of elision is the start of the third strophe (bar 61), where the opening right-hand melody is underpinned by a descending chromatic bass line instead of the expected vertical fourths. Like the 'Lokk' from the *Prillar-Guri* suite, the diatonic collection plays little structural role in the dance. But neither does Monrad Johansen appear concerned with intensifying or resolving the potential tension between the different alternative harmonic systems employed in the music. The effect is of the mosaic-like juxtaposition of small blocks of varied musical material, rather than a dynamic structural dialogue. The music's formal syntax, as Kleiberg's analysis suggests, is arguably closer to a Debussyan model than the kind of procedure developed by Grieg in his folk-music arrangements.

This sense of an essentially stable formal model based on local juxtaposition and contrast (rather than polarisation) should not be understood pejoratively: stability and balance need not necessarily be associated with a lack of depth or profundity. On the contrary, here they appear to stand for a sense of objectivity.[24] They also serve to highlight important musical differences between Monrad Johansen and Grieg. Kleiberg argues that, in comparison with Garborg,

> Monrad Johansen's concretisation of Norwegian musical elements never reached beyond the material level. He approaches folk music with his art-music conceptual apparatus and finds a limited number of characteristic features with it. The German Romantic starting point becomes 'Norwegianised' through the addition of these elements. Nationalism in music becomes a bundle of external style-clichés that will contribute to the creation of a national musical symbol, and not a genuinely musical cultural expression. That is an essential difference in attitude that underlies this musical practice and, for example, Béla Bartók's or our own Eivind Groven's, or Klaus Egge's realisation of the national in music.[25]

In other words, Norwegian folk music had a less significant structural impact on Monrad Johansen's work than *landsmål* did for Garborg's poetry. Rather, it becomes part of a process of synthesis or assimilation that ultimately rests on an art-music basis. Even if the parallels between Garborg's work and Grieg's folk-music settings are not straightforward (as Chapter 3 suggests), it is possible to point to similar differences between Grieg's and Monrad Johansen's music. Whereas Grieg's folk-music arrangements, as we have seen, are often preoccupied with feelings of nostalgia, distance and loss, there is little sense of comparable tension in Monrad Johansen's music. Rather, any sense of tension or anxiety is externalised, in Monrad Johansen's 'misreading' of Grieg's settings, rather than internalised within the pieces themselves as the expression of competing musical discourses. This is where Korsyn's adaptation of the Bloomian notion of antithetical completion could perhaps be applied to an analysis of Monrad Johansen's music. Bloom writes that:

> A poet antithetically 'completes' his precursor, by so reading the parent-poem so as to retain its terms, but to mean them in another sense, as if the precursor has failed to go far enough . . . In the tessera, the later poet provides what his imagination tells him would complete the otherwise 'truncated' precursor poem

---

[24] Kleiberg, 'David Monrad Johansens musikksyn', 150.

[25] 'Monrad Johansens konkretisering av norske musikalske elementer når aldri utover stoffplanet. Han går med sitt kunstmusikalske begrepsapparat til folkemusikken, og finner et begrenset antall karakteristiske trekk ved den. Det tysk romantiske utgangspunktet blir så "fornorsket" ved tilsettingen av disse elementene. Det musikalsk nasjonale, blir en bunt ytre stil-klisjeer som skal bidra til å skape et nasjonalt musikksymbol, og ikke en genuint musikalsk kulturuttrykk. Det er en vesensforskjell i holdning som ligger til grunn for denne musikalske praksisen og for eksempel Bela Bartoks eller våre egne Eivind Grovens eller Klaus Egges realiseringer av det nasjonale i musikken.' Kleiberg, 'David Monrad Johansen's musikksyn', 148.

and poet . . . the tessera represents any later poet's attempt to persuade himself (and us) that the precursor's Word would be worn out if not redeemed as a newly fulfilled and enlarged Word of the ephebe.[26]

Monrad Johansen's work suggests precisely such an attempt to retain the terms of Grieg's music but to mean them 'in another sense'. In that sense, his music 'completes' Grieg's work by developing certain parameters and down-playing others, and by articulating a fundamental shift in structural syntax away from issues of large-scale form to the juxtaposition of more localised elements. That Monrad Johansen believed that Grieg's music was therefore 'redeemed' (or objectified) is suggested by his writing on the broader state of Norwegian music and its future development in essays such as 'Nasjonale Verdier i musikk' ('National Values in Music'). Only through a process of renewal, Monrad Johansen believed, could the nation's true musical heritage be safeguarded. Any such attempt, however, simultaneously reveals a fear, not only of oppression through self-translation, but also of the potential loss of musical identity or voice. The tension in Grieg's folk-music arrangements between competing musical discourses is therefore superseded in Monrad Johansen's work by an even greater anxiety projected upon his construction of a Norwegian musical style. In that sense alone, the musical legacy of Grieg's work seems deeply ambivalent.

'For love I was inclined': Grieg's influence on Percy Grainger

For Bloom, influence can be understood as an 'awareness not so much of presences as of absences, of *what is missing in the poem because it had to be excluded*'. It is a process of simultaneous attraction and rejection (or, more properly, suppression). Anxieties of identity and self-censure, which underpin Monrad Johansen's music, are equally prevalent in the work of Percy Grainger, but find a different kind of musical expression. Grainger's creative relationship with Grieg offers one of the most striking examples of transcultural exchange in early-twentieth-century music. Indeed, it is harder to think of two more geographically remote figures whose work enjoyed such a close and intimate relationship. Recent scholarship has considered Grainger's reception of Grieg's music through his recorded legacy as a performer,[27] and excerpts from their correspondence have been published in a number of sources, including Finn Benestad's edition of Grieg's letters and Kay Dreyfus's seminal collection, *The Farthest North of Humanness*.[28]

---

[26] Quoted in Korsyn, 'Towards a New Poetics', 26.

[27] Eleanor A. L. Tan, 'Grainger as an Interpreter of Grieg's Work', *Australasian Music Research* 5 (Grainger issue) (University of Melbourne, 2001), 49–60.

[28] *Brev*, II, 28–34, and *The Farthest North of Humanness: Letters of Percy Grainger, 1901–14*, ed. Kay Dreyfus (London: Macmillan, 1985). See also Lionel Carley, 'The Last Visitor: Percy Grainger at

But the nature of Grieg's compositional influence on Grainger's music has not received such sustained critical attention. Grieg's influence can easily be identified in Grainger's treatment of voice leading, harmonic rhythm and register. But the process of transculturation, in Mary Pratt's words, is inevitably a tense, agonistic one, a creative passage that readily invites a Bloomian reading.[29] Grainger's first letter to Grieg, dated 14 April 1905, for example, betrays unease as much as admiration. Grainger wrote:

> What your music has meant for us English people, you naturally know: we imagine that there is something in our race which is not without kindred with the Norwegian, and perhaps not least because your glorious creations catch hold of us so much more irresistibly than, for example, German art could ever do.[30]

Grainger's comments suggest a strong desire to discover a sense of identity through association. But, like Monrad Johansen's calls for the national renewal of Norwegian music, Grainger's persistent references to ideas of race and nationhood in his letters and writings were both exclusive and inclusive. As David Pear has observed, Grainger suffered from a deep crisis of confusion in his cultural and racial background: 'he was at once a southern Englishman in temperament, a politically democratic Australian, an artistically melancholy Celt, and a morally ultra-liberal Scandinavian'.[31] Hence, though Grieg's music served to crystallise Grainger's construction of his own imaginary proto-Nordic musical voice, it also exposed the points of tension and conflict that underpinned Grainger's individual musical character. It therefore seems to have underlined his feelings of alienation and displacement, while simultaneously presenting the opportunity to create his own sense of musical space.

Grainger recalled that his first memory of Grieg's music was listening in Melbourne to the playing of his mother and Dr Hamilton Russell, whom Grainger described nostalgically as 'the first exquisite pianist in my life'.[32] Despite this key childhood experience, however, Grainger's intense

Troldhaugen', *Studia Musicologica Norvegica* 25 (1999), 189–208. My account here relies on all three sources.

[29] Quoted in Don Randall, *Kipling's Imperial Boy: Adolescence and Cultural Hybridity* (Basingstoke: Palgrave, 2000), 6.

[30] Grainger, *The Farthest North of Humanness*, 46.

[31] David Pear, 'Grainger on Race and Nation', *Australasian Music Research* 5, 25–48, here 41.

[32] 'Notes on Grieg', Grainger Museum, Melbourne, *c.* 1938, quoted in John Bird, *Percy Grainger* (London: Paul Elek, 1976), 115. 'In my childhood in Melbourne I heard a great deal of Grieg played by my mother and our dear friend R. Hamilton Russell – the first exquisite pianist in my life. Indeed my mother played more Grieg than any other music in the years 1888–95. But I did not think much of Grieg's music at that time, much as I would have liked to have admired it, for it would have suited me very well to see in Grieg's music the rebirth of the Old Norse Spirit I was worshipping then in the Icelandic Sagas. But I could not. I did not awaken to Grieg's greatness until I met Cyril Scott in Frankfurt-am-Main around 1897. He, chiding me for my then Handel-like style of composition, asked me if I didn't like modern music. 'What do you mean by modern music?' I asked him. And

admiration for Grieg's work appears to date only from his student years in Frankfurt during the late 1890s, when one of his contemporaries, the Danish cellist and composer Herman Sandby, introduced him to Grieg's newly published *19 norske Folkeviser*, op. 66. Grainger's first significant encounter with Grieg's music therefore took place in a German context. The op. 66 collection was arguably to play a central role in Grainger's subsequent compositional development, not least since it coincided with Grainger's own creative discovery of folk song. Grainger's actual contact with Grieg himself was relatively brief. Carley suggests that Grainger was first brought to Grieg's attention by Sandby, who sent Grieg a copy of Grainger's early folk-song settings for chorus in 1905.[33] Grainger wrote to Sandby on 11 November 1905:

> When you next see Grieg ask him, or if you won't very soon be seeing him write him, to tell you whether he (or whoever gathered the tunes) has the words to the Folkeviser op. 66. They must exist & be perfectly *stunning*. & MUST BE COLLECTED, if not yet done.
>
> If he didn't collect himself, find out who did & whether he got the words, or if nobody did try & get addresses of local people in the districts where the tunes were hunted.[34]

Grainger characteristically urged Sandby in the following paragraph: 'I'll look after my country if you look after yours', aligning his folk-song collecting with the broader project of promoting a national musical identity.[35] The two composers met on 15 May the following year in London, at an evening hosted by Edgar Speyer, during Grieg's last tour of the United Kingdom. This initial encounter was evidently a success, since Grieg wrote the following day to the Norwegian ambassador, Fridtjof Nansen, about a forthcoming lunch meeting:

> If you would do me a favour, invite a *brilliant* young man from Australia, Mr Percy Grainger (14, Upper Cheyne Row, Chelsea, S.W.), whom I got to know yesterday. He is mad about Norway, speaks Norwegian (Danish!) and knows everything, the sagas,

he played me Grieg's Ballade op. 24 and Tchaikowsky's Theme and Variations for Piano. But the full range of Grieg's harmonic inventivity and the adorable wistfulness and tragicness of his nature were not revealed to me until Herman Sandby showed me Grieg's "Norwegian Folksongs", op. 66, around 1899. Then Grieg joined Bach, Brahms and Wagner in the firmament of my compositional stars. My Grieg worship deepened when William Gair Rathbone put Grieg's "Norwegian Peasant Dances" Op. 72, into my hands around 1905.'

[33] Carley, 'The Last Visitor', 191.

[34] Quoted in Grainger, *The Farthest North of Humanness*, 52.

[35] Grainger wrote extensively about what he believed were the intimate connections between folk music and national (and racial) identity; see for example his essay 'The Influence of Anglo-Saxon Folk Music' (1920), in *Grainger on Music*, ed. Malcolm Gillies and Bruce Clunies Ross with Bronwen Arthur and Daniel Pear (Oxford: Oxford University Press, 1999), 113–20.

Faroese literature, Bjørnson, Ibsen, etc. He would be delighted to be able to shake your hand.[36]

Grainger subsequently visited Grieg at Troldhaugen in July and August 1907, during which time he practised a number of Grieg's works including dances from the *Slåtter*, and several tunes from op. 66. Though Grainger was engaged to play the solo piano part in Grieg's Piano Concerto conducted by the composer, as one of the highlights of the 1907 Leeds Festival, Grieg's death on 4 September intervened and the concert instead became a memorial event. Several commentators have suggested that Grainger's international career may have benefited from his perceived association with Grieg's last wishes.[37] Certainly, in the years following Grieg's death, he maintained close contact with the composer's widow, Nina Grieg, and a number of other important Norwegian musicians including the composer Sparre Olsen and the folk-music collector Arne Bjørndal. Grainger's later correspondence with Bjørndal nevertheless highlights the downturn in his career in the United States after the Second World War. Bjørndal contacted Grainger in the early 1950s to try and enlist his support for the publication of a collection of folk tunes that would eventually appear as the first volume of the Norsk folkemusikk series. In a reply dated 19 November 1954, however, Grainger wrote:

> You cannot have any idea of my helplessness in the musical world. No musicians, critics, etc. have the least respect for me or my opinions. . . . The whole stream of American musical life flows against me. No symphony orchestras perform my compositions, no eminent music societies engage me, no major papers will print what I have to say about anything or anybody![38]

There is therefore a potentially uncomfortable parallel between the critical reception of Grieg and Grainger's work in the second half of the twentieth century. Just as we have conventionally seen Grieg as a composer of picturesque lyric miniatures who was ill-equipped to deal with the rigours of large-scale symphonic form, so too the popular understanding of Grainger has often been limited by a negative perception of his folk-song arrangements as naïve, sentimental or anachronistic.[39] Grainger's bitterness

---

[36] 'Vil De gjøre mig en Glæde, så indbyd en ung *genial* Mand fra Australien, Mr. Percy Grainger (14, Upper Cheyne Row, Chelsea S. W.) som jeg igår lærte at kjende. Han sværmer for Norge, taler Norsk (Dansk!) og kjender Alt, Sagaerne, færøisk Literatur, Bjørnson, Ibsen etc.' Quoted in *Brev*, I, 532.

[37] See, for example, Grainger, *The Farthest North of Humanness*, 137.

[38] '. . . har du sikkert ikke nogen forestilling om min hjælpløshed i den musikaliske verden. Ingen Musiker, Kritker, o.s.v. har den mindste respekt for mig eller for mine meninger. . . . Hele strømmen i det amerikaniske musikalsk liv gaar IMOD mig. Intet symfoniorkester opfører mine kompositioner, intet høj[t]staaende musikselskab engagerer mig, ingen betyderlig avis vilde trykke hvad jeg skrive om noget eller nogen!' Manuscript letter in Arne Bjørndal Samling, Griegakademiet, Bergen.

[39] For a relatively recent example of this strain of criticism, see Norman Lebrecht's withering

following the commercial success of *Country Gardens* over his other work suggests that he was acutely aware of precisely this critical tendency, even to the point of over-exaggeration.[40]

Grieg's short stature and physical frailty cannot have struck Grainger as a promising model for his ideal blue-eyed Nordic racial type. And, despite his enthusiasm for Norwegian independence, Grieg did not share Grainger's radical views on nationality or gender, and never articulated anything that corresponded with Grainger's proto-racialist or anti-semitic thinking. Grainger, for his part, did not comment on Grieg's high-profile involvement in the Dreyfus affair.[41] Nevertheless, the two composers shared a number of common preoccupations, including a fascination with folk music and folk traditions, landscape and nature and Nordic mythology, and Grieg was a keen enthusiast of Grainger's playing. In an undated letter that Grainger himself translated (perhaps with an eye to the possible benefits for the future promotion of his career), Grieg wrote:

> Let me say it once: I like you! I like your unspoilt nature, which not even 'High-life' has been able to corrupt, and then I like your deep feeling for folk song and all the possibilities it carries within itself. Your conception of the English folk songs is full of genius and contains the seed of a new English style in music. And then your taste for the Norwegian folk songs and Scandinavian languages and literature proves that you are not wrapping yourself up in a cloak of onesidedness. On the top of all that there is your magnificent piano playing and – your sympathy with the *Slåtter*.[42]

Grainger recorded his visit to Troldhaugen in the summer of 1907 in precise detail in his diary and correspondence. These notes often provide striking insights into his working relationship with Grieg, not least involving the folk-song arrangements. In a lengthy letter to his mother begun 24 July, for example, he noted that:

> [Troldhaugen] drops on 3 sides to a Lake of Killarney; & who lives on the next jutting (call-overably near) tongue of rocky

dismissal of Grainger in his *Companion to Twentieth-Century Music* (London: Simon & Schuster, 1992), 140, as: 'Anguished Australian, [who] wasted a modest compositional talent on pianistic miniatures and orchestrations of folksongs. He treated jolly country frolics with utmost solemnity offset by glimpses of harmonic originality.'
[40] I am grateful to David Pear for alerting me to the dangers of reading Grainger's later correspondence on this subject too literally. Grainger certainly seems to have been somewhat melodramatic in his exchange with Bjørndal, but the broader parallels with the reception of Grieg's work are still worth drawing.
[41] On Grainger's views on racialism, see David Pear, 'Grainger on Race and Nation', 39–47. Grieg's intervention in the Dreyfus affair is summarised by Berestad and Schjelderup-Ebbe, *Edvard Grieg*, 350–2.
[42] Quoted in Grainger, *The Farthest North of Humanness*, 69. Grieg's original (in Norwegian) is reprinted in *Brev*, II, 29.

land? Fr. Beier [*sic*], the man who with Grieg collected the tunes of his op 66 (Olla Dalom, etc: to which there belongs a rare legend; all dead drowned boedees (bodies) & churchbells bimming; you'll hear it soon from me) a sort of puny Bjørnsson to look at; a good stout soul, steeped in folklore & f-music.

... After breakfast Grieg was for my playing some Slaater, so I got off to Grieg's composing-room down the slope near the fjord (on the jolly wooden walls of which hangs a likeness of "Möllergutten", who, you know, luckily was jilted by Kari & wrote *Möllerguttens bruremarsch* to bless her with) & put in a few hours practise.[43]

This letter gives some idea of the routine that Grieg and Grainger adopted during July and early August 1907. Grainger combined individual practice and rehearsals with Grieg, in preparation for their projected performance of the Piano Concerto in Leeds (which, as noted above, never took place). The two composers also exchanged compositional ideas, and though it is not ultimately clear whether Grieg's opinion of Grainger's own creative work was unreservedly positive, his initial response appears to have been enthusiastic:

... After lunch Grieg asks for English & Færoe f-songs (remembers pretty well every jolly one he heard from me last year)

Universal rapture: 'But what harmonies'. 'Das macht ihm aber gar niemand nach' (that was bobbly 'Lord Melbourne') Grieg says: 'darin leigt doch der keim zu einem grossen Englischen Styl, meinen Sie nicht.' [therein lies the seed of a great English style, don't you think?] I gave them 2 Færoes, L. Melbourne, The Nth country maid, Brigg Fair, I'm 17, Molly on the shore, Green Bushes, (just the tune) 6 Dukes, a.s.o.

... [26 July]

Today Grieg showed me [a] lot of male-chorus things of his, folk-song settings, etc.

I believe I'll get him to comply with my years-old longing for him to set some of op 66 for chorus, & that Bejer could be got to use the phonograph & bring about a gramophone recording of Norwegian folksingers & fiddlers.[44]

Beyer and Grainger never, in fact, collaborated on the collection of Norwegian folk tunes using recording equipment, even though it was a method that Bjørndal swiftly adopted. But in a letter to Herman Sandby, dated 4 October 1907 and therefore written exactly a month after Grieg's death, Grainger suggested that he still hoped to work on Nordic folk tunes the following summer:

---

[43] Letter quoted in Grainger, *The Farthest North of Humanness*, 124–5.
[44] Ibid.

Grieg was mighty keen on the phonograph. To collect *without* a phonograph (until there's something better) is mad & criminal. If I were a Scandinavian, nothing would hold me back from collecting up what yet remains in *any of the Scandinavian lands*. Even as it is I'm going over to Norway next summer & am going to do a 14-night with a phongraph & a bath chair to wheel it in; up in Jotunheim[en].

I got from F. Beyer, Grieg's friend, the words of 'I Ola-Dalom'; (you know that lovely one in op. 66) *just think*; not written down or kept or printed. But he *remembered* them still, luckily.[45]

Though the trip did not take place, Bjørndal records Grainger's return visit to Troldhaugen in 1911 at Beyer's invitation. Grainger apparently listened to a number of *slåtter* performed on the Hardanger fiddle, before playing some of the movements from op. 72 himself.[46] Beyer's pencil transcription of the words from op. 66/14 together with an explanatory note, written hastily on a folded sheet of A4 paper and dated 'Troldhaugen 1/8/07', is preserved in the Grainger Museum in Melbourne, and differs in only slight details from the version that he had originally provided for Grieg in 1895 (see Chapter 2).[47]

Among the other materials held in the Grainger museum are a two-piano transcription of 'Knut Luråsen's Halling 2', and Grainger's annotated copy of op. 66, which includes extensive indications for a 'flexible' arrangement of 'Det er den største Dårlighet' for a large room-music ensemble that Grainger never fully realised.[48] Both documents reveal much about Grainger's attitude to Grieg's work. Grainger's two-piano transcription of op. 72/11, for example, is characterised by both a textural filling out and expansion, projecting the music registrally through doubling and octave transposition, and a general smoothing over in articulation, which serves to heighten and strengthen the music's linear contrapuntal flow. Grainger commented that, 'whatever is Bachlike, Grieglike in me is mostly thickened by some sort of Wagnerlike, or Brahmslike, or Schumann sauce'.[49] The result in Grainger's transcription is that, though local moments of staccato articulation are often emphasised, the polymetric structure of Grieg's music (analysed in Chapter 4) is inevitably weakened by the thickening of individual melodic lines. Grainger may have understood this effect as a

---

[45] Quoted in Grainger, *The Farthest North of Humanness*, 144.

[46] Bjørndal, 'Edvard Grieg og folkemusikken', 15–16.

[47] Grainger Museum, University of Melbourne, box MG 13/1–4.

[48] The ink manuscript of the two-piano arrangement of op. 72/11 is dated Springfield, Ohio, 21 October 1921, and is item MG 4/13 in the Grainger archive. Grainger notes in the top left-hand corner of the front page that he '1ˢᵗ thought of it in London (1910–1913?)'.

[49] Aldridge-Grainger-Ström saga, manuscripts, Library of Congress. Quoted in Bird, *Percy Grainger*, 56

reflection of his understanding of the folk source. Elsewhere, for example, he summarised his views on articulation in folk singers, who he felt 'seldom aim at attempting anything resembling a genuine legato style, but use their breath more as do some birds and animals, in short stabs and gushes of quickly contrasted twittering, pattering and coughing sounds which (to my ears at least) are as beautiful as they are amusing'. Grainger applied a similar model to instrumental music, particularly 'the fiddling of British and Scandinavian peasants, who are as fond of twiddles and quirks as are the old singers, and do not try to exchange the "up and down" physical nature of the bow for the attainment of the continuous tone'.[50] The effect of Grainger's unrealised transcription of 'Det er den største Dårlighet' would no doubt have been similar: the impression once again is of a prevailing thickening of parts, but with attention to local highlights in individual contrapuntal lines.

Comparison with a contemporary example of one of Grainger's own folk-song arrangements, his setting of *Brigg Fair* for mixed chorus, reveals an even deeper similarity of musical approach and design that suggests a conscious imitation on Grainger's part (Ex. 5.4). Grainger may have had a number of tunes from Grieg's op. 66 collection in mind when he composed his arrangement of *Brigg Fair*, including 'Det er den største Dårlighet' or 'Ranveig'. But 'Siri Dale-Visen', discussed in Chapter 2 above, may have served as a particular model. Registrally and texturally, Grieg's setting of 'Siri Dale-Visen' is remarkably condensed: it would be very easy to imagine from the score that the piece was conceived as the piano reduction of a four-part choral setting. Indeed, Grainger had written to his mother while he was staying at Troldhaugen in 1907 that he urged Grieg to consider arranging some of the tunes in op. 66 for precisely these forces, along the lines of his own arrangements of English folk songs. As previous analysis has shown, Grieg's setting is characterised by a very strong sense of cumulative harmonic, tonal and dynamic design culminating in the powerful chain of descending parallel seventh chords that liquidate the harmonic tension of bar 17 and lead towards resolution in the final cadence. Like 'I Ola-Dalom', this formal shape may have been inspired by a simple narrative reading of the text that Frants Beyer supplied with the melody. The shifting chromaticism that begins to colour the accompaniment after the first two phrases could therefore be heard as a realisation of the emotional turmoil that underpins the song.

A similar mood of intensification, crisis and recovery pervades *Brigg Fair*. Grainger transcribed the melody himself from the singing of Joseph Taylor on 11 April 1905, following the North Lincolnshire Musical Competition that was held at Brigg. Grainger's setting for mixed chorus and tenor soloist

---

[50] 'Collecting with the phonograph' article, *Journal of the Folk Song Society*, May 1908, quoted in Wilfrid Mellers, *Percy Grainger* (Oxford: Oxford University Press, 1992), p 73.

Example 5.4. Percy Grainger: Brigg Fair, verse 4 and transition

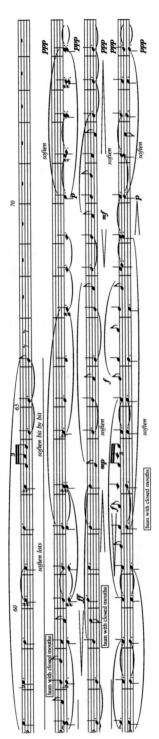

was performed at the festival the following year. A copy of the 1906 version in the British Library bears the inscription 'I Beundring / og Venskab / Percy Grainger / 2.3.06' ('In admiration and friendship'), though the individual to whom the inscription was addressed is unknown. Significantly, Grainger officially dedicated the revised version of 1911, like his other folk-song arrangements, 'Lovingly and reverently' to the 'memory of Edvard Grieg'. Grainger's setting expands on Grieg's single-strophic approach in 'Siri Dale-Visen' to five verses, but shares the same basic symmetrical arch shape: the first two strophes are set to the same music, which barely rises above a *piano* dynamic level. The folk melody is initially sung by a single solo voice above a wordless chorus: Grainger's intention here, perhaps, is to present the folk song as an individual element in its 'natural setting'. Wordless choral parts often seem to serve, in Grainger's works, as representations of nature or the natural world, and Grainger later described the kind of gently undulating polyphonic lines that characterise the arrangement as 'nature voices' representing the sound of the wind or other natural phenomena such as the sea.[51] Like the first phrase of 'Siri Dale-Visen', the simple modal style of the setting in this opening section reinforces the sense of naturalness. The third strophe is preceded by a brief four-bar introduction, in which, significantly, the choral accompaniment first emerges as an independent element in its own right. This is the point at which Grainger introduces borrowed text from a second folk-song source, 'Low Down in the Broom', a tune collected by W. Percy Merrick and previously published in the *Journal of the Folk Song Society*. Grainger's use of additional text, here and in the final two verses where he borrows words from a West Sussex tune called 'The Merry King', extends the musical narrative in his setting, and also serves to universalise the sense of utterance by elevating *Brigg Fair* from its immediate local north Lincolnshire surroundings. Hence the tune becomes an ideal type, emblematic of a collective, rather than individual folk consciousness. The gesture also serves to heighten the tension between the folk song's 'natural origins' and its 'dished-up' treatment. The raised dynamic level and greater chromatic part movement of the third verse reflects this intensification.

In the fourth stanza, the chorus finally breaks free of its accompanying role and sings words for the only time in the setting. This is the dynamic, textural and harmonic climax of the song. As Wilfrid Mellers notes, the

---

[51] See, for example, his description of similar polyphonic lines in the harmonisation of the opening melody of Grieg's *Ballade*, op. 24, in his 1943 essay, 'Grieg: Nationalist and Cosmopolitan', in *Grainger on Music*, 330. It is also worth considering his comments in the earlier essay 'Free Music' (1938): 'Out in nature we hear all kinds of lovely and touching "free" (non-harmonic) combinations of tones; yet we are unable to take up these beauties and expressiveness into the art of music because of our archaic notions of harmony . . . My impression is that this world of tonal freedom was suggested to me by wave movements in the sea that I first observed as a young child at Brighton, Victoria, and Albert Park, Melbourne', *Grainger on Music*, 293–4.

wordless entry of the soloist in bar 50 rising to the dissonant a♭ in bar 52 is the most piercing sound in the whole work, and the apex from which the rest of the setting leads away. The climax subsides through an extended nineteen-bar transition passage, dominated by a series of chromatic and dynamic descents initiated by the soloist, in which the chorus returns to its initial 'natural' wordlessness. The formal and expressive function of the transition is directly analogous to bars 17–22 in 'Siri Dale-Visen'. Both passages combine a closural, liquidating syntactical effect with a sense of temporal regression or forgetfulness, an impression reinforced in *Brigg Fair* by the diminishing chain of dynamic markings so that the song appears to die away in a series of increasingly faint echoes.

The effect of the fifth and final strophe is retrospective. The music sounds as though it is in a 'past tense'. The reduced dynamic level, sustained throughout the entire strophe, is the quietest in the piece. Similarly, the almost static choral accompaniment returns to the archaic modal style of the opening, so that the song closes with the nature sounds with which it began. As in 'Siri Dale-Visen', this strong sense of formal expressive trajectory is motivated partly by the text. Even if we hear the opening stanzas as initially sturdy and optimistic, the mood darkens from the third stanza onwards, the point at which Grainger deliberately introduces text from another folk tune. Grainger dwells on the images of the unconstant lover in the fourth stanza at which point the text breaks off, as though the emotional strain is momentarily too great for words. The extended wordless transition subsequently lends the re-entry of the soloist at the start of the fifth stanza even greater emphasis, and stresses the wintry image of withered green leaves and dead branches: the antithesis of young love and fair summer weather. Narrative readings of *Brigg Fair* might suggest that Grainger understands the final strophe as sung, perhaps, from bitter experience, or at least from a dream world, as the summing-up of the preceding verses. But the effect is ultimately one of remoteness or distance, of a lack of resolution rather than symmetrical closure, and it is in this sense that the final strophe is closest to the concluding bars of 'Siri Dale-Visen'.

Grainger's setting of *Brigg Fair* can be understood to articulate a similar syntactical or temporal conflict to that identified by Carl Dahlhaus in his analysis of 'Siri Dale-Visen', between an idealised archaic modal folk domain and modernist chromatic voice-leading, or between past and present musical tenses. But the setting can also be heard as the expression of an uneasy tension in Grainger's work between different musical domains: the world of rural folk music on the one hand, and urban Western art music on the other. *Brigg Fair*, like 'Siri Dale-Visen', represents an attempt to problematise, as well as synthesise, these opposing musical impulses. For Grainger, this is a central thread of his own colonial identity. The notion of distance is integral to a sense of remoteness, either from Australia, North America, or from centres of musical activity in Northern Europe, that seems characteristic not just of *Brigg Fair*, but of much of Grainger's work. Grainger's claim, in a letter to Bjørndal, that he wished to 'initiate and maintain as much artistic feeling between the Nordic Lands and Australia as possible',[52] takes on a greater and more poignant significance in *Brigg Fair*. Grainger's setting is not only concerned with a simple process of cultural exchange, but is an attempt to resolve the irreconcilable impulses within Grainger himself, as international composer and Australian.

Brigg Fair also invites us to contemplate Grainger's creative relationship with Grieg in a new light. The setting becomes an expression of his anxiety of influence, like David Monrad Johansen's folk-tune arrangements. The adoption and transformation of a Griegian compositional model, in *Brigg Fair*, suggests a simultaneous attraction and resistance, and (in Bloomian terms), a fear of creative isolation that is in some senses unconsiously desired. The tension in the central sections of *Brigg Fair*, particularly the wordless transition between the fourth and fifth strophes, therefore takes on the Freudian character of an Oedipal struggle. Reading the text through the music in these terms, the love for which Grainger is 'inclined' at the start of the setting could have been his desire for creative acceptance. Grainger perhaps then recognised the figure of the unconstant lover in the final strophe as representing himself, an interpretation encouraged by his subsequent dedication of the piece to the memory of Grieg. The rhetorical category to which Grainger's setting could therefore be ascribed, in Bloom's system, is that of *apophrades*, or the return of the dead. Korsyn summarises *apophrades* as the subsumption of 'two related psychic defences: introjection and projection':

> The analogical link here is that transumption is the trope-reversing trope, while introjection and projection defend against other defences. Introjection is an internalisation or imaginative identification, a 'fantasy transposition of otherness to the self', while projection is a distancing or casting-out that 'seeks to expel from the self everything that the self cannot bear to acknowledge as being its own'. In *apophrades*, the poet most often introjects futurity, identifying with the future, while projecting anteriority, through the substitution of early words for late in prior tropes. This can effect an upwards revision of the tropes, redeeming a poet's belatedness by identifying with earliness.[53]

---

[52] 'Det er mit største Ønske at igangsætte og vedligeholde saa megen kunstnerisk Føling mellem de nordiske Lande og Australien som muligt.' Letter dated 29 August 1952, manuscript, Arne Bjørndal Samling, Bergen.

[53] Korsyn, 'Towards a New Poetics', 55.

Korsyn identifies *apophrades* as the trope associated especially with closure, a syntactical function that is reinforced by the shape of Grainger's piece. *Brigg Fair* can therefore be heard, crudely, as an attempt to resurrect Grieg's creative spirit and re-project it as Grainger's own musical identity. It therefore involves a transformation, returning to a past musical work in order to articulate its own sense of musical presence. Characteristically, however, this sense of return is a process that simultaneously discloses its own impossibility. The effect of the final bars, as noted above, is ultimately of emptiness and loss. The creative spring celebrated by the opening bars swiftly turns autumnal. Grainger's attempt to assume the discourse of an earlier musical father figure, as for Monrad Johansen, therefore reveals his own sense of belatedness.

These short case studies, Monrad Johansen's folk dances and Grainger's folk-song arrangements, illustrate two different strategies adopted by composers attempting to come to terms with aspects of Grieg's folk-music arrangements. But in the context of the material discussed previously in this book, they also intensify our sense of the complexity of Grieg's work, and highlight the competing musical discourses that are one of focal points of creative tension in Grieg's music. This challenges in turn the popular received view of Grieg's work as limited in scale and musical stature. The creative problems posed by Grieg's work and addressed by figures such as Monrad Johansen and Grainger do not sit comfortably with our image of Grieg as a musical miniaturist. Grieg's critical marginalisation outside Norway therefore becomes even more unacceptable, a resolute unwillingness to understand his music in its own creative context. Wilfrid Mellers writes of Grainger that 'this aggressively personal young man taught the virtue of humility: as is most evident in the body of music wherein he is not so much transcribing or arranging folk music as effecting its ritual re-enactment'.[54] There is little comparable sense of aggressiveness in Grieg's music, but rather a rhetorical bluntness or directness that is perhaps even more disconcerting. Mellers's notion of 'music as ritual action', however, is a useful way of conceiving Grieg's work, not least since it lends his music a depth of meaning that it might not otherwise immediately suggest. Furthermore, it reinforces our sense of the way in which landscape in Grieg's music becomes abstract structure: one of the primary purposes of ritual, surely, is to embed culturally constructed meanings in such symbolic non-representational forms. The bells, echoes and mountain voices that pervade Grieg's work, and which are recalled by Monrad Johansen and Grainger, hence take on a potentially sacred, or at least spiritual, significance. Grainger appears to have sensed this quality, in a

---

[54] Mellers, *Percy Grainger*, 76.

lecture entitled 'Nordic Characteristics in Music', read at Yale University on 6 March 1921, that otherwise invoked a number of problematic racial and national stereotypes. Grainger recalled that

> One of [Grieg's] greatest favourites of his own works was 'Captive of the Hills' [Den Bergtekne], a lonely wanderer lost in the mountains, a work full of eerie northern superstition and the presentation of loneliness – a kind of exaltation in the horror of loneliness, worshipping it while hating it.[55]

Grainger's comments swiftly draw attention to his own highly ideological construction of Nordic landscape, a world view that in other senses suffered from an excessive narrowness of vision, but they also offer a perceptive glimpse of the aesthetic assumptions that underlie Grieg's landscape music. Landscape, in Grieg's work, becomes a site of heightened sensory awareness and contemplation. Closer attention to how this state of consciousness is achieved may promote a change of critical perspective, provided that we do not subscribe uncritically to the kind of generalisations offered by Grainger. Grieg's work can then take a central place in our understanding of the relationships between music and its creative and natural environments.

---

[55] Reproduced in *Grainger on Music*, 131–40, here 135.

CONCLUSION

Previous writing on Grieg has often dwelt on images of landscape and nature. Landscape, in that sense, is central to Grieg's musical identity. In extreme cases, as the iconography of Grieg's grave suggests, images of Grieg (or representations of his music) literally become part of the landscape, grounding his creativity in the Norwegian soil. But other more programmatic accounts of music and landscape are no less prevalent in Grieg scholarship. The images of sunlit fjords as a backdrop to the 'Morgenstemning' ('Morning Mood') from *Peer Gynt* promoted in the popular media, for example – a travesty of the original stage setting in the incidental music for Ibsen's play (which is located in the Morrocan desert) – simply represents the tip of one of the strongest traditions in Grieg's critical reception.[1] The association between Grieg's music and the Norwegian landscape is not a natural one, therefore, but is an ideological phenomenon, an assumption which has been culturally and historically defined.

This book has argued that representations of landscape in Grieg's music are inextricably bound to broader cultural formations of Norwegian identity. The processes through which the Norwegian landscape was framed, visualised and interpreted in the nineteenth century were part of wider European traditions of representation. Attempts to define the Norwegian landscape were shaped by a fundamental tension in Norwegian nationalism, between cosmopolitan impulses which sought to assimilate Norway within a continental European framework, and isolationist trends, which sought to achieve (and maintain) Norwegian cultural and political independence. The fact that such tensions still exist within current-day Norwegian cultural politics (as they do for other countries outside and within the European Union), is testimony to their continuing historical legacy. In Grieg's music, such tensions are articulated, at a foreground level, by the juxtaposition of elements drawn from Norwegian folk music (such as herding calls, folk melodies, modal harmonies and dance rhythms), and a conventional (mainstream continental European) diatonic harmonic syntax. As Dahlhaus has observed, the pull between these opposing musical idioms reflects the historical state of the musical material: the way in which, in 'Siri Dale-Visen',

---

[1] The CD-ROM *Edvard Grieg – hans liv og musik* produced by the Edvard Grieg Museum, Troldhaugen (Bergen: MediaVisjon AS, 1998), includes an excellent example of this strategy. A short video by Eivind Kopperdal, from a section entitled 'Norwegian Nature and Edvard Grieg's Music', juxtaposes images of fjordland waterfalls and Hardanger apple blossom with the 'Morning Mood' from *Peer Gynt*.

for example, austere modal harmonies give way to modernist chromatic voice-leading, is presented as a 'progressive' feature of Grieg's music. But such structural tensions can also be heard as an attempt to negotiate a complex sense of musical identity. The function of musical landscape devices in the very opening number of the op. 66 set, 'Kulokk', for instance, could be interpreted as means of mediating between 'Norwegian' impulses, on the one hand, and 'European' on the other. Representations of landscape in Grieg's music draw on a wider musical vocabulary, in which herding calls, harmonically static textures and registrally expansive textures are conventionally defined as landscape signifiers; at the same time, the precise configurations of such signs, the role they play within the piece, and the individual quality of the images or texts they evoke, serves as the expression of musical (hence cultural) difference. In the *Slåtter*, Grieg's most radical engagement with a Norwegian folk tradition, however, landscape arguably assumes a more antagonistic, less assimilative quality as Grieg's sense of musical individuality develops a more assertive character.

Landscape in Grieg's music therefore is a discursive, or mutable, presence. It engages in a dialogue with other elements. Indeed, there are moments, such as the final bars of *Haugtussa*, when the landscape itself appears momentarily to assume its own voice (symbolised perhaps by the way in which Veslemøy, the song-cycle's main protagonist, falls silent). Representations of landscape in Grieg's music are not necessarily tied to visual stimuli. Rather, they can refer to literary texts (which often took part in political debates about the nature and status of the Norwegian language), local musical traditions, or other phenomenological aspects (a more abstract sense of place). In works such as 'Klokkeklang' or 'I Ola-Dalom, i Ola-Kjønn', Grieg's musical landscapes can be heard as a form of acoustic ecology, the creation of a sonic environment in which man-made sounds (ringing bells) become merged with the idea of the natural world. It is this ritualistic process of transformation, and the loss of self that it entails, which appears to have particularly attracted Percy Grainger, one of Grieg's deepest and most immediate musical admirers.

Grieg's warm recollection of Bjørnson's description of the composer as a 'landscape painter', and his admission that it was his 'life's dream to be able to render the North's nature in sound', is a poignant moment of self-recognition.[2] Yet it only begins to suggest the significance that landscape gains in Grieg's music. Contemplating landscape in Grieg's music promotes a closer critical engagement with the ideologies that have underpinned Grieg's critical reception, and the broader cultural and political contexts in which has been understood. It also offers a deeper insight into Grieg's

---

[2] 'mit Livs Drøm er at kunne give Nordens Natur i Toner'. Letter to Gottfred Matthison-Hansen, dated 10 April 1869, *Brev*, II, 142.

music, an interpretative perspective that allows us to move beyond the cosy, small-scale image of Grieg that has prevailed in much Anglo-American scholarship. It is towards this larger vision of landscape in Grieg's music that discussion in this book has been directed.

Haugtussa Texts (Songs 1, 2 and 8)

1. *Det syng ('The Enticement')*

Å veit du den Draum, og veit du den Song,
so vil du Tonarne gøyma;
og gilja det for deg so mange in Gong,
rett aldri so kan dud et gløyma.
Å hildrande du!
med meg skal du bu,
i Blåhaugen skal du din Sylvrokk snu.

Du skal ikkje fæla den mjuke Nott,
då Draumen slær ut sine Vengjer
i linnare Ljos enn Dagen hev ått,
og Tonar på mjukare Strengjer.
Det voggar um Li,
det svævest av Strid,
og Dagen ei kjenner den Sæle-Tid.

Du skal ikkje ræddas den Elskhug vill,
som syndar og græt og gløymer;
hans Famn er heit og hans Hug er mild,
og Bjønnen arge han tøymer.
Å hildrande du!
med meg skal du bu,
i Blåhaugen skal du din Sylvrokk snu.

If you know the dream, if you know the song,
You will remember the sounds,
And you will hum it so often,
That you will never forget it.
O you enchantress!
You will live with me,
In the blue mountain you will turn your silver spinning
     wheel.

You shall not fear the gentle night
When Dream spreads out its wings

In a softer light than that of Day,
And sounds on gentler strings.
The slopes are still,
All strife is suspended,
And Day knows not this blissful time.

You shall not fear this wild passion,
Which sins and cries and forgets;
His embrace is hot and his heart is gentle,
And he tames the fierce bear.
O you enchantress!
You will live with me,
In the blue mountain you will turn your silver
    spinning wheel.

2. Veslemøy

Ho er mager og myrk og mjå
med brune og reine Drag
og Augo djupe og grå'
og stilslegt, drøymande Lag.

Det er som det halvt um halvt
låg ein Svevn yver heile ho;
i Rørsle, Tale og alt
ho hev denne døyvde Ro.

Under Panna fager, men låg
lyser Augo som bake in Eim;
det er som dei stirande såg
langt inn i ein annan Heim.

Berre Barmen gjeng sprengd og tung,
og det bivrar um Munnen bleik.
ho er skjelvande sped og veik,
midt i det ho er ven og ung.

She is lean and dark and slender,
With tanned and pure features
And eyes deep and grey
And a peaceful, dreaming manner.

It is as though little by little
A dream gradually envelopes her;
In her movement, speech and everything
She has this gentle calm.

Beneath her low yet pretty brow
Her eyes glint as though through a mist
It is as though they staring see
Far away into another world.

Only her bosom is strained and heavy,
And there is quivering around her pale mouth.
She is tremblingly delicate and frail,
And yet she is fair and young.

8. Ved Gjætle-bekken ('By Goat Brook')

Du surlande Bekk,
du kurlande Bekk,
her ligg du og kosar deg varm og klår.
Og speglar deg rein
og glid yver Stein,
og sullar so godt
og mullar so smått
og glitrar i Soli med mjuke Bår'.
– Å, her vil eg kvila, kvila.

Du tiklande Bekk,
du siklande Bekk,
her gjeng du so glad i den ljose Li.
Med Klunk og med Klukk,
med Song og med Sukk,
med Sus og med Dus
gjenom lauvbygt Hus,
med underlegt Svall og med Svæving blid.
– Å, her vil eg drøyma, drøyma.

Du hullande Bekk,
du sullande Bekk,
her fekk du Seng under Mosen mjuk.
Her drøymer du kurt
og gløymer deg burt
og kviskrar og kved
i den store Fred
med Svaling for Hugsott og Lengting sjuk.
– Å, her vil eg minnast, minnast.

Du vildrande Bekk,
du sildrande Bekk,
kva tenkte du alt på din Lange Veg?
Gjennom aude Rom?

millom Busk og Blom?
Når i Jord du smatt,
når du fann deg att?
Tru nokon du såg so eismal som eg?
– Å, her vil eg gløyma, gløyma.

Du tislande Bekk,
du rislande Bekk,
du leikar i Lund, du sullar i Ro.
Og smiler mot Sol
og lær i dit Skjol,
og vandrar so langt
og lærer so mangt,
å syng kje um det, som eg tenkjer no.
– Å, lat meg få blunda, blunda!

You murmuring brook,
You whispering brook,
Here you nestle, warm and clear.
And splash yourself clean
And glide over stones,
And sing so nicely,
And hum so low,
And glitter in the sun with gentle waves.
Ah, here will I rest.

You singing brook,
You rocking brook,
Here you run gaily down the bright slopes.
With chuckle and gurgle,
With song and with sigh,
With hustle and bustle,
Through a leaf-roofed house,
With strange swelling and soft flowing,
Ah, here will I dream.

You rambling brook,
You murmuring brook,
Here you make your bed under the gentle moss.
Here you dream awhile
And slip into forgetfulness
And whisper and sing
In great peacefulness
With balm for melancholy and painful longing.
Ah, here I will remember.

You wandering brook,
You swirling brook,
What have you been thinking about on your long
    journey?
Through empty spaces?
Between bushes and flowers?
When you squeeze into the earth,
When you find yourself again?
Truly have you ever seen anyone so lonely as I?
Ah, here I will forget.

You rushing brook,
You trickling brook,
You play in the grove, you hum in peace.
And smile at the sun
And laugh in your shelter,
And wander so far
And learn so much
Ah, do not sing of what I think of now,
Ah, let me slumber!

SELECT BIBLIOGRAPHY

SMN = Studia Musicologica Norvegica

Writings by Grieg (in Norwegian unless otherwise indicated)

Artikler og taler, ed. Øystein Gaukstad (Oslo: Gyldendal, 1957)

Brev i utvalg 1862–1907, ed. Finn Benestad, 2 vols. (Oslo: Aschehoug, 1998)

Brev til Frants Beyer, 1872–1907, ed. Finn Benestad and Bjarne Kortsen (Oslo: Universitetsforlaget, 1993)

Dagbøker: 1865, 1866, 1905, 1906, 1907, ed. Finn Benestad (Bergen: Bergen Offentlige Bibliotek, 1993)

Diaries, Articles, Speeches, ed. and trans. Finn Benestad and William H. Halvorsen (Columbus: Peer Gynt Press, 2001, in English)

Edvard Grieg: Briefwechsel mit dem Musikverlag C. F. Peters 1863–1907, ed. Finn Benestad and Hella Brock (Frankfurt: Peters, 1997, in German)

Edvard Grieg und Julius Röntgen: Briefwechsel 1883–1907, ed. Finn Benestad and Hanna de Vries Stavland (Amsterdam: Koninklijke Vereniging voor Nederlandse Muziekgeschiedenis, 1997, in German)

Edvard Grieg als Musikschriftsteller, ed. Hella Brock (Altenmedingen: Hildegard-Junker-Verlag, 1999, in German)

'Knut Dahle – Edv. Grieg – Johan Halvorsen', ed. Øyvind Anker, originally published in *Norsk musikkgransknings årbok*, 1943–6, reprinted in *Grieg og folkemusikken: en artikkel-samling* (Oslo: Landslaget Musikk i Skolen, 1992), 44–58

Letters to Colleagues and Friends, ed. and selected Finn Benestad, trans. William H. Halvorsen (Columbus: Peer Gynt Press, 2000, in English)

Other sources

Abraham, Gerald (ed.). *Grieg: A Symposium* (London: Lindsay Drummond, 1948)

Alter, Peter. *Nationalism*, trans. Stuart McKinnon-Evans (London: Edward Arnold, 1989, orig. publ. as *Nationalismus*, Frankfurt: Suhrkamp, 1985)

Anderson, Benedict. *Imagined Communities: Reflections on the Origin and Spread of Nationalism* (rev. edn, London: Verso, 1991, first publ. 1983)

Applegate, Celia. 'How German is It? Nationalism and the Idea of Serious Music in the Early Nineteenth Century', *Nineteenth-Century Music* 21/3 (1998), 274–96

Askeland, Jan. *Adolph Tidemand og hans tid* (Oslo: Aschehoug, 1991)

Barrell, John. *The Idea of Landscape and the Sense of Place, 1730–1840: An Approach to the Poetry of John Clare* (Cambridge: Cambridge University Press, 1972)

Benestad, Finn. 'Edvard Grieg og den nationale tone', *Musik og forskning* 19 (1993–4), 23–40

Benestad, Finn, and Dag Schjelderup-Ebbe. *Edvard Grieg: Chamber Music — Nationalism, Universality, Individuality* (Oslo: Scandinavian University Press, 1993)

Benestad, Finn, and Dag Schjelderup-Ebbe. *Edvard Grieg: The Man and the Artist*, trans. William H. Halvorson and Leland B. Sateren (Lincoln: University of Nebraska Press, 1988), orig. publ. as *Edvard Grieg: mennesket og kunsteren* (Oslo: Aschehoug, 1980)

Bird, John. *Percy Grainger* (London: Paul Elek, 1976)

Bjørndal, Arne. 'Edvard Grieg og folkemusikken', in *'Frå Fjon til Fusa', Årbok for Nord- og Midt-Hordaland Songlag* (Bergen, 1951), repr. in *Grieg og folkemusikken — en artikkelsamling* (Oslo: Landslaget Musikk i Skolen, 1992), 9–29

Blom, Jan-Petter. 'The Dancing Fiddle: On the Expression of Rhythm in Hardingfele Slåtter', in *Norsk folkemusikk serie I, Hardingfeleslåttar*. Band 7, Springar i 3/4 takt, ed. Jan-Petter Blom, Sven Nyhus and Reidar Sevag (Oslo: Universitetsforlaget, 1981), 305–21

Blom, Jan-Petter. 'Hva er folkemusikk?', in Bjørn Aksdal and Sven Nyhus (eds), *Fanitullen: innføring i norsk og samisk folkemusikk* (Oslo: Universitetsforlaget, 1993), 7–14

Boym, Svetlana. *The Future of Nostalgia* (New York: Basic Books, 2001)

Brown, Berit I. *Nordic Experiences: Exploration of Scandinavian Cultures*. Contributions to the Study of World Literature 71 (London & Westport: Greenwood, 1997)

Carley, Lionel. *Grieg and Delius: A Chronicle of Their Friendship in Letters* (London: Marion Boyars, 1993)

Carley, Lionel. 'The Last Visitor: Percy Grainger at Troldhaugen', *SMN* 25 (1999), 189–208

Casey, Edward S. *Representing Place: Landscape, Painting and Maps* (Minneapolis: University of Minnesota Press, 2002)

Corbin, Alain. *Village Bells: Sound and Meaning in the Nineteenth-Century French Countryside*, trans. Martin Thom (New York: Columbia, 1998)

Dahlhaus, Carl. *Foundations of Music History*, trans. J. Bradford Robinson (Cambridge: Cambridge University Press, 1983)

Dahlhaus, Carl. *Nineteenth-Century Music*, trans. J. Bradford Robinson (Berkeley: University of California Press, 1989)

Dahlhaus, Carl. *Between Romanticism and Modernism: Four Studies in the Music of the Later Nineteenth Century*, trans. Mary Whittall (Berkeley: University of California Press, 1980, repr. 1989)

Daniels, Stephen. 'Marxism, Culture, and the Duplicity of Landscape', in *New Models in Geography: The Political-Economy Perspective*, ed. Richard Peet and Nigel Thrift (London: Unwin Hyman, 1989), 196–220

Derry, T. K. *A History of Modern Norway 1814–1972* (Oxford: Clarendon Press, 1973)

Findeisen, Peer. *Instrumentale Folklorestilisierung bei Edvard Grieg und bei Béla Bartók:*

vergleichende Studie zur Typik der Volksmusikbearbeitung im 19. versus 20. Jahrhundert (Frankfurt am Main: Peter Lang, 1998)

Findeisen, Peer. 'Kulturell uavhengighet i speil av musikalsk etnofolklorisme' (Grieg Society, online at http://griegforum.no/griegsociety/default.asp?ka t=365&id=1392&sp=1)

Findeisen, Peer. 'Naturmystik als Kern der Einheit von Ton und Wort in Griegs Liederzyklus *Haugtussa*, op. 67', *SMN* 25 (1999), 124–43

Foster, Beryl. 'Grieg and Delius – Settings of the Same Norwegian Texts', *SMN* 25 (1999), 209–19

Foster, Beryl. 'Grieg and the European Song Tradition', *SMN* 19 (1993), 127–35

Foster, Beryl. *The Songs of Edvard Grieg* (Aldershot: Scolar, 1990)

Franklin, Peter. "'. . . His fractures are the script of truth" – Adorno's Mahler', in *Mahler Studies*, ed. Stephen E. Hefling (Cambridge: Cambridge University Press, 1997), 271–94

Frøyen, Morten Haug. 'Kulturell og politisk nasjonalisme hos Arne Garborg', in *Arne Garborgs kulturnasjonalisme*. KULT skriftserie no. 61 (Oslo: Noregs Forskningsråd, 1996), 7–103

Gillies, Malcolm, and David Pear. *Portrait of Percy Grainger*. Eastman Studies in Music (Rochester: University of Rochester Press, 2002)

Goertzen, Chris. *Fiddling for Norway: Revival and Identity* (Chicago: Chicago University Press, 1997)

Goulbault, Christian. 'Grieg et la critique musicale française', in *Grieg et Paris: romantisme, symbolisme et modernisme franco-norvégiens*, ed. Harald Herresthal and Danièle Pistone (Caen: Presses Université de Caen, 1996), 139–49

Grainger, Percy. *The Farthest North of Humanness: Letters of Percy Grainger, 1901–14*, ed. Kay Dreyfus (London: Macmillan 1985)

Grainger, Percy. *Grainger on Music*, ed. Malcolm Gillies and Bruce Clunies Ross with Bronwen Arthur and David Pear (Oxford: Oxford University Press, 1999)

Grey, Thomas S. 'Tableaux Vivants: Landscape, History Painting, and the Visual Imagination in Mendelssohn's Orchestral Music', *Nineteenth-Century Music* 21/1 (Summer 1997), 38–76

Grinde, Nils. *A History of Norwegian Music*, trans. William H. Halvorson and Leland B. Sateren (Lincoln: University of Nebraska Press, 1991), orig. publ. as *Norsk musikkhistorie* (Oslo: Universitetsforlaget, 1981)

Grinde, Nils. 'Grieg's Vocal Arrangements of Folk Tunes', *SMN* 19 (1993), 29–34

Halvorsen, William H. (ed.). *Edvard Grieg Today: A Symposium* (Northfield, Minn.: St Olav College, 1994)

Haugen, Einar, and Camilla Cai. *Ole Bull: Norway's Romantic Musician and Cosmopolitan Patriot* (Madison: University of Wisconsin Press, 1993), orig. publ. as *Ole Bull: romantisk musiker og kosmopolitisk nordmann* (Oslo: Universitetsforlaget, 1992)

Haugland, Kjell. 'An Outline of Norwegian Cultural Nationalism in the Second Half of the Nineteenth Century', in *The Roots of Nationalism*, ed. Rosalind Mitchison. Studies in Northern Europe (Edinburgh: John Donald, 1980), 21–9

Hepokoski, James. 'The Dahlhaus Project and Its Extra-Musicological Sources', *Nineteenth-Century Music* 14/3 (1991), 221–46

Hepokoski, James. *Sibelius: Symphony no. 5* (Cambridge: Cambridge University Press, 1993)

Herresthal, Harald. *Med spark i gulvet og quinter i bassen: musikalske og politiske bilder fra nasjonalromatikkens gjennombrudd i Norge* (Oslo: Universitetsforlaget, 1993)

Hobsbawm, Eric. *The Age of Capital: 1848–1875* (London: Abacus, 1997, repr. 2003)

Hobsbawm, Eric. *The Age of Empire: 1875–1914* (London: Abacus, 1995, repr. 2001)

Hobsbawm, Eric, and Terence Ranger (eds). *The Invention of Tradition* (Cambridge: Cambridge University Press, 1983, repr. 1995)

Hold, Trevor. 'Grieg, Delius, Grainger, and a Norwegian Cuckoo', *Tempo* 203 (January 1998), 11–19

Hopkins, Pandora. *Aural Thinking in Norway: Performance and Communication with the Hardingfele* (New York: Human Sciences Press, 1986)

Horton, John. *Grieg*. Master Musicians (London: Dent, 1974, repr. 1976)

Hroch, Miroslav. 'Specific Features of the Nation-Forming Process in the Circumstances of Small Nations', in Sørensen, *Nationalism*, 7–28

Hurum, Hans Jørgen. *Vennskap: Edvard Grieg og Frants Beyer* (Oslo: Grøndahl, 1989)

Hutchinson, John, and Anthony Smith (eds). *Nationalism: A Reader* (Oxford: Oxford University Press, 1994)

Jarrett, Sandra. *Edvard Grieg and His Songs* (Aldershot: Ashgate, 2003)

Johannessen, Karen Falch, and Siren Steen. 'The Grieg Collection in the Bergen Public Library', *SMN* 19 (1993), 55–8

Johnson, Julian. 'Mahler and the Idea of Nature', in *Perspectives on Gustav Mahler*, ed. Jeremy Barham (Aldershot: Ashgate, 2005)

Johnson, Julian. *Webern and the Transformation of Nature* (Cambridge: Cambridge University Press, 1999)

Kedourie, Elie. *Nationalism* (4th, expanded edn, Oxford: Blackwell, 1993)

Kent, Neil. *The Triumph of Light and Nature: Nordic Art, 1740–1940* (London: Thames and Hudson, 1987)

Kjerulf, Halfdan. *Samlede verker*, vol. III: *Samlede klaverstykker*, ed. Nils Grinde (Oslo: Musikk-Huset, 1980)

Kleiberg, Ståle. 'David Monrad Johansens musikksyn i mellomkrigstida, sett i lys av Arne Garborgs nasjonalitetsbegrep', *SMN* 10 (1984), 143–53

Kleiberg, Ståle. 'Following Grieg: David Monrad Johansen's Musical Style in the Early Twenties, and His Concept of a National Music', in *Musical Constructions of Nationalism: Essays on the History and Ideology of European Musical Culture, 1800–1945*, ed. Harry White and Michael Murphy (Cork: Cork University Press, 2001), 142–62

Kleiberg, Ståle. 'Grieg's *Slåtter*, Op. 72: Change of Musical Style or New Concept of Nationality?', *Journal of the Royal Musical Association* 121 (1996), 46–57

Knapp, Robert. 'Brahms and the Anxiety of Allusion', *Journal of Musicological Research* 18/1 (1998), 1–30

Korsyn, Kevin. 'Brahms Research and Aesthetic Ideology', *Music Analysis* 12/1 (1993), 89–103

Korsyn, Kevin. 'Towards a New Poetics of Musical Influence', *Music Analysis* 10/1–2 (1991), 3–73

Korsyn, Kevin. 'Beyond Privileged Contexts: Intertextuality, Influence and Dialogue', in *Rethinking Music*, ed. Nicholas Cook and Mark Everist (London: Oxford University Press, 1999), 55–72

Kortsen, Bjarne (ed.). *Musikkritikeren og skribenten David Monrad Johansen* (Bergen: Bjarne Kortsen, 1979)

Kramer, Lawrence. *Music as Cultural Practice, 1800–1900.* California Studies in Nineteenth-Century Music 8 (Berkeley: University of California Press, 1990)

Kramer, Richard. *Distant Cycles: Schubert and the Conceiving of Song* (Chicago: University of Chicago Press, 1994)

Kreft, Ekkehard. 'Grieg als Wegbereiter der Harmonik des 20. Jahrhunderts', *SMN* 19 (1993), 229–38

Krummacher, Friedhelm. 'Streichquartett als «Ehrensache» – Klang und Linie in Griegs Quartett op. 27', *SMN* 25 (1999), 90–107

Lebrecht, Norman. *Companion to Twentieth-Century Music* (London: Simon & Schuster, 1992)

Ledang, Ola Kai. 'Individual Creation and National Identity: On Grieg's Piano Adaptations of Hardingfele Music', *SMN* 19 (1993), 39–43

Ledang, Ola Kai. 'Magic, Means and Meaning: An Insider's View of Bark Flutes in Norway', *Selected Reports in Ethnomusicology* 8 (1990), 105–24

Lindeman, Ludvig Mathias. *Norske fjeldmelodier*, ed. Øystein Gaukstad (Oslo: Norsk Musikforlag, 1983)

Locke, Ralph P. 'Constructing the Oriental "Other": Saint-Saëns's *Samson et Dalila*', *Cambridge Opera Journal* 3 (1991), 261–302

Mäkelä, Tomi (ed.). *Music and Nationalism in Twentieth-Century Great Britain and Finland* (Hamburg: von Bockel, 1997)

Mäkelä, Tomi. 'Natur und Heimat in der Sibelius-Rezeption. Walter Niemann, Theodor W. Adorno and die "postmoderne Moderne"', *Sibelius Forum II, Proceedings from the Third International Jean Sibelius Conference, Helsinki, December 7–10, 2000*, ed. Matti Huttunen, Kari Kilpeläinen and Veijo Murtomäki (Helsinki: Sibelius Academy, 2003), 365–82

Massengale, James. '*Haugtussa*: from Garborg to Grieg', *Scandinavian Studies* 53/2 (Spring 1981), 131–53

McClary, Susan. *Georges Bizet: Carmen* (Cambridge: Cambridge University Press, 1992)

Mellers, Wilfrid. *Percy Grainger* (Oxford: Oxford University Press, 1992)

Milewski, Barbara. 'Chopin's Mazurkas and the Myth of the Folk', *Nineteenth-Century Music* 23/2 (1999), 113–35

Monrad Johansen, David. *Edvard Grieg*, trans. M. Robertson (New York: Tudor, 1945), orig. publ. in Norwegian (Oslo: Gyldendal, 1934)

Monrad Johansen, David. 'Nasjonale Verdier i vår Musikk', *Aftenposten*, 5–9 July 1924; reproduced in Kortsen, *Musikkritikeren*, 33–46

Nerbøvik, Jostein. 'Den norske kulturnasjonalismen', in Sørensen, *Nasjonal identitet*, 139–58

Niemann, Walter. *Die Musik Skandinaviens: ein Führer durch die Volks- und Kunstmusik* (Leipzig: Breitkopf & Härtel, 1906)

Olsen, Sparre. *Percy Grainger* (Oslo: Det Norske Samlaget, 1963)

Østerud, Øyvind. 'Norwegian Nationalism in a European Context', in Sørensen, *Nationalism*, 29–39

Oxaal, Astrid. 'Folkedragt som uniform', in Sørensen, *Nasjonal identitet*, 91–112

Pear, David. 'Grainger on Race and Nation', *Australasian Music Research* 5 (Grainger issue) (Melbourne: University of Melbourne, 2001), 25–48

Randall, Don. *Kipling's Imperial Boy: Adolescence and Cultural Hybridity* (Basingstoke: Palgrave, 2000)

Ranheim, Inga. 'Folkedans og disiplinering', in Sørensen, *Nasjonal identitet*, 73–89

Rosen, Charles. *The Romantic Generation* (London: Harper Collins, 1996)

Rothstein, William. *Phrase Rhythm in Tonal Music* (New York: Schirmer, 1989)

Samson, Jim. 'Nations and Nationalism', in *The Cambridge History of Nineteenth-Century Music*, ed. Jim Samson, (Cambridge: Cambridge University Press, 2001), 568–600

Schama, Simon. *Landscape and Memory* (New York: Harper Collins, 1995)

Scherzinger, Martin. 'The "New Poetics" of Musical Influence: A Response to Kevin Korsyn', *Music Analysis* 13/2–3 (1994), 298–309

Schjelderup, Gerhard, and Walter Niemann. *Edvard Grieg: Biographie und Würdigung seiner Werke* (Leipzig: Peters, 1908)

Schjelderup-Ebbe, Dag. 'Noen tankar om Edvard Griegs gjeld til Halfdan Kjerulf', *SMN* 24 (1998), 39–46

Schjelderup-Ebbe, Dag. '«Rett fra Kua» – Edvard Griegs 19 norske folkeviser, op. 66', *SMN* 25 (1999), 9–11

Schjelderup-Ebbe, Dag. *Study of Grieg's Harmonic Style with Special Reference to His Contributions to Musical Impressionism* (Oslo: Johan Grundt Tanum, 1953, Norsk Musikgranskning)

Schlotel, Brian. *Grieg* (London: BBC Publications, 1986)

Schwab, Heinrich H. '«Der Präsenz beider Elemente»: zur kompositorischen Struktur von Griegs Klavierpoesie', *SMN* 19 (1993), 155–65

Sihvo, Hannes. 'Karelia: A Source of Finnish National History', *National History and Identity: Approaches to the Writing of National History in the North-East Baltic Region, Nineteenth and Twentieth Centuries*, ed. Michael Branch. Studia Fennica Ethnologica 6 (Helsinki: Finnish Literature Society, 1999), 181–201

Skyllstad, Kjell, 'Folklore eller fremtidsmusik: kontrapunkter fra Grieg-debatten 1981', *SMN* 8 (1982), 69–75

Smith, Anthony D. *National Identity* (London: Penguin, 1991)

Sørensen, Øystein. 'The Development of a Norwegian National Identity during the Nineteenth Century: Some Aspects and Problems', in Sørensen, *Nordic Paths*, 17–35

Sørensen, Øystein (ed.). *Nasjonal identitet – et kunstprodukt?* KULT skriftserie no. 30, Nasjonal identitet no. 5 (Oslo: Noregs Forskningsråd, 1994)

Sørensen, Øystein (ed). *Nationalism in Small European Nations*. KULT skriftserie no. 47 (Oslo: Noregs Forskningsråd, 1996)

Sørensen, Øystein (ed.). *Nordic Paths to National Identity in the Nineteenth Century*. KULT skriftserie no. 22, Nasjonal identitet no. 1 (Oslo: Noregs Forskningsråd, 1994)

Steen-Nøkleberg, Einar. *On Stage with Grieg: Interpreting His Piano Music*, trans. William H. Halvorson (Bloomington and Indianapolis: Indiana University Press, 1997), orig. publ. in Norwegian as *Med Grieg på podiet: til spillende fra en spillende* (Oslo: Solum Forlag, 1992)

Steensen, Bodil. 'Borgelig nasjonalisme og bygdenasjonalisme', in Sørensen, *Nasjonal identitet*, 159–69

Straus, Joseph N. *Remaking the Past: Musical Modernism and the Influence of the Tonal Tradition* (Cambridge, Mass.: Harvard University Press, 1990)

Sutcliffe, W. Dean. 'Grieg's Fifth: The Linguistic Battleground of "Klokkeklang"', *The Musical Quarterly* 80/1 (Spring 1996), 161–81

Tan, Eleanor A. L. 'Grainger as an Interpreter of Grieg's Work', *Australasian Music Research* 5 (Grainger issue) (Melbourne: University of Melbourne, 2001), 49–60

Taruskin, Richard. 'Nationalism', in *The Revised New Grove Dictionary of Music and Musicians*, ed. Stanley Sadie and John Tyrrell, vol. XVII (Basingstoke: Macmillan, 2001), 687–706

Taruskin, Richard. Review of Joseph Straus, *Remaking the Past: Musical Modernism and the Influence of the Tonal Tradition* and Kevin Korsyn, 'Towards a New Poetics of Musical Influence', *Journal of the American Musicological Society* 46/1 (Spring 1993), 114–38

Thorkildsen, Dag. 'Skandinavismen – en historisk oversikt', in Sørensen, *Nasjonal identitet*, 191–209

Time, Sveinung. 'Språk og nasjonalitet hos Arne Garborg', in *Arne Garborgs kulturnasjonalisme*. KULT skriftserie no. 61 (Oslo: Noregs Forskningsråd, 1996), 107–95

Tønsberg, Christian. *Norge. Illustreret Reisehaandbog. Med Prospekter og Karter* (Oslo: Udgivnerens Forlag, 1874)

Tønsberg, Christian. *Norske Folkelivsbilleder, efter Maleries og Tegninger af A. Tidemand* (Oslo: Udgivnerens Forlag, 1854)

Volden, Torstein. 'Studier i Edvard Grieg's Haugtussasanger, med særlig henblikk på sangenes opprinnelse og på forholdet mellom poesi og musikk'. Hovedoppdrag (master's thesis), University of Oslo, 1967

Vollsnes, Arvid O. 'Grieg's Own Interpretations: Modern Use of Old Piano Recordings', *SMN* 19 (1993), 171–8

Walton, Benjamin. 'Looking for the Revolution in Rossini's *Guillaume Tell*', *Cambridge Opera Journal* 15/2 (2003), 127–51

Whitesell, Lloyd. 'Men with a Past: Music and the "Anxiety of Influence"', *Nineteenth-Century Music* 18/2 (Fall 1994), 152–67

Witoszek, Nina. 'Nationalism, Postmodernity and Ireland', in Sørensen, *Nationalism*, 101–21

Woolf, Stuart (ed). *Nationalism in Europe, 1815 to the Present: A Reader* (London: Routledge, 1996)

GRIEG'S WORKS MENTIONED IN THE TEXT

By opus number

op. 3	*Poetiske Tonebilder* ('Poetic Tone Pictures')
op. 6	*Humoresker* ('Humoresques')
op. 12	*Lyric Pieces I*
op. 16	Piano Concerto in A Minor
op. 17	*25 norske Folkeviser og Danser*
	('25 Norwegian Folk Songs and Dances')
op. 17/1	'Springdans' ('Leaping Dance')
op. 17/5	'Jølstring'
op. 17/6	'Brurelåt' ('Wedding Tune') from Gol
op. 17/13	'Reiseslåt' ('Recessional March')
op. 17/24	'Brurelåt' from Vang
op. 19	*Folkelivsbilder* ('Scenes from Folk Life')
op. 19/2	'Brudefølget drar forbi' ('The bridal procession passes by')
op. 19/3	'Fra Karnevalet' ('From the Carnival')
op. 24	*Ballade*
op. 28	*Fire Albumblad* ('Album Leaves')
op. 30	*Album for Mannssang* ('Album for Male Chorus')
op. 32	*Den Bergtekne* ('The Mountain Thrall')
op. 33	*12 Melodier til Digte af A. O.Vinje*
	('12 Songs to Poems by A. O. Vinje')
op. 38	*Lyric Pieces II*
op. 38/1	'Vuggevise' ('Berceuse')
op. 40	*Fra Holbergs Tid* ('Holberg Suite')
op. 46	*Peer Gynt I*
op. 54	*Lyric Pieces V*
op. 54/1	'Gjetergut' ('Shepherd's Boy')
op. 54/2	'Gangar' ('Walking Dance')
op. 54/4	'Notturno' ('Nocturne')
op. 54/6	'Klokkeklang' ('Bell Ringing')
op. 55	*Peer Gynt II*
op. 58	'Norge', *Fem Digte* (John Paulsen)
op. 62	*Lyric Pieces VII*
op. 62/4	'Bekken' ('The Brook')
op. 62/5	'Drömmesyn' ('The Phantom' or 'Dream Vision')

op. 62/6	'Hjemad' ('Homeward')
op. 65	*Lyric Pieces VIII*
op. 65/1	'Fra Ungdomsdagene' ('From Early Years')
op. 65/6	'Bryllupsdag på Troldhaugen' ('Wedding Day at Troldhaugen')
op. 66	*19 norske Folkeviser* ('19 Norwegian Folk Songs')
op. 66/1	'Kulokk' ('Cow Lure')
op. 66/2	'Det er den største Dårlighet' ('It is the greatest folly')
op. 66/3	'En Konge hersket i Østerland' ('A king reigned in the east')
op. 66/4	'Siri Dale-Visen' ('The Siri Dale Song')
op. 66/10	'Morgo ska du få gifte deg' ('Tomorrow you shall marry her')
op. 66/12	'Ranveig'
op. 66/14	'I Ola-Dalom, i Ola-Kjønn' ('In Ola Valley, in Ola Lake')
op. 66/18	'Jeg går i tusen Tanker' ('I wander deep in thought')
op. 67	*Haugtussa* ('The Mountain Maid')
op. 67/1	'Det Syng' ('The Enticement')
op. 67/2	'Veslemøy'
op. 67/3	'Blåbær-Li' ('Blueberry Slope')
op. 67/4	'Møte' ('The Tryst')
op. 67/5	'Elsk' ('Love')
op. 67/6	'Killingdans' ('Kidlings' Dance')
op. 67/7	'Vond Dag' ('Hurtful Day')
op. 67/8	'Ved Gjætle-bekken' ('By Goat Brook')
EG152d	'Sporven' ('The Sparrow')
EG152h	'Dømd' ('Doomed')
EG152l	'Ku-lok' ('Cow Lure')
op. 68	*Lyric Pieces IX*
op. 68/4	'Aften på Höyfjellet' ('Evening in the Mountains')
op. 70	*Fem Digte* (Otto Bentzon)
op. 72	*Slåtter* ('Norwegian Peasant Dances')
op. 72/1	'Gibøens Bruremarsj' ('Gibøen's Wedding March')
op. 72/2	'Jon Vestafes Springdans' ('Jon Vestafe's Leaping Dance')
op. 72/3	'Bruremarsj fra Telemark'
op. 72/7	'Røtnams-Knut. Halling'
op. 72/8	'Bruremarsj (etter Myllarguten)' ('Myllarguten's Wedding March')
op. 72/11	'Knut Luråsens Halling II'
op. 72/13	'Håvar Gibøens Draum ved Oterholtsbrua. Springdans' ('Håvar Gibøen's Dream on the Oterholt Bridge')
op. 73	*Stemninger* ('Moods')

INDEX

Printed in the United States
107189LV00001B/17/A

9 781843 832102